Beneath The Stone

Dedicated to

DAVID DRAKE
and
KARL EDWARD WAGNER

whose knowledge of history is reflected
throughout this book

Beneath
the
Stone
The Story of Masonic Secrecy

C. Bruce Hunter

Illustrations by
Phil Hawkins

WORLDCOMM
a division of Creativity, Inc.

Publisher: Ralph Roberts
Vice-President: Pat Roberts

Editors: Susan Parker, Julie Burns, Pat Roberts
Cover & Interior Design: Gayle Graham
Illustrations: Phil Hawkins
Photographs as indicated

Second Edition

10 9 8 7 6 5 4 3 2 1

Library of Congress Cataloging-in-Publication Data

Hunter, C. Bruce (Calvin Bruce), 1944-
    Beneath the Stone : the story of Masonic secrecy / by Bruce Hunter;
    illustrations by Phil Hawkins
        p.   cm. --
    Includes bibliographical references (p.).
    ISBN 1-56664-147-0
        1. Freemasonry--History.   2. Freemasonry--Symbolism.
    3. Freemasonry--Rituals.   I. Title.
    HS403.H85   199
    366'.1--dc21   98-42326
                                                            CIP

The author and publisher have made every effort in the preparation of this book to ensure the accuracy of the information. However, the information in this book is sold without warranty, either express or implied. Neither the author nor WorldComm® will be liable for any damages caused or alleged to be caused directly, indirectly, incidentally, or consequentially by the information in this book.

The opinions expressed in this book are solely those of the author and are not necessarily those of WorldComm®.

Trademarks: Names of products mentioned in this book known to be, or suspected of being trademarks or service marks are capitalized. The usage of a trademark or service mark in this book should not be regarded as affecting the validity of any trademark or service mark.

WorldComm®—a division of Creativity, Inc.—is a full-service publisher located at 65 Macedonia Road, Alexander NC 28701. Phone (828) 252–9515, Fax (828) 255–8719. For orders only: 1-800-472-0438. Visa and MasterCard accepted.

WorldComm® is distributed to the trade by Alexander Distributing, 65 Macedonia Road, Alexander, NC 28701. Phone (828) 252-9515, Fax (828) 255-8719.

Contents

Acknowledgments

Although a journey through history is a very personal thing, it can never be taken alone. This journey was made with the aid of several people whose time and ideas made it possible to reach the end. Of special importance were Inge Baum at the library of the Supreme Council, Ancient and Accepted Scottish Rite, Southern Jurisdiction; Gloria Jackson at the library of the Supreme Council, Northern Masonic Jurisdiction; and Karen Faison of Macoy Publishing Company, all of whom went beyond the call of duty in dealing with the obscure documents and extensive research that are necessary to complete a project of this scope.

Many others have assisted at various times and with various problems along the way. The list includes – but is not limited to – Susan Craven of Atkins & Craven, Saluda, North Carolina and the librarians and staffs of The Catholic University of America; Georgetown University; The New York State Historical Association; The United Grand Lodge of England; York City Library; York Lodge No. 236 (formerly The Union Lodge); and The Company of Merchant Adventurers of the City of York.

reductos in hostium numero habuit

Prologue

The Masonic lodge makes a great deal of its symbols. Since its earliest days, it has used Gothic architecture and the tools of the stone mason to teach moral lessons. The square is a symbol of virtue, while the trowel alludes to brotherly love, and the level and plumb teach equality and upright behavior.

Of these symbols, one of the most important but least known is the building stone. It appears again and again in the ritual, playing a central role in Masonic teachings. The new Mason is told that *he* is the stone, a thing to be worked and improved until it reaches its full potential. Coming from the quarry as a rough, almost shapeless lump, the stone is fashioned by the master's hand into a work of strength and beauty. Only then can it be placed on a firm foundation and joined with others of its kind to form a magnificent structure. In just this way, the new Mason is told, he must be shaped into a more proper member of his fraternity and his society. Only then will *he* be able to render the service that is expected of him.

But what lies beneath this stone? Is the foundation on which it rests merely a fraternal organization? Or is it an international conspiracy? Does it embrace moral lessons or a secret doctrine? Does it teach fellowship and brotherly love, or is a hidden agenda buried beneath its pomp and ceremony?

These questions are far from new. Rumor and suspicion have plagued Freemasonry for more than two centuries. During that time, church leaders, politicians and even the man in the street have all taken their turn at attacking the lodge.

Curiously, the order has always been reluctant to respond to the criticism leveled against it, and that has often been seen as evidence that the charges are true. But nothing about the Masons is as simple as it appears. Their silence in the face of criticism is, at least in part, the result of hard learned lessons. When Masonic bodies have tried to improve their image, their efforts have met with only limited success. In spite of their many attempts at public relations, the rumors persist. In fact, the more the Masons seek favorable publicity, the more forceful the criticism seems to become. Masonic groups advertise their charities. Critics warn of demon worship. The fraternity's official magazines promote patriotism and piety. Anti-Masonic tracts tell of political intrigue and conspiracy. In short, no claim is far from a counter claim.

In such a jumble of conflicting information, it is hard to get at the truth and even harder to recognize it. As a result, few people know what to think of this mysterious fraternity. Although most are aware of the organization's existence, few know anything about it. They see only glimpses of Masonic activities. And if they try to learn more, they quickly find that it is much easier to ask questions than to get answers. As a rule, Masonic meetings are closed to the public and, so it seems, are the lips of its members.

This is not because the Masons are publicity shy. It goes much deeper than that. Simply put, reliable and understandable information about Freemasonry is hard to find because of the phenomenon of Masonic secrecy. Indeed, the single most widely known fact about Freemasonry is that its members are sworn to secrecy. That is why most of them are reluctant to discuss their organization. And it is why the few who are willing to talk become silent when the discussion turns to certain aspects of their affairs.

Paradoxically, students of the subject claim that there are no real secrets in Freemasonry. In view of the fraternity's reputation and the behavior of its members, that is a very curious assertion. If it's true, the Masons have devoted a great deal of energy to keeping secrets that are not secret, while a curious public has expended an equal amount of energy being suspicious of secrets that never existed.

But could such a thing be true? It's hard to understand how Masons all over the world can be so mistaken as to believe that they are expected to keep secrets where none exist. And it is hard to understand why they would continue to be so misguided in the face of all the criticism their secrecy has aroused.

This book was written to address the problems that arise from such a confusing state of affairs. It is not a simple exposé. It will not, as so many critics do, reveal alleged secrets without explaining what they mean. Too often, exposés *claim* to reveal secrets that have been kept for centuries, but in the end they merely repeat isolated facts – and sometimes not-so-factual cliches – that have been published repeatedly in the past.

This "old news" contains little of importance, especially since its authors seem unaware of its significance. They take pride in publishing the notorious Mason Word but say nothing about what it means or how it is used. And all the other "secrets" get the same treatment. Unfortunately, since exposé writers never explain what they reveal, they leave their readers knowing little more than they did before.

Instead of throwing out isolated passwords and gestures with no explanation, the pages that follow will explore at the whole story of Masonic secrecy.

We will examine the fraternity's long and convoluted history and learn what lies beneath the secrets that have caused so much commotion through the years. We will show why the Masons felt the need to hide their affairs from the world in the first place. And we will see the secrets, either real or imagined, that make up the mystique which has always surrounded the organization. In this way, perhaps we can shed light on a subject that has long excelled in resisting investigation.

This volume is intended for two kinds of readers. It is designed to inform the non-mason who has heard rumors and criticism of Freemasonry and wants to understand the truth behind the commotion. But it is also intended for the Mason who does not know as much about his own organization as he should.

Both will find something new in these pages. Although their concerns and questions may be different, they will discover that Masonic secrecy is not what they thought it was. They will see that much of the commotion – from inside the lodge as well as outside – is misdirected. And, we hope, many will come to understand the real meaning of the centuries old secrets of a very misunderstood fraternity.

As we have observed, the curious non-mason trying to learn about the lodge finds barriers thrown in his way. One such barrier is the bias with which most books and articles are filled. Freemasonry is one of those subjects that is rarely discussed except by people who have strong feelings. And where feelings run strong, there is a tendency to choose selectively from the available facts.

At one extreme are the dedicated opponents who eagerly accept any criticism they can find, believing false rumor as eagerly as truth. In their rush to confirm their suspicions, they fail to sort out hoaxes and discard claims that fail the test of logic.

At the other extreme are the many Masons who are completely uncritical in defending their fraternity. They believe that anyone who berates them is an enemy who must be motivated by jealousy and malice. Conversely, anyone who defends them must be a friend and thus worthy of trust and support. No good word is discarded for fear that it might be true. No criticism is tolerated in the conviction that it is false.

It's no wonder that the facts are overshadowed by a surplus of rhetoric and prejudice. A worthwhile investigation of any subject requires a balanced approach. And that is the rarest commodity in most discussions of the lodge.

This book makes no effort to either criticize or defend the Masonic lodge. Nor does it assume that the reader has previous knowledge of the subject. It is written to be understood by the most casual observer of these matters, while delving into subjects unknown to most Masons.

Non-masons will find more than a few surprises here. The reality of Freemasonry is not at all what the public is led to believe. Its history, which stretches back for centuries, has produced a remarkably complex organization whose activities go far beyond the popular image. The rumors, as intriguing as they are, only hint at the true story. When that story is told, many will find doors opening onto vistas they never suspected were there.

But while the non-member has much to learn about this curious fraternity, its members should not feel complacent. Their knowledge of their own organization leaves room for improvement, too. Most have only a limited knowledge of the secrecy they *think* is demanded of them.

Even before he becomes a full fledged Mason, the initiate is warned that he must keep the secrets he will soon be taught. But he is never told which parts of his initiation are secret. Nor is he offered an explanation of the reasons for Masonic secrecy – or for that matter, why his organization has secrets in the first place.

Instead, the warning is so dramatic that it often has a chilling effect. Not only does it impress the new member with his lodge's desire for secrecy, it may also keep him from learning more about his own fraternity. One initiate will believe that the material is so secret it must not be investigated. Another naïvely assumes that nothing about it *can* be investigated. Both take what they have been told at face value, and neither looks below the surface to discover the "why" of Masonic secrecy. As a result, many active, longtime Masons who are adamant about protecting their organization from the public would be hard pressed to explain the purpose of their silence or what it is supposed to accomplish.

For those Masons, this book will provide perspective on a topic that is as confusing to them as it is to the public. It will show that the real problem is not Masonic secrecy but a misunderstanding of it. To grasp this important distinction, it will be necessary to deal with the origins of the secrets and the reasons they were preserved through the centuries. The conclusion will challenge the Mason who regards everything about his lodge as a secret. It will show why that attitude can actually harm the institution he is trying to protect. Perhaps, too, it will help Masons understand that knowing the "why" of their obligation can help them act more responsibly and thus chip away at the rumors that have always plagued them.

Uncovering the truth of this matter is something of a detective story. It must be, because many of the facts are hidden and clues to them are hard to find. But the clues are there, and a proper search will locate them.

The first step is to sort through six centuries of Masonic history to draw the facts from a maze of often conflicting evidence. But that will not be an easy task. The tangible evidence – what legal investigators call the "paper trail" – has suffered through the years. Many documents were destroyed by fire and flood, by riot and carelessness, by the malicious acts of foes intent on destroying Freemasonry as well as the overzealous efforts of friends trying to protect it from prying eyes.

Our study of the surviving documents will leave us with a mystery – a puzzle some of whose pieces are missing and others hidden. The complete picture can no longer be recovered. Too much has been lost, and some of it lost forever. But a careful bit of detective work can fit together what remains and fill in some of the missing pieces with reasoned speculation.

Once we have done that, we must go farther back in time, peeling away the layers of the story to discover Freemasonry's real beginnings and its original character. This will give us the key to the fraternity's rise to what it is today. Then we will finally see how Masonic secrecy evolved into the enigma it has become.

As with any investigation of the distant past, some questions must remain unanswered. But ours is far from a lost cause. In the end we will learn enough to draw conclusions and shed light on a subject that has been needlessly obscured by friend and foe alike.

Before undertaking our quest, though, we must begin with a word of caution. Not everyone will believe the conclusions drawn here. Not everyone should. The history presented in these pages is sound, the conjecture is carefully reasoned and every effort has been made to distinguish between fact and theory. But that is of little consequence.

Many people already have unshakable beliefs about the Masonic lodge, and little can be done to change their views. The dedicated critic and the Mason who is deeply entrenched in secrecy will find nothing of interest here.

This book is for those who enjoy the quest. It is for those who can believe that there is knowledge to be gained from the distant history of an enigma. And it is for those who believe that a secret must have a purpose.

Chronology

B.C.
ca. 1000 B.C. • David becomes king of Israel.
ca. 960 B.C. • David dies and Solomon becomes king of Israel.
ca. 950 B.C. • King Solomon's Temple is completed in Jerusalem with the help of Hiram, king of the Phoenician city of Tyre.
ca. 300 B.C. • Euclid is born.

FIRST CENTURY A.D. – Shortly after the crucifixion, Jesus' burial cloth is said to travel to Edessa, a city in what is now Turkey, where it disappears for nearly a thousand years.
71 • A Roman fort is established at Eboracum (York), apparently the first permanent settlement on the site. Emperors occasionally hold court there.

SECOND CENTURY – Christianity comes to York, as it does to the rest of Britain, with the Romans. This probably occurs during the second century, but the details are not known.
120 • Hadrian declares York his military capital.

THIRD CENTURY – As the Roman Empire falters and the southern and eastern coasts of Britain increasingly suffer Saxon raids, "friendly" Germans play an important role in defending the so-called Saxon Shore.

FOURTH CENTURY – The Christian Church is reasonably well organized throughout the Empire, and York is one of its more prominent centers.
306 • Roman Emperor Constantius dies during a visit to York.
312 • Following his conversion to Christianity, Constantine mandates toleration for the Christian religion throughout the Empire.
313 • The Edict of Toleration, proclaimed in Milan, makes Constantine's toleration of Christianity official.
314 • Records from the Council of Arles indicate that York plays an important role in Church affairs.

FIFTH CENTURY – The fall of Rome marks the beginning of the "dark" ages. York becomes independent, while Britain and Europe begin a period of cultural decline. Britain's best remembered hero, Arthur, dies and the Anglo-Saxon conquest gains momentum.

ca. 410• St. Honoratus founds a monastery on the island of Lerins.

428   • The Anglo-Saxon conquest of Britain begins with the arrival of three shiploads of mercenaries.

SIXTH CENTURY – Monasticism becomes a significant force in a society that is increasingly influenced by religion. The Anglo-Saxons begin to build larger and more stable kingdoms.

529   • Benedict of Nursia founds a monastery at Monte Casino and establishes the Benedictine Rule.

563   • St. Columba sends Scottish missionaries to Ireland to establish a Christian monastery on the island of Iona.

ca. 580• The Angles consolidate their power in northern Britain, creating the kingdoms of Bernicia and Deira. Ethelfrith subdues them and rules the unified kingdom of Northumbria.

590   • September 3 – Gregory I becomes pope, dies 604.

597   • Pope Gregory I sends Augustine to England as missionary to Kent. Augustine becomes the first archbishop of Canterbury, holding that office until his death in 604.

SEVENTH CENTURY – Northern England comes increasingly under the influence of Christianity. The seeds of what will become Freemasonry are sown, and Northumbrian monks provide the historic basis of the York legend.

625   • A marriage is arranged between Edwin of Northumbria and Ethelburga, princess of Kent. Paulinus, Ethelburga's chaplain, accompanies her and becomes first archbishop of York.

627   • Easter day – Edwin, with other members of his family and court, are baptized at York in a building erected for the purpose. It is possibly the first Christian church in York.

628   • Biscop Baducing (Benedict Biscop) is born, dies January 12, 690.

633   • Edwin dies at the battle of Hatfield. Ethelburga and Paulinus flee to Kent while Edwin's son Oswald seeks refuge at the Celtic monastery on Iona.

635   • Oswald regains power and invites the Church of Iona to send missionaries to Northumbria. He appoints Bishop Aidan to the episcopal see on Lindisfarne.

653   • At the age of twenty-five, Biscop dedicates his life to God and prepares for a monastic life.

664   • The Synod of Whitby adjudicates a dispute between the Celtic and Roman Churches. Its verdict increases Rome's power in Northumbria.

665 • Biscop assumes the monastic habit in a monastery at Lerins, an island near Cannes. He remains there two years.

667 • Biscop visits Rome.

669 • Theodore becomes archbishop of Canterbury and appoints Biscop abbot of the monastery of St. Augustine.

674 • Biscop establishes a monastery at Wearmouth on land donated by King Egfrid.

679 • Biscop makes a final trip to Rome to obtain relics and art for his monastery, which receives a charter from Pope Agatho.

682 • King Egfrid donates more land, and Biscop establishes his second monastery at Jarrow. Ceolfrith is its first abbot.

EIGHTH CENTURY – The Vikings move into England, while the Church holds its own. British culture continues to be strong in the western and northern parts of the island.

741 • April 23 – A church, possibly the one built by Edwin, burns in York.

767 • Albert becomes archbishop of York, serves until 780. He rebuilds a church, probably on the present site of the minster.

787 • The Viking invasion of England begins.

792 • Vikings sack Lindisfarne.

793 • Vikings raid Northumbria, operating from bases in the Shetland islands.

NINTH CENTURY – England is gradually becoming a unified nation. Alfred the Great brings a measure of peace to the land, while the Danes control large parts of northern England and Ireland.

815 • Egbert defeats the Britons of Cornwall, bringing the Anglo-Saxon conquest of England to a successful conclusion.

827 • Egbert becomes king of the West Saxons, founds the University of York, dies 839.

867 • Danish Vikings conquer Northumbria and capture York.

878 • Alfred the Great's victory at Edington results in the "Peace of Wedmore." Northumbria is surrendered to the Danes.

895 • Athelstan, grandson of Alfred the Great, is born.

899 • Alfred the Great dies and is succeeded by his son Edward.

TENTH CENTURY – The Danish Vikings, once the bane of churches and monasteries, become settled in England and many accept Christianity. Moslem rulers begin to resent European Christians who are coming to the Holy Land in increasing numbers. The shroud of Jesus reappears in Constantinople.

919 • Norse Vikings take York from the Danes.

925 • September 4 – Athelstan is crowned king of Wessex at Kingston-on-Thames and is accepted by the Mercians as their king.

926   • Athelstan annexes Northumbria after defeating kings Olaf of York and Guthfrith of Dublin. He also forces the kings of Scotland and Strathclyde to submit to his authority.
      • The traditional date of the York Assembly.

934   • Athelstan fights the Scots.

937   • The Scots form an alliance with Owain of Strathclyde and Norse forces from Dublin.
      • Athelstan defeats his combined enemies in a battle at Brunanburh and declares himself the king of all Britain.

939   • October 27 – Athelstan dies.

954   • Eadred, now Anglo-Saxon king of Wessex, captures York from Norse forces led by Eric Bloodaxe.

ELEVENTH CENTURY – While tension between Moslems and Christians increases, pilgrimages to the Holy Land become more popular. Pope Gregory VII advocates a crusade but dies before the First Crusade begins. The Norman Invasion increases the continental influence on English architecture.

1066   • William the Conqueror is crowned king of England at Westminster by Aeldred, archbishop of York.

1069   • The York minster is burned during fighting over William's claim to the English crown.

1070   • Thomas of Bayeux becomes the first Norman archbishop of York and restores the minster in the continental style.

1095   • At the Council of Claremont, Pope Urban II, believing the time for a crusade has come, delivers a sermon calling for an expedition to liberate the Holy Land.

1096   • The First Crusade begins.

1098   • The crusaders capture Antioch, their first major victory.

1099   • July 15 – The crusaders capture Jerusalem.
      • Godfrey de Bouillon, Duke of Lower Lorraine, is the first crusader to rule Jerusalem but dies within the year.

TWELFTH CENTURY – The crusaders establish a Christian and European presence in the Holy Land. The Moslems begin a prolonged struggle to liberate their territory, while the Templars become powerful and wealthy.

1100   • Baldwin, Godfrey's brother, becomes King of Jerusalem, dies 1118.

1113   • As a reward for their service to the crusaders, Pope Paschal II grants the Hospitallers a charter as a religious order to be named the Order of the Hospital of St. John of Jerusalem.

1115   • Bernard founds an abbey at Clairvaux, later becomes a major supporter of the Templars.

1118   • The Knights Templar are formed under the leadership of Hugues de Payens of Champagne. They receive a mandate to patrol the roads and escort pilgrims to and from Jerusalem.

1120 • Brother Gerard dies. His successor, Raymond du Puy, reforms the Hospitallers as a fighting force.

1126 • Hugues de Payens returns to Europe to promote his order, seek recruits and finances and gain political and church recognition.

1128 • January – Pope Honorius II calls a Council at Troyes to decide the Templars' future. With Bernard's support, the Templars receive Church sanction. They adopt Bernard's Rule and the pope grants them the white mantle as a symbol of purity.

ca.1128 • De Payens founds the Templars' first English preceptory in London and organizes Templar operations in England and Scotland.

1130 • De Payens returns to the Holy Land from his promotional tour of Europe and begins to build the Templars into a powerful organization.

1136 • Hugues de Payens dies.

1137 • The York minster is seriously damaged by fire.

1139 • Pope Innocent II issues a Bull, *Omne Datum Optimum,* allowing the Templars to recruit their own chaplains and build their own churches. In addition, they are exempted from paying tithes and allowed to receive tithes.

1140 • According to tradition, the masonic lodge at Kilwinning, Scotland is founded and operates continuously to the present.

1147 • On the eve of the Second Crusade, Pope Eugenius III grants the Templars the right to add a red cross, a symbol of martyrdom, to their white mantle.

ca.1150 • Raymond du Puy completes his reforming of the Hospitallers. They are now a military order similar to the Templars.

1154 • Roger of Pont l'Eveque enlarges and rebuilds the York minster in the Norman style. His work continues until 1181.

1169 • At age thirty-one, Saladin becomes commander of Syrian troops and vizier of Egypt. He begins a campaign to unite all Moslem territories and re-capture the Holy Land.

1184 • The English Templars move their operations to a site later occupied by the Inns of Court and Chancery. Their new headquarters building, the Temple Church, still stands.

1185 • February 10 – The New Temple is consecrated by Patriarch Heraclius of Jerusalem in a ceremony attended by King Henry II and his court.

1187 • July 4 – Saladin wins the Battle of Hattin, giving the Moslems enough momentum to gain complete victory. Within three months they take Jerusalem and break the crusaders' hold on the Holy Land.

1191 • Armies of the Third Crusade arrive in the Holy Land and begin a successful siege of Acre.
     • September – Forces led by Richard Lionheart win a major battle at Arsuf, between Acre and the strategic port of Joppa. A few days later they occupy Joppa.
1992 • September 2 – Unable to take Jerusalem, Richard accepts a treaty with Saladin. The Christians retain the coast. The Moslems keep Jerusalem but guarantee all pilgrims free access.
     • October – Richard returns to England.
1193 • Saladin dies.
1198 • Innocent III becomes pope, serves until 1216.
1199 • Richard Lionheart dies of a wound suffered in a minor battle.

THIRTEENTH CENTURY – The Templars reach the height of their power, while Europe tires of endless military campaigns. The Seventh Crusade is ineffective and is the last major attempt to conquer the Holy Land.

1204 • Constantinople is sacked. The shroud of Jesus disappears and does not resurface for more than a century.
1229 • Frederick II of Germany negotiates a treaty returning Jerusalem and other cities to the Christians. The treaty requires the return of prisoners, free access to Jerusalem and a peace to last ten years. The Dome of the Rock and former Templar headquarters remain in Moslem hands.
1243 • The Moslems capture Jerusalem.
1248 • The Templars take the lead in financing the unsuccessful Seventh Crusade, lead by France's Louis IX.
1256 • An Englishman, Thomas Berard, is elected Grand Master of the Templars, holds the office until his death in 1273.
1260 • Following a decade of political intrigue, Baybars kills his last remaining rival and assumes the Egyptian throne.
1272 • Edward I becomes king of England, chooses York as his capital, dies 1307.
1277 • After a successful twelve year campaign against the Christians, Baybars dies.
1289 • Following a long series of setbacks, the crusaders lose Tripoli.
1291 • April 6 – The siege of Acre begins.
     • May 18 – The Moslems take Acre. The Templars fall back to their castle near the city.
     • May 28 – The Templars' castle falls and they withdraw to Cyprus. According to legend, Grand Master Theobald Gaudin personally saves the Templar treasure and takes it to Cyprus.
1293 • Jacques de Molay is elected Grand Master of the Templars. He travels through Europe to promote the Order and a new crusade.

FOURTEENTH CENTURY – With the crusades at an end, the Templars are seen as a threat in western Europe. They are suppressed but, according to legend, continue to exist as an organization. The Black Plague makes skilled labor a more precious commodity.

1305 • Bertrand de Got, archbishop of Bordeaux, becomes Pope Clement V.

1306 • June – Pope Clement summons the Grand Masters of the Hospitallers and Templars to Poitiers to discuss a union of the two orders and a proposed crusade to be led by Philip IV of France.
   • Esquin de Floyran denounces the Templars.

1307 • August – Philip convinces Clement to order an inquiry into the Templars' affairs. Guillaume de Nogaret, the king's minister, heads the investigation.
   • October 13 – In a coordinated series of raids, five thousand Templars are arrested in France. They are tortured, and several confess.
   • October 14 – Nogaret meets with theologians from the University of Paris to explain the case against the Templars.
   • October 26 – Nogaret shows confessions to the University theologians. They approve his actions but insist that only Church officials can sentence the Templars.
   • November 17 – Clement agrees to let the inquisition continue.
   • November 22 – Clement issues a Bull, *Pastoralis Praeeminentiae*, ordering the arrest of Templars in all Christian lands.
   • December – Clement pressures Edward II into arresting and torturing Templars resident in England.
   • De Molay and others recant their confessions.

1308 • May – In France, the Estates-General pass a resolution condemning the Templars.
   • May 29 – Philip meets Clement at a Consistory held at Poitiers. Philip argues that the Templars have adequately confessed their guilt and defends himself against charges that he is persecuting them for his own profit.
   • June 14 – Clement agrees to hear personally the cases against seventy Templars.
   • June 27 – Carefully selected prisoners are delivered to the Church for examination. All make partial confessions, repent and are reconciled with the Church.
   • August 12 – Clement issues a Bull, *Faciens Misericordiam*, specifying charges against the Order and calling on the princes of all countries to examine Templars in their jurisdictions.

1309 • November 12 – A Papal Commission is convened to hear the Templars' defense. The Commission hears hundreds of Templars, including the Grand Master, who renounces his confession and defends the Order.

1310 • May 11 – Philip becomes impatient and orders many Templars burned as relapsed heretics. The Commission is so shocked that it adjourns.

• November – The Commission tries unsuccessfully to re-convene.

• December 17 – the Commission re-convenes but lacks the resolve to defy Philip.

1311 • May 26 – The Commission advises Clement that it can do no more.

1311 • October 16 – The Commission sends its final report to Clement, who forwards it to the Council of Vienne with his recommendation to condemn the Templars.

1312 • March 22 – Clement issues a Bull, *Vox in Excelsis*, ordering the permanent suppression of the Order. Their property is confiscated and given to the Hospitallers.

1314 • March 18 – Philip orders the Templars' Grand Master and other leaders escorted to Notre Dame for a public confession. Instead, De Molay and De Charney renounce their confessions and proclaimed the Order's innocence.

• March 19 – De Molay and De Charney are burned at the stake.

• April 20 – Pope Clement dies.

• June 24 – At the battle of Bannockburn, Scots led by Robert Bruce defeat the English forces of Edward II.

• November 29 – King Philip dies.

1349 • The Black Plague sweeps through Europe and England.

1352 • John of Thoresby becomes archbishop of York. He vaults the minster and begins rebuilding the choir.

1380 • Work on the central tower of York minster begins, continues until 1400.

1388 • Richard II calls for all guilds in England to submit copies of their charters and other archival documents.

ca. 1390• The *Regius Poem*, possibly a copy of an earlier document, is written.

1392 • Richard II, although not using York as his capital, holds a session of the Court of the King's Bench there.

FIFTEENTH CENTURY – The middle ages draw to a close and the Renaissance begins. The Northumbrian dialect, "Inglis," begins to diverge into English and Lowland Scots. The Shroud reappears.

1407 – The central tower of York minster collapses.

1453 – Marguerite de Charny, having no heirs to inherit her sacred relic, sells the Shroud to the House of Savoy. They first keep it in France but later move it to the Italian town of Turin.

1472 • Repairs on the central tower of York minster are finished, effectively completing the building's construction.

SIXTEENTH CENTURY – The building of Gothic cathedrals declines and the demand for skilled stone masons wanes. Masonic lodges begin granting honorary membership to "gentlemen" not related to the building trades. The Protestant Reformation makes it acceptable to question Church dogma.

1517 • The Protestant Reformation begins when Martin Luther protests the sale on indulgences.

1561 • Francis Bacon is born, dies 1626.

1564 • William Shakespeare is born, dies 1616.
     • Galileo Galilei is born, dies 1642.

1596 • Rene' Descartes is born, dies 1650.

SEVENTEENTH CENTURY – Gentlemen Masons appear in increasing numbers. The modern Masonic ritual is written. The concept of the divine right of kings is rejected, and modern science begins its ascendancy.

1600 • June 8 – John Boswell, Laird of Auchinleck, attends a masonic lodge in Edinburgh. He is the first documented "gentleman Mason."

1632 • Christopher Wren is born, dies 1723.

1642 • Isaac Newton is born, dies 1727.
     • The earliest surviving records of the Freemasons' lodge at Kilwinning are written. Other documents attest to its operating as early as 1598.

1696 • The *Edinburgh Register House Manuscript*, a handwritten catechism, describes the early Masonic initiation and penalty.

1698 • A pamphlet written by M. Winter appears in London warning "all godly people" against the evils of "Freed Masons."

EIGHTEENTH CENTURY – A new spirit of exploration spurs the evolution of Freemasonry into its modern form. Articles and pamphlets attacking the Craft continue appearing in London.

1700 • The *Chetwode Crawley Manuscript*, an early catechism, specifies death as the penalty for breaking the Masonic oath.

1717 • June 24 – The Grand Lodge of England is founded in London.

1723 • The Reverend Dr. James Anderson submits the first edition of his *Constitutions* to the Grand Lodge of England. It is quickly approved and published.
     • *A Mason's Examination* is published.

1724 • *The Grand Mystery of Free-Masons Discover'd* is published.
     • *The Secret History of the Free-Masons* (the Briscoe pamphlet) is published in London.

1725 • *The Whole Institutions of Free-Masons Opened*, an early catechism, gives a list of "mason words."

1726 • *Free-Masons Accusation and Defence*, an anti-Masonic pamphlet, is published.

ca. 1730• References to the Hiramic legend begin to appear in Masonic documents.

1730 • *The Grand Whimsey* is published.

1736 • Andrew Michael Ramsay delivers an oration claiming that Freemasonry evolved from the crusaders' orders of knighthood. His lecture is believed to be the source of Masonic interest in the Templars and the inspiration for the Templar degrees.

1738 • A revised edition of Anderson's *Constitutions* is published.

1774 • August 7 – William Morgan is born in Culpeper County, Virginia.

NINETEENTH CENTURY – Fire strikes the York minster in 1829 and 1840. In America, the Morgan Affair proves Freemasonry's worse scandal.

1812 • William Morgan sees military action at the Battle of New Orleans, serving as a captain in General Jackson's army.

1819 • October – Morgan marries Lucinda Pendleton.

1821 • The Morgan family moves to Toronto.

1823 • After his business is destroyed by fire, Morgan moves his family to Rochester, New York.

ca. 1824• Morgan and his family arrive in Batavia, New York.

1825 • Morgan's second daughter is born.

• February 15 – Morgan petitions to receive the Royal Arch degree from Western Star Chapter No. 33, which meets in the nearby town of Le Roy.

• May 31 – Morgan receives the Royal Arch degree.

1826 • March 13 – Morgan contracts with David Miller, a local newspaper man, to publish his expose'.

• August – Morgan and Miller recruit John Davids and Russell Dyer to finance their project. Morgan's partners post a bond of $500,000 to guarantee his share of the profits.

• July and August – Morgan delivers the manuscript of his expose' in two installments.

• August 14 – Morgan copyrights his manuscript.

• August and September – The Morgan affair is discussed in local newspapers. A notice warns members of the community to be on guard against him. Reportedly, local Masons try to buy the manuscript to prevent its publication.

• August and September – Miller's print shop catches fire at least once, possibly twice.

• September 11 – Constable Holloway Hayward, accompanied by a posse of Freemasons, arrests Morgan on a minor charge and escorts him to the nearby town of Canandaigua.

• September 11 – Morgan is arraigned before a Justice of the Peace, who drops the charge for lack of evidence. Nicholas Chesebro,

master of the local Masonic lodge, presses additional charges. Morgan is jailed.
- September 11 – Chesebro and two other Masons remove Morgan from the jail and drive him away in a waiting coach.
- September 19 – The Masons allegedly kill Morgan.
- October 4 – Miller distributes a circular to publicize Morgan's disappearance and possible murder. Governor Clinton of New York issues a proclamation calling on all citizens to help resolve the matter.
- October 26 – Governor Clinton offers rewards totaling five hundred dollars for information on the whereabouts of Morgan and his abductors.
- Criminal investigations are launched to discover Morgan's fate.
- December – Morgan's expose' of Freemasonry is published.

1827
- January – Circuit judge Enos Throop tries Chesebro and three others for abducting Morgan. Most plead guilty. All are convicted and receive jail sentences.
- March 19 – Governor Clinton raises the rewards for information on Morgan's fate to three thousand dollars.
- October 7 – A body washes ashore at Lake Ontario. It is first identified as William Morgan, later as Timothy Munroe.
- The ship *Constance* runs aground near Cuba. Survivors include a William Morgan, possibly *the* William Morgan.

1828
- Rev. David Bernard and David Miller are among forty-one former Masons who organize the Anti-Masonic Society. Thurlow Weed quickly lends his support and helps move the Society toward political action.
- July 4 – A Convention of Seceding Masons, meeting at Le Roy, New York, drafts a *Declaration of Independence from Freemasonry*.

1830
- Lucinda Morgan re-marries, dies 1856 at her daughter's home.

1831
- The "Morgan" trials finally end after fifty-four indictments and ten convictions.

1832
- The Anti-Masonic Party unsuccessfully runs a candidate for the United States presidency, its most ambitious political effort.

ca. 1840
- The anti-Masonic political movement loses momentum and fades away.

1860
- According to Thurlow Weed, John Whitney confesses that he participated in Morgan's murder.

1882
- A monument to the memory of William Morgan is erected in Batavia, New York.

TWENTIETH CENTURY – Freemasonry continues to receive criticism for its cult of secrecy and suspected immorality.

1987
- The Grand Lodge of England rewrites the Masonic ritual to describe the penalties as nothing more than "traditional" and symbolic elements.

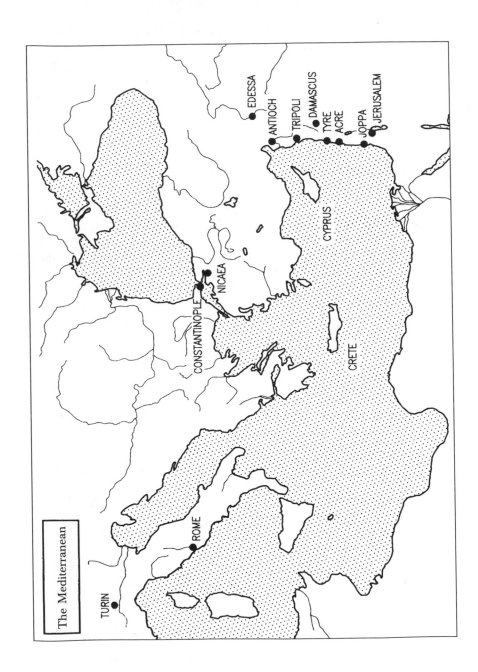

The Mediterranean

TURIN

ROME

CONSTANTINOPLE

NICAEA

CRETE

CYPRUS

EDESSA

ANTIOCH

TRIPOLI

DAMASCUS

TYRE

ACRE

JOPPA

JERUSALEM

The Controversy

In the long history of "the Craft," as Freemasonry is often called, nothing has caused more controversy and commotion than its rigid commitment to secrecy. This one thing has generated rumors so fanciful that they have become myths. It has produced suspicion and satire, mistrust and ridicule. And to this day it supports a mystique that has both helped and hurt the Masons in ways even they can only guess.

Of course, no one can deny that a little mystique helps an organization attract new members. For most Masons, curiosity was part of their reason for seeking membership in the first place. And once they joined, being privy to secrets helped strengthen the famous "fraternal bond" – the sense of fellowship that grows out of the secret handshake and whispered password. This bond is indeed a strong glue. It holds people together with their pride of being in the inner circle and a feeling of responsibility for protecting the group, a duty that is gladly assumed by those who have been granted the privilege of membership.

Unfortunately, this mystique is not entirely benign. While the members enjoy their fellowship, the public is left to imagine what goes on behind the closed doors of the lodge. Imagination is a powerful tool, and through it the very features that make Freemasonry attractive to its members – and to those who hope some day to be admitted to the inner circle – also give rise to a great variety of fantastic ideas.

Some who view Freemasonry from the outside see it as a sinister clique. In their minds, the lodge is a place where tonight's clandestine whispers become tomorrow's government policy and where men gain power by knowing the secret word, not by winning elections.

This view is not hard to understand. The mere fact that a thing is hidden spurs curiosity. And an organization that actually flaunts its secrecy will certainly conjure up images of conspiracy.

Anyone who doubts that the Masons flaunt their secrecy need go no farther than the popular press. Newspapers and magazines carry the occasional photograph of Freemasons posing in their embroidered aprons and white gloves. Chains of office hang heavily on their chests, and some wear funny hats. But the captions never explain the trappings. They only tease the reader, who is left to speculate about the meaning of these peculiar garments and the strange emblems that decorate them.

This may *seem* trivial. No real harm is done if the Masons make fleeting displays of their exotic regalia then go behind closed doors to conduct their business. But when we examine the phenomenon, we will begin to glimpse the real nature of Masonic secrecy. How the Craft perceives its relationship to the general public is at the heart of the issue, and the strange emblems they use in their rituals are enticing clues to the events that launched their commitment to secrecy in the first place.

The style of Masonic uniforms has obviously been handed down from earlier times. Tradition claims that the apron and gloves are descendants of those used by medieval stone masons, who needed leather garments to protect their clothes and hands.

Curiously, medieval illustrations do not show stone workers clothed in this way. The square, compasses and other tools were supposedly used to measure stones and architectural plans. And such implements as the trowel and mallet helped shape and assemble the masonry. But again history does not place all of these tools in the hands of the craftsmen from whom the modern Masons say they evolved.

In addition, the claim that *stone mason* became *Freemason* doesn't account for the chains of office and other emblems of which the modern Craft is so fond. Nor does it explain how the everyday gear of laborers came to be transformed into elaborate uniforms of fine leather, silk and gold braid. The pomp of today's Masonic regalia and ceremonies is more characteristic of the Renaissance than the Middle Ages. They are more the stuff of government processions and military ceremonies than of the old craft guilds.

And don't ask the Masons for an explanation. Most of them have only a vague notion of why their organization adopted such an odd collection of antiques. In fact, most know very little about the history of their fraternity. They accept its emblems as symbols of the moral values they are expected to uphold. But precisely when and how these things came to be associated with the fraternity is a mystery to them.

Moreover, the members of the Craft pay little attention to the quaint appearance of their regalia. During their initiation, they receive an explanation of the meaning of each symbol. In that setting, surrounded by artifacts of the distant past, they are given to understand that the uniforms and tools have not been modernized because of the Masons' love of tradition. Undeniably there is an air of nostalgia in the fraternity. Something about history is very dear to it. But the reason for this longing for the past is never explained to the new member. Like the origins of the emblems, it is merely taken at face value.

Since the new member leaves his initiation believing that he understands the the Craft's symbols and the traditions to which they refer, he doesn't think to question them. And while he quickly becomes comfortable with the regalia, he may just as quickly lose sight of the fact that the public sees all of this differently.

Even the most casual observer is convinced that Masonic emblems have some esoteric meaning, that they are part of some hidden agenda. But he doesn't know what that is. As a result, the emblems become a focal point for the non-member's belief that Masons are privy to knowledge – and perhaps clandestine dealings – to which the rest of the world has no access.

This kind of perception is bound to manifest itself in tangible ways. And it has. Over the years, criticism of Freemasonry has become something of a cottage industry. Dedicated critics travel far and wide, often at their own expense, to deliver anti-Masonic messages. They appear on television. They write letters to editors, and articles and books, all directed to an audience which often seems fascinated by the lurid accounts that are the stock in trade of the anti-Mason. The fruit of their efforts, of course, has been to make Masonic secrecy a houschold word. Even a passing reference to the secret Masonic handshake or password is recognized immediately by most people.

What do the Masons think of all this commotion? As we might expect, it hasn't gone unnoticed inside the lodge. In fact, they devote a considerable amount of energy to the subject. It would surprise most non-Masons to know how often these matters are discussed by individual Masons – and how sensitive they are to criticism of their order.

But this is an internal debate. They don't publicize their concern. Only the few who attend meetings or follow the discussions published in Masonic magazines are aware that the Craft pays any attention at all to public opinion. The non-Mason, hearing no reply, mistakes silence for indifference, while a real and conscientious debate is going on behind closed doors.

On one side is the argument that secrecy accomplishes nothing of importance. Its proponents question the need for keeping anything confidential and urge the organization to open itself to public view. They believe that the problem of Masonic secrecy can be cured by doing away with it. Some even propose that the public be invited to attend all Masonic meetings, while others want the rituals to be published and made available to anyone who wants to see them. (Surprisingly, these are not new suggestions. Many of the exposés that have been published over the years carry introductions stating that they were written by Masons who wanted to shed light on their fraternity.)

But this is only one side of the debate. Other Masons argue that secrecy is an integral part of the Craft. They believe that doing away with it would only hurt the lodge. The secrets, so *they* say, are symbolic elements intimately involved with Masonic teachings. Changing them would alter the basic nature of the organization.

These men value the traditions represented by an elaborate system of ceremonies. Secure in their belief that their fraternity harbors nothing sinister, they see no point in fixing what they insist isn't broken. Any problems the Craft has, according to this view, can not be solved by making a few changes here and there. Instead, those who take this side of the argument are content to leave the mystique in place, no matter how much criticism and misunderstanding it causes.

Part of the mystique, of course, has no substance at all. It arises from confusing a lack of information with an overt attempt to conceal it. Many people know so little about Freemasonry simply because they don't know where to look.

The man in the street will repeat tales of Masonic secrecy as he walks past a public library whose shelves hold several books about the Masons. He will tell of this strange organization he has heard about – whose members never write anything down – while he's standing outside a book shop whose bins offer a dozen old books on the subject. Completely unaware of how much has been written about the subject and how easy it is to find, he continues to believe that the fraternity's secrets are impenetrable.

In fact, the bibliography of Freemasonry is fairly extensive. It has been estimated that the whole of Masonic literature – including books, magazine articles and pamphlets – amounts to more than 60,000 items. This includes the many books written by the order's critics, many more by its defenders, and a slate of official and semi-official magazines, all of which are available to anyone who knows where to look for them.

The literature even includes the Masonic ritual, that enigmatic thing that many people believe is handed down orally and never committed to writing. Most editions of it are official publications that are offered only to members of the lodge. But from time to time the ritual is published independently. This is usually done by a specialty publisher who sells his books by mail. And sometimes copies crop up in bookstores, where any interested party can buy them without even showing proof of membership. (In England, the rituals are widely published and are not very difficult to find. In the United States, they are somewhat harder to locate but are still available.)

It is true that Masonic publications are rarely seen in stores. But this is not the result of a conspiracy of silence. It is simply because there is only a small market for them. Mainstream publishers don't like Masonic titles because they are less profitable than other books. The occasional exposé or tale of alleged conspiracy may bring large sales due to its appeal to prurient curiosity. But more prudent accounts, either favorable or unfavorable, based on facts that are carefully assembled and judiciously presented – these books are of limited interest to the general public.

As a result, new books about Freemasonry are usually available only from specialty stores and catalogs or on special order from major book sellers. Used books are easier to find, but they are invariably tucked away on a bottom shelf in the back of some quaint shop. Members of the public – and most Masons for that matter – either don't know that such things exist or have little notion of where to find them. If they did, the Masonic mystique simply wouldn't exist. It would quickly fall victim to the light of day.

In short, public suspicion of Freemasonry owes more to a lack of publicity than to a deliberate conspiracy. It would seem, then, that a brief look at any of the several general histories of the organization would dispel most of the misunderstanding that has built up around it. But there lies another problem. A book or two about the Craft *would* clear up a lot of misunderstanding, but only if the reader could understand and believe what they say.

Even if casual observers accept that there is no conspiracy of silence, their first attempts at reading about the Craft are likely to meet with confusing and enigmatic descriptions that are scarcely credible. Masonic literature, it turns out, can not be read; it must be interpreted. The field is so specialized that readers will likely be led astray if they don't have the proper frame of reference to judge what they're reading. And a frame of reference comes only with experience.

This may seem trivial, but it goes to the heart of the problem. A quick survey of books about Freemasonry reveals quite different and contradictory descriptions of the fraternity. One book describes Freemasonry as a noble organization that promotes the highest moral values. Another depicts it as a system of demon worship, riddled with drunkenness and debauchery. Even here, rumors and suspicions intrude. Claims that are otherwise heard only in passing are codified in Masonic books, thus taking on the aura of authority that is associated with the written word.

Still, the written word is a tricky thing. Obviously not everything that has been written about the Craft can be true. Some of it *must* be inaccurate. And just as obviously, some of it must be accurate. But anyone who does not already know at least part of the truth will be hard pressed to tell which is which.

We can now see why it is so hard to know what to believe about the lodge. Seekers after Masonic truth find themselves in the midst of what should be more than an adequate amount of information. Yet they find that they are unable to get at the facts. Innocent misunderstanding, malicious slander and unvarnished truth all blend together to form a maze that is difficult to struggle through. It is hard for novices to read far enough to get their bearings, and reading the wrong book will lead them astray.

Remarkably, this confusion does not stop at the door of the lodge room. In a strange way, members are often worse off than non-members. True, the members have the advantage of seeing the organization from the inside.

They know what does and does not take place in the lodge room itself. And they can judge whether the criticism they hear conflicts with their own experience.

But on the subject of secrecy, the Mason's experience gives him little advantage. During the initiation he is admonished to keep and protect the secrets of the Craft. Then he's told of extremely strict penalties for any failure to honor this obligation. If he reveals the secrets, he will be killed, his body horribly mutilated and buried where it will never be found. He is given to understand that these penalties are only symbolic. The worst punishment he will ever face, or so he is told, is to be expelled from membership. But he is still left with the feeling that the secrets are real and that they must be protected at any cost.

Amazingly, after all of this, the initiate is not told exactly what the secrets are or why they are so important. Nor is he told at a later date. If he is to make any sense of the matter, he must seek its meaning for himself.

Most members, even those who are very active in matters Masonic, take the lessons of their initiation at face value. Freemasonry has secrets. They understand that much. They have been admonished to keep them. That's clear, too. But they are not led to the next step – to question whether there is more to the secrets and penalties than appears on the surface.

Certainly these curious items were included in the initiation deliberately and for a specific reason. They must have some meaning. Unfortunately, few Masons take the time and trouble to look for that meaning. As a result they, like the uninitiated, see only what lies on the surface.

What, then, are we to make of an organization that has existed for centuries but is so little understood by member and non-member alike? And is there a proper role for the secrecy that has caused so many problems?

To make sense of all this, we must look at the Masonic ritual. That is where both defenders and critics believe Masonic secrecy resides.

The Ritual

T he place is Edinburgh. The time is the seventeenth century. The exact date is unimportant, because the events that will occur this night have been repeated many times before and will be many times again. A young man is escorted into a room where several others wait for his arrival. They try to scare him with threatening gestures then force him to kneel. While he is on his knees, he is told that if he *ever* betrays the secrets he is about to learn he will surely be murdered by these very men who are now bringing him into their fellowship.

To be sure he understands the gravity of that threat, they thrust a Bible into his hands and make him swear by God and Saint John that he will always keep any secrets he learns while in their company. And to drive the point home, he is even forced to describe – and agree to – his own punishment. If he betrays them, they will cut out his tongue and bury his body in an unmarked grave. Then, while he is still numb with fear, they give him the password that separates the members of this select group from the rest of society.

This young man, barely twenty-one years old and probably trembling from the experience he has just had, is now a Freemason. Nearly three centuries later young men are still going through that initiation. The procedures have changed greatly over the years. Even the password is not the same as it was then. But every Mason must submit to the initiation through which the other members of his lodge first entered the Craft, and in that way he becomes part of a tradition that has existed for uncounted centuries.

The thing that holds this tradition together is the ritual, a document that spells out the procedures used to open and close meetings and to initiate all new members. It is the ritual that contains the Craft's infamous oaths of secrecy and the even more controversial penalties. These are the first things the critic seizes upon, just as they are the source of the Mason's commitment to secrecy. It is the ritual – and the ritual alone – that makes the new Mason believe he must never reveal any of the secrets he may learn as a member of the Craft. Clearly, then, we must begin our investigation of Masonic secrecy by focusing on this peculiar document and the way it influences the attitudes of the world's Freemasons.

The ritual is wrongly called the Bible of Freemasonry. No doubt this perception is based on the notion that the fraternity contains some creed to which all its members must subscribe. If such a dogma existed, it would certainly be contained in codified form, and members would certainly be required to swear loyalty to it.

But in fact, the beliefs demanded of a Freemason are remarkably few. The new member is only required to assert that he believes in a Supreme Being. Everything else, including how he perceives that Being, is left to his own conscience. The Jewish Mason may believe in the God of Israel, the Christian in the Trinity and the Moslem in Allah.

Some of the "higher" degrees *are* explicitly Christian, and the candidate for them must profess a belief in the Christian faith. But even then he is required to make only the most general statement of what he believes. The specific doctrines to which he subscribes are no concern of his lodge.

Beyond these few points, the Mason is not required to accept any creed or dogma. He is, in fact, specifically admonished to interpret the Craft's symbols in the light of his own beliefs.

Obviously, then, the ritual falls short of being a Bible. It is not regarded by the organization's members as a sacred book. It is not worshiped. Nor is it *treated* by the Masons as if it were a sacred book.

One of the main characteristics of a holy writ is that it is handed down unchanged from each generation to the next. Anything that contains the word of God, or basic and eternal truths of any sort, is not to be tampered with. Historically, those to whom a sacred book has been entrusted see themselves as custodians, not as editors. Biblical scholars can attest to the errors that crept into the sacred writings and were left uncorrected for centuries because later scribes were afraid to correct what appeared to be errors. Even in places where the document they were given to copy seemed to make no sense, the scribes copied the text exactly as they found it.

The Masonic ritual, on the other hand, has been altered repeatedly over the years. Efforts are made to preserve the spirit of the ritual, but this is done more to maintain the organization's traditions than to preserve a sacred truth for future generations. Minor changes in wording are commonplace and can be authorized by any of Freemasonry's many ruling bodies. Consequently, the ritual now exists simultaneously in a wide variety of versions.

In the United States, each of the fifty-one Grand Lodges (including one in the District of Columbia) has its own version of the ritual. All are basically the same, but each Grand Lodge can – and occasionally does – change portions of the text that is used within its jurisdiction.

In the British Isles, several more versions are in use. Local lodges may choose the version they prefer. As in the States, the workings of the various rituals differ, and the custodians of each version may make changes as they seem appropriate.

The same is true of other jurisdictions throughout the world. Some use the official versions of their "mother" jurisdictions (British colonies, for example, use one of the British rituals), while others have developed their own. The farther from his home lodge a Freemason travels, the more variation he will find in his fraternity's most basic document.

Still, though it is not in any sense sacred, the Masonic ritual does preserve remnants of something that has existed for more than three centuries. A careful examination of its pages reveals things that apparently make no sense *unless* we assume that their purpose is to preserve a message hidden in the ritual by the early Masons. If the secret password and handshake are more than an initiation stunt, it is those curious remnants in the ritual that will tell the story, and that is where we will find the basics of Masonic secrecy.

The ritual itself is a small volume. It is generally published in pocket-sized editions that are barely half an inch thick. Their covers are plain, often blue and often decorated only with the famous "square and compasses" emblem.

This book does not contain the procedural rules for conducting the lodge's day to day business. For Grand Lodges, those rules are in volumes variously called a *Book of Constitutions* or *Code*, and local lodges have their by-laws. The ritual merely specifies the order of events in the so called "degrees" of the initiation. It contains the words spoken by the various participants and stage directions to guide them in their actions. It also includes lectures and catechisms that reinforce and explain the Masonic teachings.

At the beginning of the ceremony, the initiate is brought into the meeting room blindfolded. Since he can not see what is going on around him, he is escorted by a lodge officer called the Junior Deacon.

The initiate is led through a carefully rehearsed series of steps. Although the precise content of the ceremony varies from place to place, each lodge adheres strictly to its own ritual. Everything that is said and done during the ceremony goes according to an established formula. The members of the initiating team either memorize their parts or read them verbatim from a copy of the ritual. And if anyone falters in reciting his part, he is prompted by another member.

The first thing the initiate experiences is a warning against revealing "the secrets of Masonry." This occurs while he is still blindfolded. And since he doesn't know what's going to happen next, the warning is quite impressive.

He is then led to various parts of the lodge room, where he is asked a series of questions to determine if he is qualified for membership. This is not an informal conversation. It is all part of the strictly observed procedure, with both questions and answers rigidly specified. The Junior Deacon either answers for the initiate or prompts him when he is expected to answer for himself. These questions are really just a formality, since his application for membership has already been approved, but they are always recited without variation.

The initiate is then given the obligation, an oath taken with his hand on the Bible or other sacred text of his choice. The oath is read to him, and he repeats it word for word. As soon as he has finished reciting the obligation, the initiate's blindfold is removed. He is presented a white lambskin apron and is shown passwords and signs of recognition. Then various symbols are explained to him.

In the early stages of the initiation, most of the symbols have to do with "operative" masonry. Operative is a term used to denote the masons who actually worked in stone, as opposed to the "speculative" Masons, who are members of the modern fraternal organization. To avoid confusion, key words relating to the operative craft are traditionally written in lower case, while those relating to the modern fraternity tend to be capitalized.

Many of the "operative" elements of the initiation have to do with Gothic architecture – the building style of the medieval cathedrals – and with the tools used by the stone masons who erected those cathedrals. But along with these elements are others that are taken from the Bible, along with references to the seven Arts and Sciences, especially mathematics and astronomy. As the initiation progresses, these non-architectural elements seem to take on more and more importance, as if the references to architecture were only an introduction to the lodge's *real* symbols. It's a peculiar mix, and the initiate is given no explanation for the combination of such apparently unrelated items in a single ritual.

All of this is new to him, but he is given ample time to adjust to it. His initiation into Craft Masonry consists of three "degrees," which are conferred at three different meetings. After finishing each degree, and before proceeding to the next, the new member is expected to learn a catechism that summarizes parts of his initiation. Only when he has completed that task can he proceed to the next level of membership.

Apparently the degree system was created by the speculative Masons. The operatives used a single initiation ceremony. But when the modern fraternity was hammered into shape, its leaders expanded the procedure, partly to stress the symbolism of the number three, and partly to make room for the moral teachings they wanted to include and to give new members time to absorb them.

The ceremonies for the three modern degrees all follow the same pattern. But at each level, different symbols and lessons are presented. At first a foundation is laid. Then new courses are added. And at the conclusion of the third degree, the initiate is considered a full fledged Mason.

This is very much the stuff of fraternity initiations. It uses symbols to communicate the virtues promoted by the organization. And the symbols are fitted into a framework designed to make them more impressive and palatable. But there is a curious scene at the end of this ritual. Scholars believe that it was not part of the original masonic initiation but was added later, because it seems unrelated to what has gone before, as if it were included as an afterthought.

The almost casual addition of one more piece to the ritual is peculiar, because this "afterthought" goes to the very heart of Masonic secrecy. Although the new Mason has already sworn three oaths of secrecy by the time he is shown the last part of the ritual, he is given the impression that *this* is the culmination of his initiation, that it is what the entire process has all been about. And if he goes on to study the history and philosophy of the organization, he realizes how intimately this afterthought is connected to the Craft's secrets.

This final part of the ritual is a story that tells of secrets dating to the earliest operative period. It goes back to a time before the Gothic cathedrals were even imagined, to a time when men labored with tools of wood and bronze to erect the magnificent temples of antiquity. The masonic secrets of that era, the story claims, were known only by the most skilled masons and enabled the workers who knew them to earn the wages of a master mason.

It was in those days that King Solomon decided to build a temple in Jerusalem. To direct the work he enlisted the aid of a man named Hiram, a skilled worker in bronze. Hiram was appointed the chief architect of the temple, and he oversaw its construction with skill and cunning.

As the craft's Grand Master, this Hiram was the only one who knew the master mason's secret, sometimes called the Master's Word. But it was not an ordinary word. Knowing it was a necessary part of attaining the high rank of master mason.

Naturally, the workers who were building the temple wanted to know the word so that they, too, could receive higher wages. The Grand Master was a man of great wisdom and was sensitive to their wishes. So he promised to communicate the secret to those who were found worthy when the work was completed.

It was a fair deal, and all the masons labored hard to complete their work and receive their reward. But shortly before the temple was finished, a group of workers became impatient and entered into a conspiracy to compel the Grand Master to give them the word before the appointed time.

Unfortunately for them, the conspiracy went wrong. Hiram refused to reveal the word, and in desperation the conspirators murdered him. Although they quickly fled the scene of their crime, they were later caught and punished, but when Hiram died, he carried the Master's Word with him to the grave, and since that time no one has known the real secret of a master mason. It has, according to the story, been replaced by a substitute word that is to be used until such time as the original might be rediscovered.

Clearly this is more than a piece of unvarnished history. Even a superficial look is enough to convince the observer that this last part of the Masonic initiation is loaded with religious and moral symbolism. But neither is it merely a parable. It has the tone of a cautionary tale, a story designed to convey a warning.

Just as clearly, the story also has something to do with the essence of Masonic secrecy, whatever that is. Although it may serve other purposes as well, at its very core this is a story about the importance of keeping a secret. It is the story of a man who voluntarily laid down his life to protect a small bit of knowledge from those who were not worthy to receive it.

But what is the secret? Why is it so important? And what are we to make of an organization that has taken upon itself the responsibility of protecting not a secret but the *story* of protecting a secret?

The first step in unraveling this puzzle is to look at the story in its original version. The original is in the Old Testament, which is obviously where the Freemasons found it. The Biblical account of the building of King Solomon's Temple does mention a craftsman named Hiram, and he does correspond roughly with the Hiram of the Masonic ritual. Undoubtedly, the early speculative Masons extracted this character and used him to communicate something they considered important.

Where their version of the story differs from the original, that difference will give us a clue to the meaning the story held for them. So if we compare the "original" and "Masonic" versions of the story, perhaps we can discover why they considered it important enough to add to a ritual that already contained the threat of a hideous punishment for anyone who revealed the Craft's secrets.

As we have seen, the Masonic version of Hiram's story is heavily laced with symbolism. The original is much simpler. The little information we have about the historic Hiram comes from the books of *First Kings* and *Second Chronicles*. There we read that Solomon was determined to build the temple his father David had dreamed of. David had been unable to build it himself because he was constantly preoccupied with struggles against his enemies. But Solomon administered Israel during a reign of peace and prosperity. He had time and money to spare, so he was able to realize his father's dream of building a magnificent House of God.

Solomon turned for assistance to Hiram, the king of the Phoenician city of Tyre. Earlier, Hiram had supplied timber and workmen for the construction of King David's palace. Now he would help David's son build a temple. In return for a yearly payment of wheat and oil, he supplied timber and skilled carpenters and stone masons.

But King Hiram was not to be the central figure of the third degree. The *Masonic* Hiram was a different character altogether. He was a metal worker whose mother was a widow from the tribe of Naphtali and whose father had been a Phoenician from Tyre. According to the seventh chapter of the book of *First Kings,* he was filled with wisdom, and understanding, and cunning to work all works in brass. And he came to King Solomon and wrought all his work. For he cast two pillars of brass, of eighteen cubits high apiece . . . and he made two chapiters of molten brass, to set upon the tops of the pillars. . . ."

The rest of the chapter describes how Hiram decorated the pillars, which were set on the porch of the temple, and the brass lavers, basins and shovels he made for the temple.

The *Second Book of Chronicles* repeats the story, describing Hiram more effusively as,

skillful to work in gold, and in silver, in brass, in iron, in stone, and in timber, in purple, in blue, and in fine linen, and in crimson: also to grave any manner of graving, and to find out any device which shall be put to him. . . ."

This is a description of a skilled craftsman and almost certainly an overseer. But there is no indication that Hiram was the chief architect of the project. Nor is he identified as a Grand Master, either of a group of workers or of a secret society. Further, the Bible says nothing about Hiram's death shortly before the completion of the temple. It mentions no conspiracy to gain knowledge of a secret, nor does it say that there ever was a secret to be gained.

A comparison of the two versions makes it clear that the Freemasons greatly embellished the Biblical story. They expanded an historic character, of whom little is known, into the major character in a pseudo-documentary drama. The historic Hiram *was* an important man. He was brought in from abroad to fabricate several large implements for the most important and sacred building in Jerusalem. But the *story* the Masons tell about him does not come to us from the Bible. It is, quite simply, a different story.

It is not surprising that the writers of the Masonic ritual departed from the bare bones of history in adapting characters and events to their needs. It was never their intention to write history. The purpose of their drama was to help transform outsiders into members of a fraternal organization. In order to perform that function, an initiatory drama must convey moral symbolism (in order to teach the lessons fostered by the organization). It must promote a sense of belonging (to develop a fraternal bond among the members). And it must distinguish the organization from other similar organizations (to show how it is different from other groups the initiate might have joined).

This is a key point and one which is necessary to a proper understanding of the Hiramic story. In adding it to their ritual, the Freemason created a legend. But a legend is not an arbitrary thing. It arises from history. Although the stories told in legends always stray from the facts, they grow out of a particular time and place. It is their function to tie together two times; they convey lessons that are important in the present, while preserving something that was important in the past.

At the very least a legend reveals the moral and cultural values of the setting in which it developed, perhaps centuries before it became formalized. But it may also contain something that lies just below the surface and thus reveals something very intimate about the time in which it was created.

Certainly there is glamour and mystery in all of this. The Masonic ritual conjures up images of ancient history and faraway places. Set as it is in Biblical times, the story of Hiram carries with it the aura of religious authority, and it hints at a secret that is of great value, a secret that was once lost but may someday be found again.

But what does this story have to do with the Masons? Does it point to something real and important in their history? Did they really have a secret that was worth dying to protect? Or is the story of Hiram just an allegory, a nice little drama borrowed from history for its symbolic value? Does this story embody an *original* Masonic secret – handed down from antiquity? Or is it merely a modern innovation designed to have the appearance of something old?

Unfortunately, the ritual is not the place to look for the answers to these questions. It is the nature of a symbol that it does not explain itself. It merely hints at the meaning of something else, and that meaning must be sought elsewhere.

And while the Masonic ritual is admittedly a collection of symbols, it goes a step further. It seems deliberately enigmatic. Students of Masonic arcana know that the story of Hiram was added to an already established ceremony. But the ritual gives no indication of when or why it was added. Nor does it offer any clues to tell us where symbol ends and history begins. To learn that, we must examine the historical context in which the ritual developed.

A Problem with a History

The enigma of the Masonic ritual is not a problem for the casual observer. Although the ceremonies are peculiar and quaint, their real esoteric nature is concealed with great skill. The more unusual parts of the ceremony are designed to seem, at least at first glance, to be nothing more than odd bits of fraternal symbolism. Outsiders see only an initiation they are not supposed to understand because they aren't members. The new member, in turn, accepts the various elements of the initiation without questioning them. He trusts the wisdom of his Masonic ancestors and assumes that he will come to understand the Craft's symbolism at the appropriate time.

But a critical examination of the ritual quickly uncovers a series of curious features. Parts of the ritual are not as easy to understand as they should be. Bits of the ceremony don't quite seem to fit together. And the more closely they are examined, the more questions they suggest.

Perhaps, the reader begins to think, this is part of some master plan. Both the outside observer and the new Mason are given the impression that these ritual elements point the way to something. It is almost as if they are pieces of a large and curious jigsaw puzzle. It just could be that if enough clues are found, and if they are viewed the correct light, something of great importance will be revealed.

Looking at this matter in the context of the mystique of Masonic secrecy, it is easy to believe that the authors of the ritual had just such a thing in mind. The ritual itself speaks of lost and hidden knowledge. It hints at a quest for that knowledge and the promise of finding it at the end of a diligent search. This could be the essence of the great Masonic secret. If it is, the most important question becomes "what is the solution to the puzzle?"

To find out, we must broaden our investigation. Since the ritual by itself will not provide the answers, we must see how the ritual fits into a larger picture. And that will take us back in time.

People, being creatures of habit, tend to see the things around them in the present tense. It's a pleasant enough trait but sometimes makes it difficult for us to look beyond our own horizons.

Since most people know little or nothing about Freemasonry, they lack the historical knowledge to place what they hear about the fraternity in its proper context. Therefore, when they encounter criticism of the Craft – a word here or an anti-Masonic pamphlet there – they may think they are dealing with are purely contemporary remarks about a contemporary organization. In fact, the commotion is as old as the speculative Craft. Perhaps it is older.

The debate over Masonry is a perennial thing. It has been going on so long and is now so entrenched that it has become a ritual in its own right. The anti-Masonic arguments of today are almost identical to those of a century or two ago. They deal with the same issues and are often couched in the same language. Laid side by side, it is hard to tell the difference between a recently written anti-Masonic tract and a reprint of its century-old counterpart.

How far back criticism of the Craft goes can not be determined precisely. Like everything else in Masonic history, it trails off into a blur of incomplete records and missing evidence. Much has been lost and much more was never committed to paper in the first place. But there is reason to believe that the commotion began as the organization evolved into its modern form during the seventeenth and eighteenth centuries.

Today's Masonic ritual dates from the years following the establishment of the Grand Lodge of England in 1717. It was then that the ceremonies were hammered into their present form by the "gentlemen" Masons of the day.

These gentlemen Masons were prominent citizens who had been granted honorary membership in the lodges of the operative masons. When they entered the lodge, they brought new blood and fresh ideas with them. What had been a professional organization now took on the character of a social club. It lost much of its practical, workaday nature, taking on a more cosmopolitan character. And in the process, the straight forward initiation of the old craft evolved to include a large dose of moral symbolism.

Gentlemen Masons began to appear in the seventeenth century. The first documentary evidence of this phenomenon *may* have been penned on June 8, 1600, when one John Boswell, Laird of Auchinleck, attended a masonic lodge in Edinburgh. As a Laird, Boswell would not have been a working stone mason. He might not have been a member of the lodge, either. He may have attended the meeting merely as an invited guest or to conduct business with its members. Still, history credits him as probably being the first gentleman Mason.

Although we have no details of his reason for being there, what we know of Boswell's visit to the lodge does not have the feel of an historic occasion. If he was a member, it is likely that others came before him. Certainly hundreds came later. As the seventeenth century progressed, the lodges admitted honorary members in increasing numbers. And by the end of that century the practice was well established.

In those days, the need for skilled stone masons was on the decline and the lodges that were organized to support the craft had apparently come on hard times. They were still prestigious organizations. Their ranks were filled with skilled craftsmen, and the masonic lodge had assumed an important position in the community. But now that operative masonry was dying, the lodges were desperately struggling to sustain their membership rolls at a time when new operative masons were in short supply.

Fortunately, membership in their ranks was still very desirable. The town's prominent citizens would pay for the privilege of being honorary masons, and that proved to be the craft's salvation.

As things turned out, those honorary members would do much more than just save an obsolescent organization. The evolution of the stone mason's craft into the speculative Craft came during an age of intellectual change. Church dogma and the authority of Scripture were giving way to reason and scientific method. This was the century when Galileo, Descartes and Newton rewrote the rules for acquiring knowledge.

Those great thinkers were not scientists in the modern sense, and their enterprise was not a lofty pursuit confined to the cloistered halls of academe. In their day science was not a profession. It was a hobby, pursued by people who had the money and time to explore the mysteries of nature. Suddenly, science and philosophy were much more available than they had been during the Middle Ages, which had just recently come to an end. And more and more people developed an interest in them.

The gentlemen of the day eagerly embraced the new avenues of exploring and communicating knowledge. For them, speculating about nature and the human mind became a popular pastime, and through them the new freedom to ask questions gained an even wider following.

These enlightened men found something in the lodges of the operative masons that appealed to them. Although history is vague about it, the gentlemen of the Enlightenment obviously saw *something* in masonry that they could use to build a philosophical society, something that lent itself to their new explorations in science and philosophy. They sought membership in steadily growing numbers. And as they gradually became a majority, they changed the organization to suit their own interests.

Energized by new members, the lodge grew and evolved into a social and fraternal organization. But when this transition occurred, other things began to change as well.

It does not appear that the operative masons inspired much criticism. Nor would we believe that they should. Those early craftsmen were skilled professionals who attended to their own affairs. Their code of ethics called for high standards of behavior and cordial relations with the community. It is unlikely that they would incur the hostility of their neighbors. By all accounts they were an honorable group who made a special effort to stay on good terms with the members of the communities in which they worked.

Then all of that changed. For some reason the transition from stone mason to gentleman Mason altered the way the lodge was seen by the world. Freemasonry began to experience both suspicion and ridicule. What had once been a society of skilled craftsmen meeting to attend to the business affairs of their profession became an assembly of men who met in secret for no known reason. That in itself was suspicious. To make things worse, it was understood that these men swore an oath of secrecy. They practiced a peculiar loyalty to their own kind – and to the exclusion of all who were not members of their group. They even devised special gestures so they could recognize their own without betraying their secrets to the public.

It is not surprising that people became suspicious of such an organization, but the intensity of their feelings is curious. In 1698 – nearly two decades before the establishment of the Grand Lodge in London – a pamphlet appeared in that city to warn "all godly people" against the evils of "Freed Masons." The author of the pamphlet, one M. Winter, went so far as to call them the Anti-Christ and a "devellish Sect of Men." He was alarmed because Masons convened in closed meetings and took oaths against outsiders. "For how should Men meet in secret Places and with secret Signs taking Care that none observe them to do the Work of God; are these not the Ways of Evil-doers?"

A few years earlier, these men were honest craftsmen. Now the community was beginning to see them as perverse and sinister.

A recurring feature of this new criticism was the suspicion that the Freemasons were custodians of hidden knowledge. Either they had some worthy information that was denied the general population, or perhaps it was evil knowledge ill suited to the light of day. This, in turn, produced theories about Masonic activities that ranged from demon worship to political manipulation on an international scale.

Reputable men, the critics of the period reasoned, would operate openly. If an organization hid its dealings from the public, there must be a reason. And the reason could only be that those dealings were abhorrent to honorable men and women.

But this was only one view of Freemasonry. While some saw the Craft as an elite group of conspirators, others took an even less flattering view. A pamphlet published in 1726 describes the fraternity's members as,

> the very Scum and Dregs of the Common People, idle, indigent Wretches, the Scandal of humane Society. . . ."

If the Freemasons were not involved in demon worship or political intrigue, the critics claimed, their peculiar activities had to be the frivolous revelries of intemperate men. Such men could have no legitimate secrets.

Although they might profess a long history and privileged knowledge, they were only making a show. The secrets they kept were trivial and their rituals nothing more than tongue-in-cheek parodies.

These contrasting perceptions tell us something of the state of the Craft at that time. The criticism it received came from people who saw it as peculiar, as outside the mainstream of society. But the strikingly different views of the organization suggest that the critics based their judgments on partial and inadequate information. Apparently outside observers were able to glimpse only bits and pieces of Masonic activities, often distorted and culled from second and third hand sources. Lacking an accurate picture of what the Masons were actually up to, the critics found themselves focusing on the superficial and guessing about the things they couldn't see.

The Masons of the day were not unaware of this problem. They knew they were being criticized, but their response is something of an enigma. The record shows that they made little effort to dispel the false statements and rumors that were now being aimed at them. Occasionally pamphlets appeared with the avowed purpose of setting the record straight, but they have the feel of individual efforts, tracts that were published without official sanction and perhaps against the wishes of the fraternity's leadership.

Indeed, the Masons seemed primarily concerned with protecting their meetings from impostors who might learn enough of their secrets to infiltrate a meeting. There is reason to believe that the Masons bought up copies of one exposé to keep it out of the hands of the public. And another exposé was apparently published by the Masons themselves to discredit a pamphlet that had hit too close to home.

As peculiar as this behavior is, it is not the only curiosity we discover when we study the early Masons. Surviving documents indicate that the controversy over the lodge had taken shape by the first few decades of the eighteenth century. We might assume that it ran its course and died out, eventually to be replaced by a new criticism of twentieth century Freemasonry. It didn't happen that way. Those critics of three hundred years ago fired the opening shots of a battle that has gone on continuously from their time to the present. Like other battles, there have been lulls and surges of activity, but the suspicions that were voiced then have never been resolved.

Considering the distant origins of that battle, and the fact that it never stopped, we must wonder why the gentlemen Masons allowed it to continue so long. And if we ask that question, we soon have to ask why they felt a need for secrecy in the first place.

We will not find the answer to either question in the eighteenth century or even in the seventeenth. One of the first "official" documents of the Grand Lodge, a *Book of Constitutions* compiled by Dr. James Anderson, suggests that Masonic secrecy had its roots in something that existed long before the watershed date of 1717.

Anderson's history of the Craft is admittedly fanciful. It tells of things that can't be true. But it also suggests something that may be true – the possibility that Freemasonry's character was shaped eight centuries earlier. If that is true, Masonic secrecy could have been inherited, not invented, by the gentlemen who took over the old operative lodges. In fact, it may have been well established when the fraternity entered the modern period, and the origins of Masonic secrecy may well be the product of a very dark period of the Craft's history.

The Early Days

The history of Freemasonry has not always been told the same way. In the early days of the Grand Lodge era, it was fashionable to claim that the Craft was literally as old as the human race. Adam was its first member. He and King Solomon were Grand Masters, as were Noah and Moses. Their names formed part of a list of Masonic dignitaries that extended through all of antiquity, into the Middle Ages and right up to the modern period.

This was only one of several theories advanced during the eighteenth and early nineteenth centuries by people who might have called themselves "historians" but would scarcely be recognized by that name today. Most of their theories claimed great antiquity for the order and nobility for its founders. They fabricated stories that were glamorous and appealing. Unfortunately, they were scarcely in touch with reality and have since fallen by the wayside. They are now dismissed as fanciful attempts to imbue the Craft with the prestige that is afforded by a long pedigree.

Modern historians take a more practical view. They generally agree that Freemasonry can trace its roots no farther back than the late Middle Ages. This version of the story has been told with more or less accuracy and in more or less detail in the many Masonic histories that have been written since the middle of the nineteenth century. But the true facts of the fraternity's evolution are still hard to separate from the jumble of myth and legend.

No matter. We are not concerned here with a detailed account of Freemasonry's evolution. Our interest is in the particular bits of the fraternity's early history which produced its cult of secrecy. That's a much more manageable task.

We have seen that a small part of the history we're looking for is contained implicitly in the ritual itself. And we have seen that the ritual currently used in the English-speaking world was written during the eighteenth century.

But the gentlemen Masons of that period did not invent their ritual. Instead, they borrowed large portions of it from a ritual that was used in the Middle Ages.

Presumably, the *original* version of the Masonic initiation was created by the same men who crafted the Gothic cathedrals into wondrous expressions of fantasy and imagination. These were not mere stone cutters. They were artists whose work on religious buildings mirrored God's own creation and pointed the way to heaven.

Not surprisingly, the nature of their work influenced the ceremony that initiated new members into their craft. Religion became an integral part of their ritual, as it did in so many aspects of medieval society. The masons saw themselves not only as builders in stone but also as custodians of pious values, and they tried to convey that spirit to each new member of their craft.

Even now – centuries after the last of the old Gothic cathedrals was built – the ritual contains traces of the operative masons' ancient ceremony. But as we have seen, the modern ritual is such a blend of symbol and legend and history that it simply can not give us the answers we need.

For our purposes an even more important source is Anderson's *Constitutions*. This is one of the fraternity's earliest surviving documents. It was commissioned by the newly formed Grand Lodge. And since they gave it their official sanction, we can rely on it to show us a good picture of the Craft at that particular moment in history – the moment when modern Freemasonry was born.

Like many historic events, the start of the modern Craft was a relatively modest affair. There was nothing about it that foreshadowed the massive fraternity which was to grow from such humble beginnings.

Simply put, on June 24, 1717 four London lodges got together and organized a Grand Lodge to oversee their affairs. That was nothing unusual. These lodges had apparently been in existence for some years, meeting quietly and preserving an old tradition but with a difference. By this time, Masonic lodges were no longer purely operative. They had become primarily a social group, and like other such organizations, they met at the local tavern. There, they assembled at regular intervals for an evening of fellowship. They took an upstairs room where they could conduct their business in relative privacy. Food and drink were brought in, and the meeting proper was held during or after the meal. This is very similar to the procedures followed by present day clubs and societies, and it was quite ordinary in eighteenth century England.

By 1717, Masonic lodges had been meeting in this way for some time. They had settled into a routine. Their procedures were fairly uniform, but the lodges themselves seem to have been independent.

Surviving records identify the four London lodges only by the names of the taverns where they met. Apparently they did not feel the need to use names or numbers, as today's lodges do, to distinguish themselves from each other. A lodge was simply a lodge. Any unity the Masons enjoyed was the product of a common heritage and cordial relations among the lodges rather than the influence of a higher authority holding them together.

This has the air of something quite informal. At the start of the eighteenth century, Freemasonry by all accounts was a relatively small enterprise with no great pretensions. The formation of a Grand Lodge, for that matter, was apparently not regarded as an momentous event. Members of one lodge could and did visit others, and Freemasons throughout the area recognized themselves as members of the same organization. The evidence suggests that the four lodges merely wanted a more formal organization to oversee and coordinate their affairs.

But the establishment of a governing body had ramifications that went far beyond anything its members could have expected. In the beginning, the four lodges intended the Grand Lodge to supervise only their activities. However, other lodges soon joined, and in a few years Freemasonry in England changed from a loose confederation to a single, organized body.

Over the next several decades, that one innovation was to produce a more standardized Craft and give it an added potential for growth. Of more immediate concern, though, was its effect on the way the Masons told their own story.

It soon became obvious that a beginning had been made. If they had not already done so, the Freemasons realized that they would have to turn their attention to the future. That meant more conscientious administration, better record keeping, and documenting the Craft's history for the benefit of later generations.

One of the Grand Lodge's first acts was to mandate a book of constitutions. This was to embody the history and regulations of the Craft in a form that could be circulated to all the lodges and updated from time to time. Such a document already existed in the *Gothic Constitutions*, which had apparently been used by the operative masons of the medieval period. But that document was seriously out of date. The Grand Lodge now oversaw a fraternal organization, and a lot had happened since the old constitutions were written. The new organization needed something tailor-made for its changing and expanding role.

The Grand Lodge appointed the Reverend Dr. James Anderson to assemble their constitutions. We know little of this Presbyterian minister or why they chose him for the job. He was well educated and by all accounts an active Mason and lodge officer. Beyond that, we know nothing of any special qualifications he brought to his task. We do know that he threw himself into the work with some enthusiasm. He drew heavily on the *Gothic Constitutions* and added new material to produce the thin volume that still bears his name. Anderson submitted the first edition of his work to the Grand Lodge in 1723. It was quickly approved and published, and a revised version appeared in 1738.

This is where we will get our first look at the medieval organization from which the Craft is believed to have descended. Anderson's work is certainly not a modern history. The good doctor must be numbered among the fanciful historians of the Craft. In fact, he went beyond the call of duty on that count. Not only did he preserve the legends he found in the documents he was copying, he also brought his own imagination to bear, created new stories of mythic proportion and presented the whole as if it were unvarnished truth.

Admittedly, Anderson will lead us astray if we read him uncritically. Still, his *Constitutions* does give us a valuable look at the Craft of his day. And more to the point, it gives us insight into the largely undocumented history of Freemasonry before the Grand Lodge era.

For the purposes of our investigation, the most important thing about his work is that it establishes the regard in which the eighteenth century Masons held the *Gothic Constitutions*. The Grand Lodge's acceptance of material from that older document in its official history confirms that the Freemasons of Anderson's day believed its history to be *their* history. The fact that the speculative Masons adopted this "operative" document as their own gives us our first circumstantial link between the modern fraternity and the medieval craft.

More than that, the early speculative Craft did not merely recognize the old *Constitutions* as an artifact that had something to do with their order. They saw it as one of their basic documents. Copies were handed down and carefully preserved by local lodges. They were, in short, given the treatment due an historic treasure, a relic of an earlier time.

By the eighteenth century the *Gothic Constitutions* had been copied and recopied until it existed in several versions. Some included material added to satisfy the needs of an evolving organization. They show what Masonry was becoming. But all retain material from the document's first writing, when it was new and told only what the craft had been. We see something of the nature of medieval masonry in the various versions of the *Gothic Constitutions*. And the older the version, the more medieval it is.

The earliest surviving copy, known as the *Regius Poem*, dates to about 1390. There is every reason to believe that it is a copy of an earlier draft; the original may have been written at the mid-point of the fourteenth century, or perhaps a few decades earlier. But the *Regius* copy is certainly close in time to the very first draft, and its content can not have strayed far from the original.

We need not be distracted by the fact that the *Regius Poem* is written in verse. In those days information was routinely versified to make it easier to memorize. Our concern lies in what the poem says, and it begins with words that all Masons will recognize.

> "Here begin the constitutions of the art
> of Geometry according to Euclid."

References to Euclid still appear in the ritual, although his connection with the Craft is left vague. In the old constitutions, it is spelled out very clearly.

> In Egypt he taught it full wide,
> In divers lands on every side;
> Many years afterwards, I understand,
> Ere that the craft came into this land.
> This craft came into England, as I you say,
> In the time of good King Athelstane's day;

This is where we will pause in our journey back in time. It is a moment that is neglected by the ritual and overlooked by most Freemasons. But it was distinctly remembered by the custodians of the old constitutions. To them, it was important to recall the beginnings of masonry in England. And the *Regius Poem* told them how it all started.

Certainly neither Euclid nor Athelstan was the founder of stone masonry. The craft of building in stone had existed for thousands of years. It passed through golden ages, witness the appearance of the pyramids of Egypt, the temples of Greece and the magnificent work of the Roman architects. And it was often neglected, as in the dark ages when a collapse of social organization made large construction projects impractical.

But we are not looking for the origin of stone masonry. Our quest is for a single moment when the ancestors of the modern Freemason entered history. When we find that moment, we will be able to follow its consequences forward in time until we locate the genesis of Masonic secrecy.

If Anderson and his contemporaries were right, that moment occurred centuries before Freemasonry evolved into a social and philosophical society. It occurred when operative masonry was the whole of the story. True, the craft in those days had more in common with the builders of the pyramids and the Coliseum than with the well dressed men who attend lodge meetings today. Its people did not see themselves as a part of anything that even remotely resembled modern Freemasonry. But it is to them that Anderson and the *Gothic Constitutions* direct our attention.

Historically, the old and new constitutions give us an unbroken trail of evidence that goes back to 1390. From there we have only a legend to follow, and legends both exceed and fall short of the truth. But the *Regius Poem*'s reference to Athelstan, though it may be only legend, at least gives us a real person who lived in a real time and place. Athelstan was once a king in the city of York. And that is where we will look next in our quest for masonic origins.

The City and the See

A thelstan, a member of the Anglo-Saxon nobility and grandson of Alfred the Great, was born in A.D. 895, reared in the Mercian court and ruled England from 925 until 939. As a young man he followed the course expected of him. He led men into desperate battles; that's always the curse of those who would rule a divided land. But Athelstan was a man of vision as well as a warrior chieftain. After a series of military victories he declared himself king of all Britain and established his court in Northumbria, where he made himself known to history as a wise ruler and lawgiver. According to Masonic lore, he also convened an assembly of masons there, and the modern Craft descended from that one event.

History is silent about Athelstan's assembly. No details of its proceedings survive. In fact, the meeting itself may never have taken place. The story is only a legend. But it does give us a starting point for masonry in England, and since it constitutes our earliest clue to the origins of Freemasonry, we are compelled to investigate it.

It is important to remember that legends are based on actual events. Although the story of the York assembly can not be regarded as unvarnished history, it almost certainly contains some element of truth. Perhaps that truth is veiled and distorted, but if we can sort it out from the layers of embellishment that are always found in legends, we may be able to learn something very significant about the early days of the Craft. And since the *Regius Poem* is the earliest of several versions of the story, it is the one least likely to have been corrupted with material added by later writers who had lost track of the truth. Legend or not, it is the best account we have of Freemasonry's earliest history.

When we look at the *Regius Poem*, however, we must be aware that, like any legend, it has two parts. One is the story itself. The other is the instrument that records it.

Ordinarily, there is little point in distinguishing between the two. But in this case the difference is critical. Although the *Regius Poem* contains the

King Athelstan
Reproduced from the Corpus Christi College MS 183. Photo courtesy of The Master and Fellows of Corpus Christi College, Cambridge, England.

legend of masonic origins, it does not — as do most legends — stand on its own. It is embodied in a larger work that claims to record the history and rules of a real organization. This places the York legend a little closer to history than most legends, and we must therefore be especially careful in distinguishing between the story and the medium that brings it to us. Although one may be quite reliable, the other may not.

The story of Athelstan could be a deliberate flight of fancy thrown in to add spice to an otherwise mundane document. Perhaps it is a fairy tale known at the time for its lack of authenticity. Or quite possibly it is a vain attempt to recall a long forgotten history whose true facts could no longer be recovered. (Even if it was intended as a true history, we must not forget that this story and the poem that tells us about it are separated by four and a half centuries. During that time, at least some of the details certainly drifted from their original form.)

We do not know how the story of Athelstan's assembly was transmitted during those centuries. It may have been preserved in documents now lost. More likely it was either passed down as an oral tradition or, alternatively, created from whole cloth in the fourteenth century. In any case, it is unlikely that the version we now have is a completely accurate account of something that happened centuries earlier.

Nor is it likely that we will ever find the missing pieces. Any oral tradition that might have spanned those centuries is now lost and will remain lost forever. And there is little hope that documents misplaced so long ago by a largely illiterate society will resurface after all these years. In short, the story as we now have it can not be considered reliable.

In the absence of records from those lost centuries, the *Regius Poem* in and of itself can tell us little. To make proper sense of its legend, we must look at the story and its telling separately. If we can find confirmation of one in the other, we may then be able to judge how much of the legend is fact and how much is fiction. Only by doing that can we hope to find the grain of truth that must be hidden somewhere in the legend.

First, we will look at the story. This is the story of a time and a place and a king. It tells of a time when something changed. And that change, according to the later telling of it, started a chain of events that led from the distant past to the present. At least, that's the way it appeared when the story teller looked back at it from a distance of four centuries.

The complete text of the *Regius Poem* is reprinted in Appendix I of this book. It contains a history of the craft of masonry and rules for governing it, and only a small portion of the document is devoted to an account of how Athelstan became a patron of the masons and revived their craft.

Unfortunately, this brief "Athelstan" passage contains little detail. It does not, for example, tell us where the assembly occurred. Masonic tradition places it in York, Athelstan's capital city. That would certainly be a logical site, but it was obviously attached to the story at a later date.

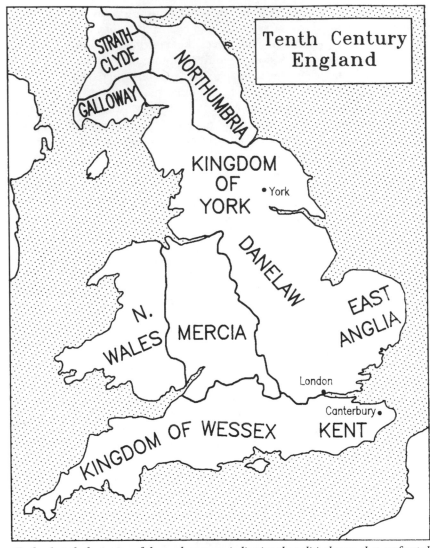

England at the beginning of the tenth century, indicating the political scene that confronted Athelstan when he began his reign.

As we will see, York enters Masonic lore more than once. Apparently, the masons of the fourteenth century knew, or at least believed, that *something* of importance to them had once happened there. They assumed it was Athelstan's assembly, and that makes the city a focal point for our investigation.

To determine how much of their assumption is history and how much is wishful thinking, we must go to York and see if the assembly could have happened there. At first glance, the idea seems credible. The city does contain a magnificent cathedral, the largest Gothic church in England. The building certainly had a connection with the medieval stone masons. But was it in fact the site of an assembly that gave birth to modern Freemasonry? The answer to that question lies somewhere in the history of the place.

York is an ancient city. It is located in the north east corner of England, not far from the Scottish border, but its people have always been drawn into the affairs of the south.

Geography and history conspired to make Britain a cultural melting pot. The island, or parts of it, were occupied by successive waves of immigrants from the earliest times. These influxes produced turmoil for the people who had to live through them, but the influence of their various cultures produced a moderation and toleration among the people. As a result Britain lacks the extremes often found in more homogeneous and isolated cultures.

York in particular was destined to be a microcosm of the island's evolution. A prime location and the lay of the land made it inevitable that an important city would develop there. The site is in the middle of the island, on a large plain that opens to the north and south to give easy access to both ends of the island. This makes it a suitable mid-point for travelers moving north or south. Through the plain runs a navigable river that opens into the North Sea, providing an avenue to international trade. And at the center of the plain stands a bit of high ground bounded by the confluence of two rivers. Such a place is easy to defend and just as easy to re-supply by land or sea.

All things considered, the site was ideal for a major city. As Britain emerged from prehistoric times and moved toward the Middle Ages, the area's assets became more and more obvious, and it was only a matter of time until someone came along to exploit them.

The more patriotic of Yorkshire's historians claimed that York is an immemorial city – that it has existed forever. That is a romantic notion but an unlikely one. More probably, there was no permanent settlement in the area until the Romans established a fort there in A.D. 71.

This was still early in the history of the western world. York was founded only a few years after the Emperor Nero committed suicide. While the Romans were still building their fortifications there, another fortress, Masada, fell to the legions in Palestine. The *Gospel According to Luke* was not yet written. Vesuvius still smoldered above the thriving town of Pompeii. And *The Book of Revelation* would not be committed to paper for another two decades.

It was in this historic context that the Romans arrived in Britain and established a settlement they called Eboracum. Centuries later, when the Anglo-Saxons came, they named the town Eoferwic. The Danish version of that word was Jorvik, and in time the name evolved into its present form.

The Romans came to northern Britain as part of their empire's invasion of the island. They established their camp to the east of the river Ouse, in the triangle formed by the joining of the Ouse and the river Foss. There they occupied about seventy acres situated on a low hill which is now occupied by the minster (cathedral). Modern visitors who walk along the streets named Petersgate and Stonegate are treading on the ancient roads that serviced the Roman camp.

After the army pacified the southern parts of the island, the greatest need for a military presence was in the north, and for this reason Eboracum became the most important military post in Britain. Of four legions resident in the island, two were stationed there. Hadrian declared it his military capital in A.D. 120, and for a time the Emperor Severus held court at Eboracum. In fact, Severus was in residence there at the time of his death, as was Emperor Constantius. Clearly Eboracum was an important place. It was so important that the Romans considered it the capital of Britain during the whole of their occupation.

But the area's strategic location was only part of the story. It was a pleasant place to live and was well suited to serve as a river port to exploit the resources of the surrounding countryside. With these advantages, it is not surprising that what started as a military outpost gradually developed into a much larger undertaking.

At first, merchants and other camp followers settled outside the fort to provide goods and services to the soldiers. Their settlement soon grew into a town. It was not a bad place to live and work, and as the town grew larger, it offered more and more attractions to its residents. In addition, many of the soldiers retired there, contributing even more of a Roman influence. Thus the Britons became Romanized, and the Romans became locals.

A melding of cultures was inevitable during the first few centuries of Roman rule in the island. But it wasn't only the Britons and Romans whose cultures influenced the area. Rome routinely employed conquered peoples as auxiliary forces to strengthen her legions. As the Britons resigned themselves to playing the role of Roman subjects, it became increasingly necessary to protect them from the barbarians (anyone not a Roman subject) who had begun to maraud the island's eastern shores.

It was largely to Germanic tribes on the continent that Rome turned for this service. During the third century, as the Roman Empire faltered and the southern and eastern coasts of Britain became increasingly subject to Saxon raids, "friendly" Germans played an important role in defending the so-called Saxon Shore. Through the years, these German mercenaries blended more and more into the mainstream of the culture they served, until eventually they ceased being residents abroad and became British citizens.

Meanwhile, the religion of York's future was beginning to take shape. For our purposes, this side of the city's history is at least as important as its politics. Since Freemasonry is heavy laden with religious symbolism, we may reasonably believe that early masonry, too, was strongly influenced by church and chapel. If so, we may well find in the distant past some clue to the origin of Hiram's story. And if the Craft had its birth in York, we must look there for the origin of its view of religion.

Christianity came to York, as it did to the rest of Britain, with the Romans. This probably occurred during the second century, but the details are not known. Until the beginning of the fourth century Christianity existed as a minority religion. It was tolerated as long as it posed no problems for the establishment, and quite sensibly the Christians of York maintained a low profile. Their faith had no official status until the reign of Constantine the Great.

According to legend, Constantine was born in York. This is somewhat doubtful, but the residents of the city did feel a strong affinity with him. So when the emperor Constantius died in York during a visit in A.D. 306, Constantine was enthusiastically proclaimed emperor by the troops stationed there.

Following his conversion to Christianity in 312, Constantine mandated toleration for the Christian religion throughout the Empire. The policy was made official by his famous Edict of Toleration, proclaimed in Milan in 313. This allowed Christian communities, including the one at York, more freedom to practice their faith.

Although the surviving records are scant, there is reason to believe that the Church prospered in Britain during this period. By the fourth century, it was reasonably well organized throughout the Empire, and York may have been one of its more prominent centers. Of the three British bishops who attended the Council of Arles in 314, the one from York is described as the most important. Even at this early date, it seems that the Church had been quite active in the city for some years.

The Church in York might have developed differently if the city had continued to operate under the political influence of Rome. But the world was changing. After more than three centuries in the island, Rome finally lost her hold on Britain.

The decline of Roman power was a gradual process, not a sudden event. The Empire simply expanded until it was too large to manage then remained in that over-extended condition for generations. While it struggled to hold its territories, its enemies probed at every weakness they could find. In time, the relentless battering proved too much for a culture that no longer had the will to renew itself, and the Empire started to crumble.

The struggle came to a head at the beginning of the fifth century. That was when the German tribes of northern Europe mounted a renewed series of attacks that threatened to destroy the Empire. With resources stretched to the breaking point, Rome found herself increasing unable to administer law and order in the outlying provinces. Finally in 410, the year Rome was sacked by the Goths, Emperor Honorius yielded to the inevitable and advised the people of Britain that his government could no longer help them.

If there was still any doubt, it now became clear to the inhabitants of the island that they would henceforth be left to their own resources. As part of the Roman retreat, the troops occupying York pulled out, leaving behind the community of locals that had built up around the fort. At that point, York ceased to be a military town and became a city in its own right.

It was a new day for the city, but the withdrawal of Roman power from Britain brought about more than political changes. Just as the Romans were capable administrators, they were also excellent builders. Their stone structures, always erected with an eye to defense, were designed to last. Some of their fortifications in the island still stand, and many more would have survived if they had not been destroyed by war or pulled down to obtain stone for other buildings. But when the Romans withdrew, construction declined drastically and remained in decline for several centuries.

While little of Roman York's stone work remains, its less tangible fabric did survive. The settlement was well established and had all the characteristics necessary to make it a prominent city. The site was well suited to serve as a seat of economic, political and military power, and the British kings who were left to rule the area seemed to favor York as their capital.

Unfortunately for them, York was not destined to remain a British city. As the first quarter of the fifth century came to an end, it was clear that the island's inhabitants no longer had the resources to defend themselves. In desperation, and with few other options available, the Germans immigrants invited more of their people to join them from the continent.

According to tradition, this influx began about 428 with the arrival of three shiploads of mercenaries – the first wave of what was to become an invasion. It was less violent than is often imagined, but the arrival of new German tribes, notably the Angles and Saxons, worked significant changes on the culture of the island.

The newcomers found a nation that had disintegrated into warring factions. The most powerful of the land owning families had asserted their authority with varying degrees of success. But without the Roman army to back them up, nowhere was there enough military force to resist a determined onslaught.

Encouraged by this power vacuum, the Germans moved in and established a dozen petty kingdoms across the island. The British resisted, and the Anglo-Saxons brought in reinforcements.

The resulting struggles created both history and legend. It was toward the end of the fifth century that the island's best remembered hero, Arthur, entered British lore. Although the legendary king is remembered as living in the much later age of knights in shining armor, the real Arthur was a British warlord who fought in the shimmer of chain mail.

Under his leadership the Britons fought valiantly and with some success, but the tide of history was against them. Arthur was killed at the Battle of Camlann, which presumably occurred some time between 515 and 540. After that time, the Anglo-Saxons were unstoppable. They imposed their will through a combination of combat and intermarriage. And of these two, the violence of combat played the lesser role.

While the Germans knew how to fight, they were primarily farmers. In Britain they found fertile fields for their crops. They came for land, not for pillage, and their "invasion" of the island seems to have involved considerably less conflict than it might have. The Germans of that era had a tribal society. It was common for them to conduct feuds with their neighbors, but it was not in their nature to harbor dreams of empire. They wanted only enough land to provide food and comfort for their families.

In keeping with their lifestyle, they built simple homes. Some were long houses that ran up to sixty feet in length. They were often divided into smaller rooms, but they were not built of stone. Most were wattle or timber structures with thatch roofs. Buildings used as workshops and for storage were similar. These people were, after all, farmers and their lives were not pretentious. In fact, it was not uncommon for the Anglo-Saxons to build small wooden houses rather than move into the grander and more spacious villas that had been abandoned by their former owners and were free for the taking.

German tribes continued moving into Britain in this manner for several generations. And as they settled in, they established borders and fought for the control of territory.

About A.D. 580, the Angles made their move in northern Britain. Now a time of consolidation was at hand. The area between the Humber and Tweed rivers had evolved into two kingdoms, named Bernicia and Deira. They, in turn, were subdued by Ethelfrith (593-617). He and his successor, Edwin, ruled them as the unified kingdom of Northumbria, a name that is still used in the area. At last an Anglo-Saxon chieftain had become so powerful that he was, in effect, the king of England, and York was his capital.

During this period Christianity did not fare well at York. The Anglo-Saxons brought in their own religion. They did not come, as had the earlier German mercenaries, to be subjects of another culture whose rules and values they were willing to adopt. These Germans came as colonizers intent on retaining their own culture in the lands they chose to occupy.

Of course, Christianity did not vanish completely. It probably coexisted with the worship of Woden and Thor. But it no longer had the official support it had previously enjoyed and certainly suffered a drastic decline during the next few centuries. Now lacking the powerful support of the Romans, the religion the Empire had brought into Britain withered, and the organized church may have disappeared entirely in Northumbria. But efforts to correct that problem were on the way.

A new pope, Gregory I, was about to change the history of England. He was well suited to assume leadership of the Church. Born into an aristocratic family, he had quite naturally entered the Roman civil service. By age thirty, he was prefect of the city of Rome and presided over the senate. Clearly a promising career in government lay ahead of him, but it was soon cut short. When his father died, Gregory turned his back on secular politics and became a monk.

The future pope took well to the monastic life, going so far as to turn his family home into a monastery dedicated to St. Andrew. Later, he built six more monasteries on his family lands in Sicily. When he was called to serve as the papal ambassador to the court of Emperor Tiberius in Constantinople, he took several of his monks with him and continued to pursue a monastic life. But his experience with administration and his knowledge of the ways of government could not be ignored. The Church was in desperate need of strong leadership.

On September 3, A.D. 590, Gregory inherited the papacy at a time when the Church was under pressure on both secular and religious fronts. Natural disasters and waves of invasion had weakened the society, and the Church had a severely strained relationship with a state that was jealous of the power the pope might someday acquire.

While dealing with all these problems, the bishops of Rome had struggled for some time to establish their primacy against the claims of the eastern Church in Constantinople. Now they faced yet another danger. German tribes from the north threatened to subdue Italy and perhaps extinguish the Roman Church altogether.

It was in this setting that Gregory assumed the papacy. Faced with immense challenges, he moved decisively to improve the fortunes of the Church. One of his more important steps was to encourage the monastic life he knew so well. But this was not simply an act of patronage to his friends. It was a very deliberate part of his strategy. He realized that the monasteries would someday be a powerful tool for the papacy.

The pope's support of monasticism also set the stage for an important element in Masonic lore, the Crusades. But that story would not unfold for several centuries. Of more immediate concern to us is the effect his actions had on the religious history of York.

What might have been an isolated episode in Roman history turned out to be critical for the beleaguered Christians of the British Isles. Since the Church was experiencing severe problems in the north and east, the new pope decided to expand to the west.

Gregory was determined to re-establish the faith in England. To that end, in 597, he sent Augustine into southern England as a missionary to Kent. This Augustine is not to be confused with the better known St. Augustine of Hippo, who was born in Nubia and spent his life in Roman Africa. Augustine of Canterbury lived more than a century later and served as prior of the Benedictine monastery of St. Andrew in Rome until Gregory sent him on the mission to England.

Augustine lost no time getting to know Ethelbert, the king of Kent and the most powerful prince in southern England. Although Ethelbert resisted at first, he soon converted to Christianity, and Augustine went on to establish an abbey and later a cathedral at Canterbury. Of course, the pope rewarded Augustine by naming him first archbishop of Canterbury.

Gregory quickly authorized his new archbishop to appoint other bishops for England. Revival was under way, and since York was the most important city of the north, it was an obvious choice for one of those bishoprics. But that would have to wait. The deaths of both Gregory and Augustine in 604 delayed the re-establishment of the Roman Church in England. The revival faltered, and the appointment of an archbishop in York would not occur for another two decades.

Sometimes the momentum of history has a way of accomplishing things that elude the strongest and most determined of men. What happened next was a case in point. For nearly a century, a process of consolidation had been going on in the island. The petty kingdoms of the Anglo-Saxons had slowly come together, much to the detriment of the Christian faith. Now that same process was about to give Christianity an opportunity to expand its influence into northern England.

The north was still under the control of Edwin, who had inherited a unified Northumbria from Ethelfrith. Edwin continued to increase his power and now ruled almost all of England. Only Kent did not recognize him as king, and he was eager to extend his influence to that southern region. To that end he arranged to marry Ethelburga, the princess of Kent. It was a peaceful way for him to get what he wanted, and everyone else benefited enough to find the proposal agreeable.

As a Christian, Ethelburga insisted on bringing a chaplain with her when she moved to York to live at the royal court. Edwin saw no problem in that. And Justus, the fourth archbishop of Canterbury, jumped at the opportunity to do what his predecessor had not lived long enough to accomplish. He quickly consecrated Ethelburga's chaplain, one Paulinus, as bishop of York.

Paulinus originally came to England to assist Augustine. Now he was to establish a dynasty of his own. No matter that it would be founded on a stroke of good fortune. Justus' hastily assembled strategy worked, and Paulinus took full advantage of it. Within two years Edwin, along with other members of his family and court, agreed to be baptized into his wife's faith. The baptisms were performed in a special ceremony held on Easter day, A.D. 627, and the Church at York was off and running.

The first specific record we have of a church building in York refers to a wooden structure erected especially for this ceremony. It was built with some haste, suggesting that the city at that time did not have any other religious building suitable for so important a baptism. The use of wood instead of stone, however, was not part of the haste. The Anglo-Saxons were still building mostly with wood, a practice fostered by the vast quantities of timber available in the island.

A few years after the historic baptism, when the sense of urgency had died down, a stone structure was built around the wooden baptistery. This church was dedicated to St. Peter and is perhaps the earliest example of a stone church built by the Anglo-Saxons. The most likely site for this early church building was at the center of the old Roman city, a spot now occupied by the minster. But the seventh century structures have apparently vanished without a trace, and their exact location will never be known.

In keeping with Pope Gregory's plan, the bishop of York was authorized to consecrate new bishops, and the city became an important center of Christianity in the island. In fact, York was soon embroiled in a long running dispute with Canterbury over the issue of precedence, in other words, which would be the number one church in England.

The relationship between York and Canterbury was soon to be complicated even further. Edwin was killed at the battle of Hatfield in 633. With the loss of its king, the government in Northumbria fell apart, and Christianity again lost its hold on York. Ethelburga and Paulinus returned to Kent while Oswald, one of Ethelfrith's sons, fled with his brother to the Irish monastery on Iona, an island in the Inner Hebrides.

Although this was a Christian monastery, it was not associated with the Roman Church. Iona was part of the Celtic church; its monastery was founded in 563 by St. Columba, who had sent missionaries from there to Scotland. The two churches were similar in most respects, but they differed in the way they calculated the date of Easter. This one issue was enough to keep them in conflict with each other. And York found itself embroiled in that conflict.

Apparently an ambitious and impatient man, Oswald did not stay in exile long. He soon returned from Iona and regained the Northumbrian throne. But his reign marked a shift in the religious climate of the area.

In 635, he called upon the Church of Iona to send in missionaries to re-convert the Northumbrians. The task was entrusted to Bishop Aidan, whom the king appointed to the episcopal see on the island of Lindisfarne, since known as Holy Island in honor of this event. Oswald then completed the church building Edwin had started and placed it under Aidan's control.

Since Rome was no longer well represented, the Celtic Church became the major religious force in Northumbria, but it did not replace the Roman Church. For more than a century dissension plagued the affairs of both church and state. This allowed the archbishops of Canterbury to increase their influence in the rest of England, and York became relatively less important as a religious center.

About A.D. 650, the Roman Church received another boost from a man named Benedict Biscop. He was a member of the Anglo-Saxon nobility who, like Pope Gregory, turned his back on secular politics and entered the monastic life. He imported stone masons from Gaul to build two monasteries near York and furnished them with books and works of art he had acquired during several trips through Europe.

For the rest of his life, Biscop maintained close ties with Rome. As a leader in Northumbrian Church affairs, his work was oriented toward religion, but it had far reaching effects for the secular society as well. He became a serious patron of the arts, reviving skills that all but died out in England. His influence in this field was so strong that most of what is now known as Anglo-Saxon art and architecture bears Biscop's mark if not his name.

Thanks in part to Biscop's efforts, the fortunes of the Roman Church improved so significantly that by 664 it was in a position to re-assert its authority in Northumbria. A Synod held that year in the North Yorkshire town of Whitby adjudicated the claims of the two Churches. Both sides got a fair hearing. Cuthbert, abbot of Lindisfarne, argued for the Celtic Church. Wilfred, bishop of Ripon and a close friend of Benedict Biscop, represented the interests of the Roman Church. And when the proceedings reached their conclusion, the Synod's verdict in favor of Rome helped restore that Church to its position of prominence in the area.

Now Wilfred was the man of the hour in York, and he took full advantage of the fact. He quickly turned his attention to undoing the neglect his Church had suffered since Paulinus was forced to abandon the bishopric. High on the list was Edwin's church building. It had been allowed to fall into disrepair and was in serious need of aid. Near the end of the seventh century Wilfred restored the building, an operation that consisted largely of placing glass in the windows and repairing and whitewashing the masonry.

The results of his effort may have been short lived. Contemporary records indicate that a church burned on April 23, 741. It isn't clear whether this was Edwin's church or another in the area. But a separate document records that a new church was built by Albert, who served as archbishop of York from 767 until 780. This church is described as being very tall and having many porticoes and thirty altars. If it was Edwin's church that was destroyed several years earlier, this is almost certainly a record of its rebuilding.

As the pre-eminent town in the area, York could be expected to have the grandest church, and now it did. The church of St. Peter was famous.

Because of it, the city hosted tourists and became a burial place for local kings and bishops.

But York was more than a religious center. The cultural revival Benedict Biscop had started in the seventh century continued to bear fruit, as well. Just one example: the University of York was founded by Egbert, king of the West Saxons. Egbert was encouraged in this undertaking by the work of Bede. And Bede, in turn, was trained by Biscop.

York had come a long way since its days as a Roman fort. It was now a major center of learning with an international reputation. When no less a figure than Charlemagne needed an advisor, he turned to York and recruited Alcuin, one of the city's pre-eminent scholars.

The maturing of the area's culture was reflected by political developments, too. Egbert's victory over the Britons of Cornwall in 815 marked the conclusion of the Anglo-Saxon conquest of the island. Theirs was now the dominant culture, except in the far north and west and across the water in Ireland, where the Britons continued to hold sway. It was in those rather remote areas that the old British culture and the particular brand of Christianity it had inherited from the Romans were preserved. Elsewhere, the island was English and Roman Catholic.

Egbert is often called the king of all England. That's a peculiar title, since England was nothing like a unified country. But it does give Egbert credit for what he had accomplished. For the first time, the island was "anglicized" and operated more or less under the control of a single king.

But more trouble was on the horizon. Norwegian Vikings had already begun to expand their influence to the islands around Scotland. The Vikings were driven by overpopulation and a custom that gave inheritance to the eldest son of each family. This left the younger sons without means and free to seek their fortunes in foreign lands.

It was the same system that would play an important role in the Crusades a few centuries later. However, unlike the crusaders, the Vikings were not interested in religious conquest. They wanted land and wealth. Many of their expeditions were mere hit and run raids in search of plunder. But others left permanent settlements on English soil.

The Anglo-Saxon Chronicle relates that the Viking invasion began with an incursion of three Danish ships in A.D. 787. In 792 the Vikings sacked Lindisfarne. And a year later they were expanding from their bases in the Shetland islands to make raids on Northumbria.

At first they didn't stay. They staged lightning raids, attacking where they found defenses weak and booty worth the trouble. But this limited their targets to places near the water. In time the Vikings began setting up temporary base camps from which they could venture farther inland. And eventually their camps were replaced by permanent settlements. They continued expanding their territory in this way until, in 867, the Danish Vikings conquered Northumbria and captured York.

Under Danish rule, the archbishops of York operated more or less independently of – and as rivals of – Canterbury. But this was a time of turmoil. Political changes occurred in quick succession.

Alfred the Great, the king of Wessex, fought the Danes back. He was not strong enough to defeat them, but he did force them to the bargaining table. In 878 his victory at Edington enabled him to hammer out a treaty with the Danish Guthrum. Under this "Peace of Wedmore," Northumbria became part of the Danelaw, a territory surrendered to the Danes.

When Alfred died in 899, his son Edward took over. He ruled Wessex for a quarter of a century and continued the struggle against the Vikings.

Meanwhile, the Vikings were fighting everyone, including their own brothers. In 919 the Norse took York from the Danes. This didn't involve any serious religious or cultural change. It was merely one more inconvenience for a city that had changed hands several times during its history. But it was a prelude to the next development.

By 920 Edward had taken substantial territory and obtained concessions from the Danish and Scottish rulers. At that point, he was the most powerful man in England. Then he died in 924, leaving his work unfinished. His son, Athelstan, was now king of England.

Athelstan and the Masons

It was now left for Athelstan to deal with his father's enemies. Athelstan was crowned king of Wessex at Kingston-on-Thames on September 4, 925 and at the same time the Mercians accepted him as their king. Determined to continue Edward's aggressive policies, he quickly engaged the northern rulers in battle. In little more than a year he added Northumbria to his territory by driving out Olaf, King of York, and Olaf's uncle, Guthfrith of Dublin. He forced the kings of Scotland and Strathclyde to submit to his authority. Then he turned his attention to the petty kingdoms of Wales and subdued them.

By 934 Athelstan was fighting the Scots again. He won some early victories in this campaign, but his enemies soon joined forces. By 937 an alliance that included Constantine of Scotland, Owain of Strathclyde, Olaf and Norse forces from Dublin were massing against him. They invaded England but lost a decisive battle at Brunanburh.

It was after this victory that Athelstan styled himself *rex totius Britanniae*, the king of all Britain, and he is recognized by modern historians as the first who really deserved that title.

Although men of Athelstan's stature have a great influence on their society, they are also greatly influenced by the times in which they live. His reign in particular came at time of religious change. For several generations, the Church had endured a period of decline and corruption. But by the ninth century it had begun to right itself. A monastic reform based on the teachings of St. Benedict helped spur a revival. And by the early tenth century morality was much on the people's minds.

Athelstan thrived in this setting. He developed a reputation as a pious ruler and a good administrator. He was especially concerned with fighting corruption and lawlessness. To that end he enacted a sizable body of law and, although the record is sketchy, seems to have created an efficient civil service to administer his government. He was also adept at international relations, as demonstrated by the royal marriages of five of his sisters to European princes.

More to the point of our investigation, Athelstan was a patron of the arts and religion. He restored monasteries that had fallen into disrepair. He collected relics, giving many of them to local churches. He donated money and land to the minster at York and to libraries. It is even claimed that he translated the Bible into the Saxon language.

On the whole, King Athelstan appears to have been an enlightened ruler for his time. Unfortunately, he is now known only by historians. He might have been better remembered if he'd had time to amass a longer list of accomplishments, but that was not to be. After a reign of only fourteen years and ten weeks, Athelstan died on October 27, 939. The events that underlay the York legend were now history.

The struggle against the Vikings continued, now led by Athelstan's successors, Edmund and Eadred. York fell again. In 954 it was recaptured from the Norse Eric Bloodaxe by Eadred, who followed Edmund as the Anglo-Saxon king of Wessex. Eadred reunited Northumbria with the rest of England, and York continued to prosper as a northern center of commerce.

Although the chronicles might make the period seem one of incessant strife, the people always had time to conduct business. From the beginning of the ninth century York was a trading center, and from the end of that century until the middle of the eleventh, it rivaled anything in Europe.

At the end of the tenth century, York boasted a population of 30,000, a large city for the time. It had come a long way from the scattered huts of traders and craftsmen who had attached themselves to the Roman camp nearly a thousand years before. Still, the charm of the land was always much the same. Time and the English countryside have a way of tempering new arrivals. The Danish Vikings, for a long time invaders, had now settled in the island. They found life comfortable and eventually felt the need for protection against the Norse, who continued to menace their settlements in northern England. After all, the Danes, like the Angles and Saxons before them, had come to farm the land, not to destroy it. They allied themselves with the Anglo-Saxons against their common enemy, and thus the Danes became English, too.

As was the case with the others who moved into the island, their assimilation began quickly and progressed slowly. In the early years of this period, the Danes had concentrated their efforts on stealing from churches and monasteries, simply because those targets were easy and profitable to raid.

Then, after they settled in the land, the Danes soon accepted Christianity. Their conversion was well under way at the beginning of the tenth century, and in a few generations a substantial majority of them were Christians. This allowed York to continue its tradition as an ecclesiastical center.

But the course of history was about to change again. In 1066 William the Conqueror came on the scene. Although the population of York had dropped to about 7,000, it was still an important city and quickly became entangled in the events that followed the invasion.

William was crowned King of England at Westminster by Aeldred, the archbishop of York, but that event was not without incident. The Norman invasion was not at all popular in England, and Aeldred was severely criticized for giving allegiance to the Conqueror. In fact, feelings ran so deep that York rebelled, and it took repeated attempts to bring the city under control.

During the fighting, many of York's buildings were severely damaged, by either the Normans or the rebellious Danes. The minster was among the casualties and may have been completely destroyed. The library and university were destroyed, too, in an upheaval that might be considered symbolic of the cultural changes that were to follow.

Although the common people continued to speak English, Norman French became the official language. But the Normans brought more than their language across the Channel. They were skilled in building with stone and spurred an abrupt change in architectural style.

Thomas of Bayeux, the first Norman archbishop of York, found the minster in ruins. It had suffered fire damage during the fighting in 1069 and burned again in 1075, soon after he arrived on the scene.

Following his appointment in 1070, Thomas could do little more than put a roof over what was left of the building and make temporary repairs. A decade later, when things were more settled, he rebuilt the minster from the ground up. Though the resulting structure was smaller and simpler than the present minster, it was in the new continental style and was aligned to point true east.

Thomas also renewed the diocese's rivalry with Canterbury, but unfortunately the tide of history was now against York. During the following centuries the city lost much of its religious power and authority until, in the middle of the fourteenth century, Pope Innocence VI finally settled the issue of precedence in favor of Canterbury.

During those years, the minster continued to have an eventful history. It was again damaged by a great fire in 1137. Roger of Pont l'Eveque, a contemporary and rival of Thomas a Becket, rebuilt the eastern part of the building in the Norman style, but he didn't stop there. By this time several grand cathedrals stood in England and Europe, and the building at York compared unfavorably with them. Since the minster was now in serious need of repair, Roger took the opportunity to enlarge as well as rebuild it. His work lasted from 1154 until 1181.

Another round of construction began around 1230 with the enlargement of the transepts. Later the nave was rebuilt to match the scale of the new transepts, and a chapter house was added, the whole of this work ending by 1330.

During the reign of Edward I, York regained its status as the capital of England. Thus began one of the most important periods in the city's history. With York once again the most important place of England, major construction was the order of the day. Not the least of this period's beneficiaries was the minster. The magnificent structure that now stands was begun then and built at a leisurely pace over the next one and a half centuries.

This is not to say that peace had finally come to the area. For a while it was Scotland's time to shine. After the battle of Bannockburn in 1314, the Scots had a freer hand in northern England, and any student of English-Scottish relations knows what that meant. A generation of turmoil followed. Although the Scots had little interest in the southern parts of the island, they did move on York and at one point defeated the archbishop and his army in a battle at Myrton.

The fighting took its toll on the city as it did on the rest of England. When John of Thoresby became archbishop of York in 1352, he inherited a diocese that had fallen into disarray. Those citizens who escaped the Scots had to contend with plague of 1349, and the combination of the two was very depressing. The people were thoroughly demoralized, and the city suffered neglect from a populace that had given up hope.

As soon as he assumed his duties, the new archbishop set about the task of repairing the damage – to both the diocese and the minster. His efforts were fairly successful. He restored the people's faith in their future and set them to work rebuilding the city's grand symbol of hope. Under his direction, they vaulted the minster in 1354 and seven years later began the work of rebuilding its choir.

Richard II was another of York's patrons. He considered making it his capital but in the end settled for visiting the city repeatedly during his reign and holding the Court of the King's Bench there in 1392.

Work on the minster continued for less than a century after Richard's time. The central tower was built from 1380 to 1400. It collapsed in 1407 and its replacement was finished in 1472. Bell towers were also added during the fifteenth century, but there was little more to do. Eight and a half centuries after King Edwin accepted his wife's faith in a small wooden baptistery, the masons' work was finished.

Although the minster has been considered complete since 1472, its history did not stop then. Fire struck again in 1829, 1840 and 1984. The damage caused by all three fires was repaired in due course. But the events of the fifteenth century and later have little to do with our investigation.

By 1390, about a century before construction of the minster ended, the *Regius Poem* was written and the city of York had entered Masonic lore. There is some reason to believe that the verse was composed during Richard's reign, though that's a debatable proposition and one we won't stop to examine.

Our inquiry into the history of northern England was prompted by the observation that the York legend, like any legend, is made up of two parts: the story and the instrument that records it. And the first part of our quest has been a search for the *story* of Athelstan and his assembly.

By the end of the fourteenth century, that story, whether fact or fiction, was a matter of record; it was contained in the pages of the *Regius Poem.* We have now surveyed the span of history that was known by the scribe who wrote the poem. Whatever that document has to tell us about the origin of Freemasonry can now be found in the lines of the poem itself and somewhere in the long history that led up to its writing, and we are thus left to ponder the facts of Athelstan's life, for that is where we will find the truth behind the York legend.

This man was a builder, but only in the symbolic sense of that word. He did more to make England a single nation than did any of his predecessors. He fashioned a system of law to hold the country together. And he tried to improve the lives of his people by promoting the arts and crafts that by his time were well established in the island. In short, he did not build in stone but was an architect of things that improve the soul.

If the gentlemen Masons of eight centuries later had not chosen Hiram to represent their Craft, they might well have used Athelstan instead. The Masons held many values in common with him, and he was already proclaimed in the old constitutions as their founder. They certainly knew the story; it was preserved in their most basic documents. But they ignored him.

Perhaps he was not a tragic enough figure. Perhaps they could not tie him to their cult of secrecy. Or it may be that a king was simply not suitable for their purposes. In addition to Athelstan, they also eliminated Solomon as a candidate for the main character of their drama, when either would have been a fine example of Masonic principles.

For some reason the Freemasons of the seventeenth century chose not to feature the legendary founder of their Craft in their degrees. Nevertheless, the legend of Athelstan and the masons does exist. It ties the man and the organization together, and we must believe that it has some basis in fact.

The truth of the story, if it is there at all, is somewhere in the history of the city of York. But if it is there, it must lie below the surface. It seems that once again the Masons have hidden their secrets well.

The Legend Writers

S o far our quest has not led us to the origins of Freemasonry. A document written in the fourteenth century took us to the tenth. But we did not find evidence there that King Athelstan was the patron of Freemasonry the *Regius Poem* says he was. It's true that he was a patron of the arts and religion, may have translated the Bible into his people's language, and did give a grant of land to the minster, but none of that was unusual for a king in a time when all strata of society were dominated by religion. And it certainly doesn't prove that the historic Athelstan was a major patron of the stone masons, that the craft came to England during his reign, or that he reformed it. The facts, at least the ones we have seen so far, simply do not bear out the Masonic legend of the York assembly.

If we are to make sense of this story, apparently we will have to examine its *telling* and the people to whom its authorship has been credited. After all, if the legend of Athelstan's assembly was written either by or for the medieval stone masons, it may tell us more about them than about their presumed antecedents of four centuries earlier. Legends often do reveal more about the people who created them than about the stories they tell. It is just possible that the story of Athelstan is not real history but an allegory for the time in which it was written. To find out, we'll take a look at the *Regius Poem*, the stone masons of the fourteenth century and the age that produced them.

The fourteenth century was a time of drastic change. Its early years were more a part of the ancient world than of the modern — it was more contemporary with the black death and the Crusades than with the modern world of science and technology.

Since commerce had largely ceased to exist in medieval Europe, most people lived and died within a few miles of their birth place. When the Roman Empire retreated in the fifth century, the benefits it had brought with it disappeared, too. The result was a very local economy. Wealth was reckoned by the owner-ship of land and by the labor of serfs who were bound to the land.

This was not the system of near slavery it is often supposed to have been. All parties received some benefit from the social arrangement. They all gave and took, but the serfs had very little to bargain with, and the system clearly favored the landed gentry.

Then the Black Plague swept through Europe. It is well known that the plague decimated the populations of the western nations in the middle of the fourteenth century. But its real consequences were more subtle and far reaching than the immediate tragedy of the deaths it caused. The plague wiped out a large part of Europe's work force. And that was to change the basic nature of society.

Suddenly labor was in short supply. For the first time the people who provided it were in a position to bargain for their services; now they actually had something to bargain *with*. Naturally, those in authority fought the changes, as they would be expected to do. But the tide of history was against them. Although the aristocracy would survive as a class, they would increasingly have to share the good life.

This occurred just as commerce was on the increase and the feudal system had started its decline. Towns were becoming dynamic places where things could be bought and sold. At the same time the people were becoming individuals. They were no longer, as had been the case for several centuries, merely articles of property that virtually belonged to the local nobility.

Of course, the towns were slow to respond to these developments. Social change came gradually, and the towns' buildings – the most tangible aspect of any society – could not adapt very quickly. Architecture always reflects the society it serves, and the towns of Europe and Britain had been laid out to serve the old feudal way of life. They were small by modern standards, consisting mainly of houses clustered tightly together.

The slow moving economy of the period could not support stores in the modern sense. In those days, a shop consisted of the front room of the family's living quarters. A window was opened to allow customers to see the wares, and the residents attended to their household chores until a customer arrived.

In this system, there were few buildings that could be thought of as belonging to the community, with one spectacular exception: the cathedral. The first cathedrals were their towns' only architectural expression of a developing civic pride. They were large and beautiful structures that could be admired by visitors as they approached the town from a considerable distance. In addition, they could hold the entire population of the town at once.

These buildings were truly for the whole community. They were used not only for worship but also as community centers and markets where the town's people came to buy and sell their wares.

The appearance of cathedrals on the medieval landscape was certainly a matter of worship and civic pride. It was also a complex phenomenon that affected the society in many ways. Not the least important of these had to do with the building itself. The Gothic style of the cathedrals marked a departure from earlier forms. It was based on new theories and new methods that created a different *kind* of structure.

Ancient stone construction used massive walls and columns topped with stone lintels. The result was a very sturdy building, but the natural properties of the materials placed limits on its style and appearance. Large spans of unsupported stone will not stand. They crack and crumble under their own weight. Thus, columns had to be placed close together, and walls had to be thick to support the weight of the large masses of stone that rested on them.

Gothic architecture left brute force behind. It used new principles. By balancing forces, it was possible to raise taller and lighter buildings. Stone was used only where it was absolutely required. Elsewhere, air and glass replaced stone. The result was a tall, graceful building whose surfaces virtually demanded intricate carving and decoration.

Making those cathedrals a reality required skill and understanding that were certainly uncommon at the time. We don't know precisely how much theoretical knowledge the Gothic architects had. They worked in an illiterate society and left few documents to record the details of their profession. We do know that their plans were much less detailed then modern blueprints, and much of the actual work was done by trial and error.

While that might seem to detract from their accomplishments, it actually makes them even more impressive. Their enterprise was not only an expression of faith, it was also an act of faith. Such a profound advance in style, done on such a large scale, required a strong belief in the human potential to achieve great things, a belief that was well ahead of its time.

When we see the cathedral in that light, it becomes obvious that its physical construction was only part of the picture. The cathedrals were more than magnificent buildings that have stood for over half a millennium. They were the product of something quite new in European history. The people who built them reflected an unusual set of cultural developments. And it is generally believed that those were precisely the developments that gave modern Freemasonry its start.

The early Middle Ages were characterized by harsh conditions and a fatalistic view of life. Many believed that the world would end after the first thousand years of the Christian era. When it didn't, and when the people began to realize that they had survived the darkest part of the Dark Ages, they began to look forward. Now there was some point to building things of stone, so they could last for centuries. There was a point to building something that would not only continue to exist long after its builders were dead, but in fact wouldn't even be finished until long after the first generation of its builders had passed away.

Unlike anything else that had occurred in European memory, erecting a cathedral was a truly massive project that required the cooperation of large numbers of workers, often over a period of centuries. And unlike most

York Minster
As it appears today.

events of European history, there was a place in it for everyone. Much of the work was unskilled labor that could be done by anyone who wanted to render service to the Church. The rest, especially shaping the building stones and doing the decorative carving that is everywhere apparent in a cathedral, required the skill of an artist.

The key to success in cathedral building lay in keeping all these people under control. Recruiting, training and supervising so many workers required quite a bit of organization. And continuing organization was needed to keep the unskilled volunteers productively employed while maintaining discipline among the artisans who came to the work as professionals.

Dealing with the volunteers was straightforward enough. The chief architect and his assistants could tell them where to go and what work to do. That was a simple matter of logistics. But the professionals, well, they presented a different set of problems. And the solution to those problems was to establish the first masonic lodges.

These lodges are often confused with the medieval guilds, but they were not precisely the same. A guild was a permanent organization, located in a particular city and established to oversee the affairs of a particular trade or profession. The masonic lodge performed similar functions but, unlike a guild, it did not serve the interests of the craftsmen in a particular city. It was an *ad hoc* organization set up to deal with the stone masons working on a specific construction project.

Lodges of this sort became necessary fixtures of the economy that developed in the later Middle Ages. As the early medieval village gave way to the modern town, the need for new construction overwhelmed the resources of local craftsmen. Major projects like cathedrals, castles and abbeys required more skilled labor than the community could provide.

The obvious solution to that problem was to bring in more workers. With the assurance that construction would continue for the foreseeable future, that was not hard to do. Adventuresome young men were glad to join the craft. They learned the necessary skills by working on one project. Then, when the job was finished or when they became impatient, they could move on. They might have to travel great distances to find other work, but the pay was good and as skilled craftsmen they were respected wherever they went.

Local guilds, organized as they were to serve the routine needs of their own people, did not lend themselves well to dealing with itinerant craftsmen who were no part of the community. It was more politic and more convenient for these craftsmen to have their own "guild," located at or near the building site to serve their needs and to organize and discipline them.

Just such an organization still exists in the Scottish town of Kilwinning. Like the rest of Freemasonry, it has lost its connection with the operative craft, but it traces its roots directly to the abbey whose ruins can still be seen in the town, and it still meets in the shadow of those ruins. We will pause to

Abbey at Kilwinning
The ruins as they appear today.

look at this lodge, partly for what it tells us of the operative craft, and partly for the bit of Masonic history it represents.

The Freemasons' lodge at Kilwinning claims to be the oldest lodge in existence. Its records go back to 1642. Other documents attest to its operating in 1598. But tradition insists that the lodge in that town has existed continuously since 1140. It was then that Kilwinning Abbey was built, and the Freemasons who now meet in an upstairs room near the Abbey's ruins claim to be heir to the lodge that was established by the stone masons who built that venerable structure.

The history of that affair is worth noting. Hugh de Morville, whose descendants continue to hold land in Scotland, came into the Highlands at the beginning of the twelfth century. He was presumably a Norman and may have come to the island with William the Conqueror. It is said that he founded a monastery in Kilwinning and, like Benedict Biscop some centuries earlier, imported stone masons from the continent to build an abbey.

De Morville naturally had his abbey executed in the Gothic style. It was a major undertaking, and the French masons augmented their work force by admitting some of the locals to their ranks.

Since the records of that era have been lost, it is impossible to tell precisely how the lodge of stone masons became a permanent fixture of the community. The French craftsmen might have been expected to return to their own country when they finished their work. But apparently some of them stayed on. It was not the first time people came from abroad for a specific purpose and became permanent residents. In this case, though, one result of their presence was that the stone masons' lodge they founded did not cease to exist when its work was finished. Along with its members, it became part of the town. In time its operative function was replaced by a fraternal one, and its connection with the abbey became only a remnant of its history. The lodge building houses a museum that pays tribute to its past, but in all respects it is very much an active and contemporary organization.

How the Kilwinning lodge evolved over time may be a mystery, but the way it served its original members is not. The medieval stone masons were organized and trained according to the practical requirements of the job.

Operative masons were divided into specialized groups. The setters were assigned to the building site. Their job was to set the cut stones in place according to the plan given them by the architect. Setters could work outdoors only in moderate weather and were employed only during warm months, except when the building was far enough along to allow them to work under shelter.

The hewers were in the quarries, cutting the stone to shape. Their work was more skilled, since they needed to have an understanding of the physical properties of the material. This knowledge was necessary both to get the stone out of the ground and to prepare it for the various building uses to which it would be put – paving, vaulting, and so on.

St. Barbara
By Jan Van Eyck. 1437. Note masons' lodge on the right of the Cathedral.
Photo courtesy of Koninklijk Museum, Antwerpen, Belgium.

Some of the stone was set aside for decorative work. After it had been rough cut, it would be handed over to the free-stone mason – apparently the earliest namesake of the modern Freemason. The free-stone masons were skilled craftsmen who required serious training. This, too, was a largely practical matter. Skills were learned by example. Workers began as apprentices and advanced in their craft as their skill and knowledge increased.

The organization and training of the various classes of stone masons was not in itself peculiar. But their work did set them apart from other workers of their time, and for that matter from the secular group of laborers we would see on a construction project today. True, they were skilled workers, but they had come together to erect a building of spiritual importance, a building deliberately designed to be more magnificent than anything else in the community. And that determined both the niche into which they fitted in the community and the learning to which they were exposed.

Medieval peasants needed no formal education. They were well versed in the things that mattered to them – the seasons, signs of coming weather, the skills needed to fashion tools and bring food from the earth. They had no need of reading and writing.

The nobility, too, were illiterate. Their function was to provide stability in an uncertain world. They protected the peasants from attack and administered local justice. In practice, the petty wars and feuds of the local nobles often produced more threat than protection, but that is another story. The nobility's place in society was well defined and required only a knowledge of military skills and the money to hire enough soldiers to keep the peace. They had no need for schooling.

In the Middle Ages, it was to the Church that the preservation of literacy fell. Anyone who received an education was closely connected with the organized Church. Not all who sought an education came from the nobility. Some were low born, but all had chosen a life in the Church. It was in that capacity that they received schooling, and by receiving education they became part of an elite. It was the churchmen who argued philosophy and theology, who taught reading and writing and accounting. It was they who provided any service that required literacy and knowledge. The advisors to the rulers and nobles were clerics, as were the scribes who prepared the few legal documents that were needed in such a basic society. Even the architects were clerics.

This established a connection between the masters of the stone mason's craft and the Church at the beginning of the cathedral age. While the local stone mason might be merely a craftsman, the "Master" who supervised the cathedral builders would have been educated in Church schools and would be a cleric himself. In that role, his duties went further than those of the modern foreman or architect.

The Master was responsible for preparing the site, organizing the workers and materials. And when the actual construction began, he was the architect who designed the building. This was a simpler operation than it is today. The Master drew a design on paper, showing the ground plan and elevation of the projected structure. Based on that drawing, a full scale version was laid out on the ground with pegs and string, and at that point the work could begin. Most of the details were finalized as the construction progressed, using trial and error to see what worked and what didn't.

As the building rose, the Master continued to be in charge of administration and logistics. He supervised the flow of finances, the transportation of materials and the work of the laborers. Sometimes he was assisted by a clerk; sometimes he handled all these duties himself. But whatever authority he delegated to others, the success of the project rested on his shoulders.

In much of this, the medieval Master was very similar to his modern counterpart, but his concerns did not stop with the performance of the men who worked under him. As a representative of the Church in a time when religion was an all pervasive force, he was concerned with their spiritual welfare, too. His duties went so far as to see that moral instruction and religious services were provided for the workers.

This blend of secular and churchly duties may seem odd to modern readers, especially in the United States where the separation of the two is considered a basic principle. In the Middle Ages, combining them was not only logical but commonplace.

The welfare of the soul was then a major preoccupation for the people of Europe and England. It was the Church that spoke for the soul. And since the Church was also the custodian of literacy, the line between religion and education was by no means distinct. Knowledge, like everything else, had been created by God and flowed from Him. Therefore, the educated churchmen who possessed and transmitted knowledge were a special class in a class-riddled society. They were a true elite.

The free masons, like their Master, were a part of this elite. There is some question about what types of craftsmen were included in the craft that eventually became Freemasonry. It has been argued that the word "free" simply meant they were free to travel from place to place to find work. In an age when most people were bound to the land, freedom of that sort was in itself something of a distinction.

It has alternatively been suggested that the free masons were those who worked free-stone, the soft, fine grained limestone from which elaborate decorations were carved. If that's the origin of the word, they were called "free" masons after the material they worked, or perhaps because the artistic nature of their work freed them from the restraints placed on those who cut and set the plain, rectangular building stones.

Whether the earliest lodges of free masonry included only the most highly skilled sculptors or the itinerant masons as well, these were the professionals of their industry. They were not called upon to provide brute force. That could be had from men who had volunteered or been pressed into service at the king's order. These free masons were the men who had special skill and knowledge, and who were one step closer to God by virtue of their connection with their Master and, through him, with the Church.

The medieval free masons thus enjoyed the respect and prestige due a skilled elite. And they were obviously concerned to guard their position in the community, as indicated by the code of ethics found in the *Regius Poem.*

It is interesting to note that the code seems to have been designed more to protect the lodge than to benefit its members. This is not hard to understand. It was the craft, more than the individual craftsman, that had earned a privileged status. The craft, as a group, worked on religious buildings at a time when life was dominated by religion. It had knowledge that went beyond the rudiments of construction and well beyond the knowledge of the other ranks of society. And its lodges were dedicated to the welfare of the members' souls as well as to their employment. All things considered, the masonic lodge held a special position in medieval society and was determined to protect it. Its code of ethics and the loyalty it expected of its members speak eloquently to that point.

These, then, were the people who traced their roots to Athelstan's assembly. Apparently it was a member of their ranks who committed the story to paper at some point in the fourteenth century. The author of the document is not identified. We don't know who he was or why he penned his poem. The best guess is that he was a monk. He may have been a Master architect or a free-stone mason. He may have written the free masons' story at their request. Or possibly he was just an aspiring writer who assembled material from various sources and fashioned it into a manuscript he could call his own. Whoever he was and whatever his reasons, all we can conclude about him is that he was concerned with preserving a story for the future, and it was a particular kind of story.

In its medieval form, the *Gothic Constitutions* appears to be, in effect, a professional manual for a working craft. It gives a history of the craft as well as rules of behavior. But there are important differences between its account of the craft and the one that survives in the modern ritual.

As we have seen, the cathedral builders of the *Regius Poem* took Euclid as the founder of their craft. They did not, as they might well have done, claim to be the direct descendants of King Solomon's builders.

The ritual, on the other hand, bases *its* story on the events surrounding the building of Solomon's Temple, and much of the tradition of present day Freemasonry recalls those early times. But the Hiramic story is a cautionary tale. It is the stuff of fraternities, not of a group of operative craftsmen. Its absence in the *Regius Poem* suggests that it was not part of the operative craft. At least, it was not part of the face the craft showed to the public. If the story did exist in the fourteenth century, and if the free masons considered it part of their lore, its absence in their manual would indicate that it was part of their inner workings, something for the use of members only.

Another difference between the old and the new is that the history presented in the *Regius Poem* is not the fanciful sort of tale that was employed by the eighteenth century Freemasons. The older version shows all indications that it was an honest effort to present the actual history of a working craft.

This is an important point in shaping the direction of our inquiry. Since the Hiramic story is symbol, there would be little point trying to find it in the pages of history. Conversely, since the *Regius Poem* appears to be history, it would be wrong to treat it as mere fable and ignore the kernel of truth it must contain.

It is reasonable to believe that the *Regius Poem* was written for a specific purpose. According to one theory, it was a response to Richard II's call for all the guilds in England to submit copies of their charters and other archival documents. This decree was issued in 1388, and presumably the free masons' lodges would have felt obligated to respond to it. But they were not a guild and had not been granted a charter. Nor were they likely to have extensive archives on hand.

When the king called for documents, they might well have considered the occasion a suitable opportunity to commit their history to writing. If so, the *Regius Poem* was the result. Whether the document was actually submitted to the crown is not known. It does, however, set out the history and constitution of the stone masons' craft, precisely the sort of thing the king had called for. If they did prepare it in response to Richard's decree, it was certainly a work of history – as opposed to a fable – and would have been the product of the best documents and oral tradition the craft had available at the time.

Perhaps an oral tradition was the only source the masons could draw on for a reconstruction of their history. Considering the illiteracy of the time and the lack of a national organization of stone masons, it is reasonable to assume that their history had never been committed to paper. This would help to explain the verse form of the *Regius Poem.* In those days it was customary for anything that was handed down orally to be in rhyming verse as an aid to memory.

This gives us some perspective on the telling of this story of masonic origins. If we grant that it was originally prepared as a record of the craft's actual history – either to send to the king or for the craft's own purposes – we have no reason to discard its story as a mere fabrication. Some bits of the story may be in error. Some may simply be untrue. But we must accept them as at least an honest attempt to tell the truth.

With this perspective, we can return to the story to see what it tells us. The *Regius Poem* gives us the name of a real person. This implies that the story it tells is literal and accurate. Still, the telling of the story poses problems.

The most obvious is that the poem gives us what appears to be contradic-tory information. It states that masonry came to England during the time of

Athelstan. There could be some truth in this. We have seen that groups of stone masons were at least occasionally imported from Europe both before and after Athelstan's time. But the story later states that Athelstan found problems with the craft,

> "For divers faults that in the craft he found."

To remedy these faults, he called a meeting of masons from all parts of the island to review and reform the way the craft was governed.

> "He sent about into the land
> After all the masons of the craft,
> To come to him full even straight
> For to amend these defaults all
> By good counsel, if it might fall."

The king also invited members of the nobility, including knights and squires, to help establish a new set of regulations for the craft.

> "Fifteen articles they there sought,
> And fifteen points there they wrought."

The story of this effort at reform suggests that masonry had been active in England for some time, since it would have taken many years for the craft to degenerate enough to need reforming. We may assume that the continental masons knew their craft. They might have had to make some adjustments to conform to the English way of doing things. But this would not likely have been recorded as a major reform of the craft.

If the English found it necessary to import skilled artisans, they would hardly have been in a position to dictate reforms to craftsmen who were more accomplished in their specialty than were the English. It is much more likely that importing the craft and reforming it were originally two different stories separated by a considerable amount of time.

This apparent contradiction gives us an important clue to the truth behind the legend. If there are two stories of events widely separated in time, they could not both have occurred during Athelstan's short reign of only fourteen years. Not in the slow moving world of the Middle Ages. If Athelstan re-introduced the craft to England, it would not have had time to degenerate enough to need a major reform before his death.

But if Athelstan was the historic subject of only one of these stories, we must next decide which occurred during his time. And for this, we must return to the history of that era.

The Romans were certainly masters of stone masonry. As long as they were in the island, the craft prospered. Only when they left did the crafts they practiced fall into disuse.

The British chieftains, on the other hand, spent most of their time squabbling among themselves, neglecting most constructive pursuits in favor of military matters. Needless to say, architecture was one of the first casualties of the Roman withdrawal.

When the Angles came into the area, they brought with them no more than the rudimentary crafts of the farmer and the warrior. With particular reference to masonry, we have seen that they built in wood and had little interest in grander structures. It is even recorded that they left Roman villas empty while living in the simple wooden houses they built literally next door to the abandoned structures.

This confirms part of the story. Masonry did as a matter of historic fact degenerate so much that the English no longer knew how to erect a large stone building. The mason's skills died out to such an extent that restoring the craft really did require importing skilled craftsmen from Europe.

But these conditions did not exist in Athelstan's time. By the tenth century, stone masonry had already been revived in the island. While the craft still awaited another revival, which the Normans brought with them, building in stone was far from unknown in Athelstan's time. While he may have reformed the craft, he could not have revived it. We must, therefore, look to an earlier time to find the the reintroduction of masonry described in the legend.

For that, the regulations listed in the *Regius Poem* give us an important clue. To the modern mind, these regulations seem peculiar for a group of craftsmen. But we must remember that the architects of the middle ages were monks. As such, they were subject to monastic discipline. When a group of monks was organized, it was customary for a Rule to be written to govern their behavior. Then could Athelstan's regulations have something to do with a monastic Rule that governed the affairs of craftsmen who were imported to work in England?

Athelstan was indeed a law giver. The body of law he left behind attests to both his ability to rewrite the law and his desire to reform a society with which he found fault. We can easily believe that he saw fit to institute reforms in the building trades as well. Perhaps his real contribution to Masonic lore was to revise a centuries old monastic Rule that was no longer suited to the regulation of the stone mason's craft as it existed in his day.

We know that it is the nature of legends to have some historic content, although they are always garbled. Sometimes they attribute to a single person a litany of deeds that were in fact performed by more than one. We may easily believe, then, that someone else revived masonry in England, that Athelstan later reformed the craft, and that the chronicler of an even later time combined the events into a single story.

The Truth Behind the Legend

I f we accept the idea that Athelstan did not revive masonry in England, then to whom does the legend really refer?

Legends have a way of distorting time. It is their nature to build on some event from the past to satisfy the needs of the present, and that often requires changes in the facts of the story. The exploits of prehistoric kings are retold as the dealings of gods at the dawn of time. The history of a tribe is personalized as the deeds of a single hero. Regional figures are brought forward in time and glorified as national leaders.

It was in just this way that the Arthurian legend transfigured a military leader of the fifth and sixth centuries into the gallant king of a much later time. Perhaps the York legend was the result of a similar transformation. It may well have embellished the career of someone who was less than regal. Then, centuries after the fact, when the masons tried to reconstruct their *real* history, they mistakenly chose Athelstan as the one who best fitted the story as it had come down to them. If that's what happened, the real founder of Freemasonry is not Athelstan but the man for whom he was mistaken.

In seeking that figure, we need not look into prehistory. As we have seen, the York legend does not deal with the first stirrings of stone work in England. It does not draw us to the builders of the ancient stone circles or prehistoric tombs. Nor is it a tale of the coming of the Romans with their engineering feats. In fact, it is not *just* a story about the architecture of any age. The York legend is keyed to a revival in stone building, but it is about something else, too. A look at Freemasonry's earliest document implies that the organization was built on a complex foundation of which architecture was only a part.

While the *Regius Poem* speaks of Euclid as the founder of the stone mason's craft, it also credits him with teaching the seven Arts and Sciences. In the ancient world, the seven Arts and Sciences were the components of a complete, well rounded education. Their mention in the York legend suggests a revival of more than architecture. It seems to point to a broader

Benedict Biscop
Taken from an old, but not contemporary, rendering

cultural phenomenon. The image presented here is of a post-Roman revival, perhaps spurred by an advance in architecture, in which arts and crafts were brought back to England after a period of inactivity.

The decline that followed the withdrawal of the Romans was just such a period of inactivity. Political disintegration and successive waves of invasion did little to help the arts and crafts. The Anglo-Saxons of the time lived practical lives that stressed utility, not elegance; it was a world in which art would not soon flourish again.

But the York legend does not tell the story of a gradual evolution of culture. It describes a deliberate reintroduction of skills under the direction of a single patron. It was an event, not a lengthy process.

The patron of that event – the man we seek – would have to bear enough resemblance to Athelstan to confuse future generations. Like the historic Athelstan he would probably be a member of the Anglo-Saxon nobility. He could well be a Northumbrian. At the very least he did some of the things that the masons would attribute to a future king.

Starting in Athelstan's reign, let us go back in time, peeling away layers of history and legend. Our task is to find a man who fits this description well enough to be the start of it all.

In the history of English architecture, we do in fact come to a time when masonry was reintroduced. And at that moment in history we find a candidate for its patron.

A man named Biscop Baducing lived in the post-Roman period, at a time before the austerity of that age had run its course. Like Athelstan, he was an Anglo-Saxon and a member of their nobility. He was a Northumbrian. He imported builders whose crafts did not exist in the island, or barely existed. And he became a patron of the arts and learning, which he imported enthusiastically from the continent.

All of this seems to fit the York legend and what it implies. But to see how well Biscop fits the story, and whether he might be the historic figure behind the legend, we must examine his life and times more closely.

Biscop Baducing was born in A.D. 628. He was highly placed in the Anglo-Saxon nobility and served as an officer in King Oswy's court. The details of his service are not known, but he apparently rendered military service and may have received land from the crown in payment. (Such exploits, in future years, could well be confused with Athelstan's military successes.)

In 653, at the age of twenty-five, Biscop decided to dedicate his life to God. To that end, he severed his ties with the secular world, returned his lands to the king (as Athelstan would later donate land to the minster) and prepared for a monastic life.

In those days, pilgrimages to the shrines of the apostles at Rome were popular with the Anglo-Saxons. Not to be outdone, Biscop followed the fashion enthusiastically. He set out on his first trip in the company of Wilfred, another Anglo-Saxon noble.

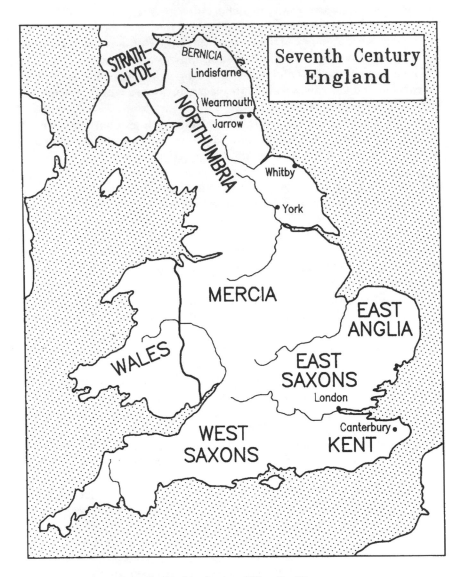

England in the time of Benedict Biscop.

Wilfred had chosen the same course for his life, and the two youths wanted to learn about the Church and its leadership in Rome. While we know little of their journey, we may assume that they took the seventh century equivalent of the "Grand Tour," which by the standards of the day gave them the rare distinction of being world travelers.

When they returned to England, undoubtedly with many marvelous stories to tell, King Oswy's son Alcfrid was so impressed and inspired that he asked to tag along on the next trip to Rome. But Oswy was reluctant to let his son undertake such a journey. In the Dark Ages any long trip was both difficult and dangerous. So when the time came, Biscop had to make his second pilgrimage alone.

From Northumbria, Biscop traveled to Rome and then on to the famous monastery at Lerins, an island off the southern coast of France near Cannes. This monastery had been founded by St. Honoratus around A.D. 410. It was well known for the discipline it imposed on its monks, and Biscop assumed the monastic habit there. He spent two years at the monastery, beginning in 665. During that time, he observed the monastery's Rule strictly and attended to his spiritual development.

While at Lerins, Biscop took the name Benedict in imitation of the monk who founded the monastery at Monte Casino. It had been more than a century since St. Benedict established the monastery in the Italian mountains and developed a set of rules to govern the lives of his monks. But his efforts had a profound impact on Church affairs from that time forward.

Like everyone else in the seventh century, Biscop was strongly influenced by the Benedictine Rule, and its influence was to follow him for the rest of his life. It would be some time, though, until the forces that were now shaping Biscop's life would bear fruit. Still more adventures had to unfold before he could make his big contribution to the Anglo-Saxon culture.

By 667, he was becoming impatient to see Rome again. There is some question about what happened next. We know that the English monk had attracted the attention of Pope Vitalian. Perhaps the pope called him to Rome for a special mission. Or perhaps Biscop decided for himself to move on, an energetic man who had simply stayed too long in one place. In any event, he obtained passage on one of the merchant ships that occasionally put into Lerins and left the island.

Once in Rome, he was chosen to assist in the consecration of Wighard, the archbishop-elect of Canterbury. This episode came soon after the Synod of Whitby, which had adjudicated the dispute between the Celtic and Roman churches. So the new archbishop of Canterbury would have the responsibility of resolving the array of problems that inevitably remain after a decision of such magnitude.

It was a delicate task, and one that required a capable leader. Kings Oswy of Northumbria and Egbert of Kent had agreed on the appointment of

Wighard. (Egbert, especially, felt that an an English archbishop was needed to do the work properly.)

Biscop may have been a part of that plan from the beginning. He was well connected, being both a friend of Oswy and an old friend and traveling companion of Wilfred, who had argued Rome's case at the Synod. As both a cleric and a member of the Northumbrian nobility, Biscop would certainly have been a valuable member of the team.

Unfortunately, Wighard died before he could be consecrated, and the pope appointed Theodore of Tarsus to take his place. That might have ended Biscop's role in the matter, but it seems that he was destined to return to England. Since Theodore was Greek and not well versed in the English language, he needed a guide and interpreter. And since Biscop was available and still the best man for the job, he was sent to Canterbury to serve as the new archbishop's aide.

When they arrived in England, Theodore appointed Biscop to the post of abbot of a monastery near Canterbury. The monk dutifully served in that capacity but was impatient to found his own monastery. His opportunity came when Adrian, one of Theodore's old advisors, arrived at Canterbury. Biscop had spent two years in Kent studying under Theodore. Now he resigned his office in favor of Adrian, and that left him free to establish a monastery under the patronage of the king of Wessex.

Then, for the second time, death delayed Biscop's pursuit of his destiny. The king died before plans for the new monastery could be finalized. Temporarily at a loss, Biscop paid another visit to Rome. Always eager to improve his understanding of the monastic discipline he had chosen for his life, he now took full advantage of the resources that could be found there.

On earlier trips to the continent he had assembled a small library. He'd entrusted his books to friends while he continued his geographic and spiritual explorations. That was typical behavior for a young man. But now in the fifth decade of his life, he was ready to settle down. During this trip he added a large number of books to his library. Then he packed them up, along with a collection of relics and icons, and brought everything back to England.

With little hope of establishing a monastery in southern England, Biscop returned to his native Northumbria. The king there was now Egfrid, another of Oswy's sons. Egfrid welcomed this well traveled monk to his court and, like others who had dealt with him, found Biscop a very impressive character.

What we know of Biscop suggests that he was indeed a man who would impress kings and popes. Contemporary accounts picture him as intelligent and energetic. His love of religion matched his affection for his homeland, and he had acquired a great appreciation for art, which at that time could be found much more on the continent than in Northumbria.

King Egfrid took favorably to Biscop's energy and zeal. No doubt the king also appreciated the political advantages of a warm relationship with the papacy. He granted Biscop a piece of land – large enough it was said to support seventy families – at the mouth of the river Wear in Durham. The plan was for Biscop to establish a monastery to be dedicated to St. Peter.

Biscop launched into the project with great enthusiasm. It didn't take long for him to get organized. No doubt he had seen his monastery in his mind many hundreds of times. Now he had only to lay it out on the land that waited for him. It would stand on the north bank of the river. The monastery complex and a church to go with it would be built in the Roman style he had grown to love. But that posed a problem. The building he wanted would have to be done in stone, and the Anglo-Saxons built in wood. Even the grand church in Lindisfarne was a wooden building with a thatch roof.

Still, a determined man on the verge of realizing his dream is not to be deterred. Since Northumbria could not supply workers who knew how to build his church, he went to the continent to enlist stone masons from Gaul. And since the English did not have glass windows, he imported glaziers from the continent, too.

Work on the first building started in 674. The church was substantially complete a year later. It and the monastery came to be called Wearmouth because of their location at the mouth of the Wear. As Biscop had intended, they were done in the Roman style, making them a peculiar addition to the countryside since they employed arches, which were not then used in England.

Some of the work at Wearmouth still stands, a tribute to the French masons who built it. The actual stone and mortar they left beside that river, however, may have been their least permanent contribution to England. When the work was completed, many of them did not return home. They stayed in the island and taught their craft to others. This was more than they were required to do. They could have moved on, but in staying they gave birth to a tradition that would long outlive them.

Biscop, too, did more than was required of him. He had built his monastery, but that was not enough. He made one more trip to Rome, this time in search of relics and art to furnish his church and monastery.

His need to look abroad only partly reflected his love of all things Roman. It also underscored the relative shortage of artistic masterworks in England.

Here, once again, the record is sketchy. Biscop did bring back a great deal of art. But we have an enticing suggestion that he brought back more. Contemporary descriptions of his buildings indicate that their walls were decorated with murals. That sort of thing would have to be done on the spot, and Anglo-Saxon painting was not well developed at the time. The obvious conclusion is that he imported painters and other artists to decorate his churches and to teach their skills to the Northumbrians. This conclusion is guesswork, of course, but it is born out by one of the known facts of Biscop's career.

At Rome, Biscop obtained a charter for his monastery from Pope Agatho. That was to be expected. Then he took the additional step that is always the mark of a wise man. Biscop understood well that a religious institution is, and must be, more than its physical trappings. While he still had the pope's ear, he convinced Agatho to lend him the services of a monk named John, who was then the abbot of St. Martin's and arch-cantor of St. Peter's in Rome.

It was a simple arrangement. John would return with Biscop to England. There, he would compose music for the services at Wearmouth. But it must have been agreeable duty, because John went on to teach the liturgy and chants in Wearmouth and throughout Northumbria.

Now Benedict Biscop had land. He had mortar and stone. And he was acquiring art and music. The fabric of his monastery was almost complete. Still, there's always one more thing to do.

Another of Biscop's passions was collecting books. He already had a fine library, but that was for his personal use. He was determined to furnish his monastery with a large library, too. This, he felt, was necessary for an orderly monastic community. He believed that monks should spend their time inside the monastery, and a good library would help keep them in their cloisters and out of mischief. In addition, the learning that could be gained from books would contribute to an orderly and well run monastery.

Before leaving Rome, he assembled a library for Wearmouth. Then he returned to Northumbria. His trip to Rome provided all the things he needed. All that was lacking now was a set of regulations to guide his monks' conduct.

Biscop lost no time establishing a Rule for his monastery. Not surprisingly, he based it on the Rule of the Benedictine monastery at Monte Casino. But with characteristic thoroughness, Biscop studied the Rules of the seventeen monasteries he had visited during his life. Only then did he select what seemed to him the best of their regulations to compose his own Rule.

King Egfrid must have been pleased to see how well his gift of land had been used, because he now gave Biscop another piece of land nearby, this one consisting of forty "ploughs," for a monastery to be dedicated to St. Paul. Biscop began work on his second monastery at Jarrow in 681 or 682 and appointed a close friend, Ceolfrith, as its first abbot.

Soon these monasteries were home to more than 600 monks. Although the two establishments were six miles apart, Biscop conceived of them as a single institution, and he built them into the largest and most important monastery in England.

The size of Biscop's monastery gives an indication of its influence on the community, but only an indication. The forces he set in motion took on a life of their own, and their total effect can hardly be estimated. For a start, he did nothing less than spur the development of Anglo-Saxon art. The objects he brought from the continent undoubtedly excited many of the Northumbrians. But the artists and craftsmen he imported were the key to the cultural revival that followed. For the first time in memory, Biscop's people could not only see and touch art – something many of them had never done before – they could actually learn to *create* their own art.

Sometimes genius lies in nothing more than grasping a simple solution that has eluded everyone else. When Benedict Biscop solved his own problem by importing the craftsmen he could not find locally, he set an entire culture on a new course. The illuminated books produced in Northumbrian monasteries provide the first examples of Anglo-Saxon painting. The fine jewelry and tapestries that came next owe much of their beauty to the start Biscop provided. And, perhaps most important, a new appreciation – a new way of thinking – developed alongside the skills of the Anglo-Saxon artists. They not only learned to do art, they also learned its value.

Having set all of this in motion, Biscop merely went on with his work. Now that he was building a small empire, he needed to spend a substantial amount of time away from Wearmouth. So he appointed his nephew, Easterwin, to serve as abbot there in his absence.

Ironically, the time he spent away from the monastery may have contributed to its downfall. Or, just possibly, his absence may have prolonged his own life.

When he returned from a final trip to Rome, he found the monastery devastated. An epidemic had killed King Egfrid, abbot Easterwin and most of the monks. In fact, there were only two survivors at Jarrow – the abbot and a youth named Bede, who would later set to paper the primary record of Biscop's life and work.

Having escaped the epidemic, Biscop was virtually the only one left to salvage his work. He quickly set out to recruit more monks for his monasteries.

Unfortunately, his days of triumph had ended. He was an old man and his health soon began to fail. Before he could rebuild what Wearmouth and Jarrow had lost, he fell victim to an incapacitating illness that kept him bed ridden for most of his last three years. But even this did not weaken his concern for his monasteries. During his illness he specified that the libraries he had assembled not be dispersed and that his Rule be continued. Then he died at the age of sixty-two, after receiving a last communion on January 12, 690.

At first glance, all of this might seem a mere bit of ecclesiastical history that has nothing to do with Freemasonry. But the parallels become obvious when this story is compared with the legend of the *Regius Poem* and with some of the elements of the modern ritual.

In a very real sense, Biscop was the one who re-established the craft of masonry in England. The stone mason's skills had disappeared from the island long before his time, and they had not been revived. The revival of masonry is the critical element of the York legend, and Biscop, more than any of his contemporaries, deserves the credit for that. In addition, he was a patron not only of masonry but also of the arts and learning. This calls to mind the Masonic emphasis on the seven Arts and Sciences, which survives in the ritual and, as the *Regius Poem* attests, was a very early fixture of the craft.

Less obvious but just as important, Biscop's Rule foreshadows the free masonry of later centuries. It gave the craft a code of ethics from the earliest time. As we have seen, the old constitutions went beyond purely craft-related matters in a way that suggests it may have been derived from a monastic Rule. If Athelstan did reform the craft, if he did rewrite its regulations, we almost certainly see his work reflected in the pages of the *Regius Poem*. In the distant memory of Biscop's Rule, we may see the regulations that needed reforming.

By Athelstan's time, a seventh century monastic Rule would no longer serve the needs of operative masons whose ancestors, we must assume, had borrowed it from their patron. Newly settled in England, with no Rule of their own, Biscop's masons would likely look to him for guidance. He, in turn, would certainly frame a set of rules for them. It didn't have to be the same Rule he wrote for the monks of Wearmouth and Jarrow. Perhaps it was, perhaps not. Either way, it would have been suited to their needs at the time but would not have suited a craft that two and a half centuries later had evolved into an organization capable of erecting Gothic cathedrals.

Here, at last, we see the origin of Freemasonry. As the *Regius Poem* says, Athelstan reformed the stone mason's craft, but he did not bring it to England. Benedict Biscop did that.

This is not to say that Biscop created the organization that is now known as Freemasonry. It is one thing to trace the cultural roots of an organization to an earlier time. It is quite another to claim that it has an unbroken history that spans several centuries.

We need not waste time with the futile task of trying to establish an unbroken line of descent from the monasteries of Wearmouth and Jarrow to the modern Grand Lodge. That is probably impossible and certainly unnecessary.

Modern historians have learned the difficulty of trying to trace the Craft's history. As we go back in time, Freemasonry becomes more and more fragmented. Before 1717 it was not even a single organization. In the medieval period it was a different *kind* of organization. And by the time we reach the seventh century, we lose track of discrete organizations altogether.

What Benedict Bishop created was a *tradition*. He imported relics to give his monks an appreciation of the Church's history, art to make them appreciate the beauty of the world, and a craft that would eventually grow into a brotherhood. That, pure and simple, was the birth of Freemasonry.

A New Direction

We have pinpointed the origins of modern Freemasonry, and it might seem that we now have enough information to start drawing conclusions. But we are far from reaching the end of our quest. Parts of the puzzle still remain beyond our grasp, and we will not understand Masonic secrecy until we deal with them.

In the next part of our journey, we will encounter something unexpected. Of course, that's the way of Freemasonry. Its history, like its ritual, contains many surprises. Any Mason can attest to the surprises his initiation held for him. And he can verify that the farther he went in Masonry, the more surprises he encountered.

When an initiate becomes a full fledged (third degree) Freemason, he may think he has learned all the secrets and lessons the Order has to offer. Then he discovers that he has only begun. If he did not already know it, he soon finds that there are more degrees. He is not required to apply for them but is encouraged to do so. And he is led to believe that there is much more to learn – that he will better understand the things shown to him in the first three degrees if he continues his quest for Masonic knowledge.

Perhaps, then, it's fitting for our investigation of the Craft's secrets to unfold in the same way Masonry reveals information to its initiates. We have looked at the three degrees and traced the fraternity to its historic beginnings. But the origin of its secrecy still eludes us. Now we discover that we must see what is contained in the higher degrees before we can understand what Hiram gave his life to protect.

There are several advanced degrees from which to choose. At various times and places, more than a thousand of them have been practiced. They were especially popular in eighteenth century France, where systems of Masonry proliferated. Most of them have become extinct. In many cases, historians know only their names. The rituals have vanished completely. But a handful of these degrees have survived and are regularly offered to

Knight Templar
A medieval Templar in full battle dress.

people who have completed the basic initiation. They include the well known Scottish and York Rites as well as more obscure offerings like the Royal Order of Scotland and the Royal Ark Mariner.

When the Master Mason begins to investigate these degrees, he finds another legend at every turn. The use of legends is a recurring theme in the higher degrees. Some are based on the story of Hiram Abif. Others deal with matters that seem, at least on the surface, completely unrelated to what the new Mason discovered in the first three degrees. We will soon see, however, an enticing hint that somehow it all ties together.

The advanced degrees tell a hodgepodge of stories that are hard to keep track of and even harder to understand. The ones that deal with King Solomon's Temple are the least enigmatic of the lot. Since they build on the story from the third degree, they can at least be recognized as part of the same system of instruction. But what of the others. They are of a very different nature. They span thousands if years and are set not only in the Holy Land but across Europe as well.

Among these are the stories of the Knights Templar. Soon after a Mason begins moving through the higher degrees, he encounters the Templar legend. This may seem curious, since he has been given to understand that his fraternity dates back to the medieval stone masons — or perhaps that it goes back in that same tradition all the way to King Solomon's Temple. Now he discovers hints that it descended from a group of medieval knights who presumably had nothing to do with architecture.

But that idea is not as unbelievable as it might seem. The Templar degrees are based on historic fact. They tell of a military and religious order that was wrongly persecuted. At that time, some of its members fled, taking refuge where they could, and eventually, according to Masonic legend, they became Freemasons.

The historic events that underlie this legend occurred in the fourteenth century. They are fairly well documented. Certainly we know more of this episode than we do of the building of Solomon's Temple. And we can easily compare the Masonic legends with a large body of contemporary documents and historic interpretation.

We would not be the first to make such a comparison. Over the years, many writers have spent a great deal of effort trying to prove that modern Freemasonry descended from Templars who fled the persecution in France and took refuge in Britain. Some have even argued that the Templars provided the *real* origin of the Craft's symbolism.

These theories are romantic and intriguing. Moreover, they seem to explain some things that are otherwise very confusing. Unfortunately, at least for their proponents, there seems to be no evidence to confirm that there is any truth in them. The events that could prove the Masonic Templar theories lie on the extreme fringes of history. They might have happened, but it is very difficult to tell if they did. In fact, it may no longer be possible to sort through the vagaries of history to determine what did and did not happen so long ago.

In view of these problems, many Masonic writers have concluded that the task of proving a connection with the Knights Templar is impossible, while others insist that the theory was nonsense in the first place. They point out that the Masonic legend of King Solomon's Temple at least has some logical connection with the medieval stone masons. The Templar legend, on the other hand, seems completely unrelated to the operative craft. The only thing they have in common is their appeal to secrecy, and that is not enough to establish an historic connection.

Still, as we have seen, Masonic legends have something to do with historic fact. They have certainly drifted far from the genuine past. Not all of the events they describe are recorded by the historian and some are at odds with the way history has come down to us. But they do retain at least a trace of history.

Trying to sort out the facts from the Masonic jumble of myth, allegory and play acting is not easy. But history of the Templars contains something that will point the way for our investigation. In their final days the Templars did become fugitives. The king of France ordered five thousand of them arrested in one night. Later, he had dozens put to death, while those who escaped continued for years to live under the threat of torture and execution.

Men in such peril understand the value of secrecy. Their very lives depend on being able to recognize their friends and avoid their enemies. Keeping their identity, their comings and goings and the details of their meetings hidden from prying eyes takes on the utmost importance.

But isn't this curious? If it were not an account of the Templars, it could easily be mistaken for a description of the Masons. Their cult of secrecy and the severe penalties that go with it do have a medieval air. Is it possible that they were originally designed to satisfy the needs of a band of fugitive knights?

Although evidence for a connection between the Freemasons and the Templars is elusive, it is a simple fact that secrecy lies at the heart of both organizations. This, combined with the fact that the rituals of the higher degrees contain repeated references to the Templars, now sets the direction for our quest. In our effort to understand Masonic secrecy, we can not ignore such an obvious parallel. It may prove to be nothing more than a coincidence, but we would be remiss if we did not investigate it.

The Templars

W hat if the early free masons were not simply stone carvers? What if they were something else, something much more mysterious and glamorous than a mundane group of craftsmen? These have become perennial questions for an organization whose legends often have a grim ring of truth. Since the details of the Craft's early history have never been deciphered, such questions as these are not merely possible. They are wide open to speculation.

Indeed, speculation has become a preoccupation for students of Masonic history. The many unexplained bits of the ritual provide a fertile ground for breeding theories. During the early Grand Lodge period, curiosity about the fraternity's origins was widespread, and the minds of the enlightened gentlemen of the day took pleasure in concocting stories – the more elaborate the better – to explain the exotic aspects of the Craft. Then, as the field of Masonic history matured, the romantic stories of the Craft's origins came under rational scrutiny. Many were found too fantastic and most were discredited in favor of a more mundane view of Masonic origins. But one in particular has survived all attempts to debunk it.

Prominent among the theories that arose in the eighteenth century, the Templar story has attracted more than its share of attention. Lovers of conspiracy theories are strongly attracted to it. And although historians are reluctant to take it seriously, the idea that the Freemasons descended from the Templars simply refuses to go away.

As we have seen, the operative masons had one level of initiation, one degree. Historians believe that a second degree evolved in the late seventeenth or early eighteenth century and was soon followed by a third. At that point, what is called "blue lodge" Masonry was essentially complete. The three degrees were – and still are – the basic system of initiation, but others were soon to follow.

As the eighteenth and nineteenth centuries progressed, a large number of Masonic and pseudo-Masonic rites appeared. Some were legitimate, others a little shady, and many were downright fraudulent. Freemasonry, it seems, had become popular enough to attract the odd confidence trickster. Since the Craft operated behind closed doors, few outsiders knew what a *real* Masonic lodge was like. Consequently, it was easy for charlatans to invent and stage bogus degrees just for the money they could obtain from initiation fees. And bogus degrees did appear – by tens and hundreds.

The legitimate side of the Craft was by no means idle during this period, either. The Grand Lodge of England was soon joined by grand lodges springing up in other countries. As they spread their influence, and as ruling bodies arose to govern the higher degrees, the excesses died away and a limited number of degrees became standard. Some of these are still obscure, but the main ones are well known to Masons if not to the general public.

Among these higher degrees, more than a few deal with the Knights Templar. Both the York and Scottish Rites have them. And the Order of Demolay, a youth organization founded early in the twentieth century and sponsored by Freemasonry, is based on the authentic history of the Templars.

These degrees form a Masonic legend that presents moral lessons by recalling the exploits of a medieval band of knights. Curiously, though, the Masonic version of the story seems to have been developed in the eighteenth century. There is nothing to prove that the Masons had anything like a Templar legend before then.

The apparent absence of Templarism at an earlier date makes us wonder whether the Templar degrees are records of a real historic connection or just the product of a fashion that developed several centuries after the fact. Although this may seem to be a trivial question – and one of interest only to academics – it is in fact one of the most important questions the modern Freemason can ask. It goes right to the heart of his organization's origins.

Masonic literature is filled with attempts to show an actual connection between the medieval Templars and the Masons. Historians can point to intriguing parallels. And they can talk about what might have happened in the distant past. But they are consistently thwarted when they try to *prove* that one organization actually evolved into the other.

Proponents of the Templar theory are frustrated by the lack of evidence that the medieval Templars joined forces with the cathedral builders of their day. And there is no evidence that the Templars evolved into modern Freemasons independently of the medieval craft of stone masons.

Plagued by the lack of evidence, the theory's proponents have slowly died away. Modern writers, taking pride in their sober approach to historiography, settle for tracing Masonic Templarism to the eighteenth century and leave it there. They find no evidence of an earlier connection, so they conclude that there was none.

But the theory can not be disposed of that easily. If there were a connection so many centuries ago, it might have left no traces in the documentary record. In an age of illiteracy, information often does not survive the last person who considers it important enough to remember. Only a small part of any society's knowledge is committed to writing. Much more is forgotten, and in the case of the Templars much was forgotten on purpose.

We know that modern Masonry is a secretive organization. As we will see, the Templars were even more so. And when history turned against them, they suddenly found an urgent need to increase their already strict rule of secrecy. If Freemasonry's antecedents were indeed the fugitive knights the Templars had become, Masonic secrecy could well have had its origins four centuries before the first meeting of the Grand Lodge of England. According to that scenario, it is reasonable to believe that there was a concentrated effort to keep the facts from being preserved. And if that is so, anyone who tries to uncover the truth of this story must contend with a conspiracy of silence from a period that, under the best of circumstances, yielded a scarcity of historical evidence.

To get to the bottom of this, we must take a hard look at the medieval Templars, the early free masons and the times in which they lived. If we find enough similarity between the two organizations, and if we find that they had both a reason and an opportunity to join forces, then there may be some substance to the theory.

The most obvious point of departure is that the Templars were more or less contemporary with the early masons. Their order was founded in the twelfth century, a time when cathedral building was in flower and stone masonry was developing into a highly organized craft.

The Templars and the free masons were born into the same world and were shaped by the same society. But in many ways the society they shared was different from ours. It was a time in which religious fervor blended with an amorality that shocks the modern mind. And it was a time when blame had to be assigned to actions that to the modern mind would appear trivial and accidental. Everything that happened was caused by God or man or the devil. Someone had to accept the responsibility, and where the buck stopped was usually decided by those individuals who had wealth and power.

In the Middle Ages, the measure of wealth was land. The pre-industrial world took everything it needed from the land. Food was harvested from field and pasture. Wool and cotton for clothes were fruits of the land, as were wood and stone for building. Even ink for the few who could read was ultimately an agricultural product.

The more land a man controlled, the more wealth and power were at his disposal. But land was not easy to hold. Large landowners faced the perennial danger that their estates would become fragmented into smaller and smaller lots as the property passed to successive generations of heirs.

To avoid this problem, the entire estate was left to the first born son. This was a common sense solution to an age old problem. It kept property relatively intact and under the control of the oldest and most experienced heir. A dowry was given to daughters to insure that they married into desirable families. But the younger sons were routinely left with no estate to manage and little to do.

In a simple, rigid society, there were few opportunities for young men who had no land to provide them even a small income. The military and the Church were the best places for them to seek a career, and that is where the younger sons of landed families usually ended up. That tradition has survived well into modern times. In recent generations it became a matter of convenience. In the Middle Ages, it played a more important role. It provided the manpower and motivation for a marvelous adventure that became the Crusades. But that is a complex story.

As the second millennium got under way, Europe was still divided into small kingdoms. With no strong central authority to maintain order, the petty princes were left to protect their own interests as best they could. The result was strife with no end in sight. In this world, the concept of "might makes right" prevailed.

That notion was a little more involved than it may seem. It was only partly based on a belief that God would give strength to the just in their struggles against the unjust. It was also a recognition of the practical state of the society. Modern nations did not yet exist. Some nobles did claim authority over large areas, but their power depended on the aid of vassals to whom they granted land – the only source of wealth – in return for support. The vassals frequently granted some of their land to vassals of their own. And those vassals granted serfs permission to use bits of land in return for specified payments. The entire society was a network of contractual arrangements that, at least in theory, benefited everyone.

In the absence of a central authority, a well developed system of laws and an independent judiciary to enforce them, the nobles had no choice but to administer justice on their own. And the only way they had to do it was to rely on the force of arms. In that setting, it was a very obvious and practical principle that right was determined by whomever had the might to enforce it. There was simply no higher authority to which the dissatisfied could appeal.

One of the forces that operated in this political patchwork was the Church. During the first thousand years of its existence, the Christian Church worked out its doctrine and organization. Monasticism carved out a niche for itself. And religion become a dominant force in the lives of people at all levels of society.

During its second millennium, the Church began to pay attention to its position as a temporal power. It had occasionally involved itself in political matters, but now the time was right for it to take important new steps. The papacy had long wanted sovereignty, at least in spiritual terms, with all princes and kings paying allegiance to the Church. That had been an impossible dream in the chaotic world which emerged from the fall of the Roman Empire. But Europe was changing. The means for improving the Church's fortunes were now at hand, although they were to come from an unexpected quarter, and the occasion to use them was taking shape in the east.

The Holy Land had been in the hands of Infidels since the seventh century. That was something of an affront to most Christians, but it wasn't worth fighting over. Most of the time, relations between East and West were fairly normal. Christian pilgrims traveled to Jerusalem with little hindrance. The Infidel saw them as relatively inoffensive tourists who caused little trouble and added to the coffers of the local merchants. For their share of the pie, the Eastern rulers imposed a tax on pilgrims. That made the trip more costly, but the pilgrims had little to fear from the Infidel. As a rule, it was business as usual.

This is not to say that all was well. The life of a pilgrim was never easy. The trip from Europe to the Holy Land could take years. It was a grueling journey through strange lands where travelers could easily fall victim to bad food, disease, fatigue or bandits. And anyone fortunate enough to survive all of that faced a similar ordeal on the return journey.

The Europeans knew very well that the pilgrim's enterprise was long, hard and dangerous. But merely living in the Middle Ages was a perilous adventure, and the added hardships of a journey to the Holy Land were a perfectly acceptable price for the spiritual rewards the pilgrim expected to receive in return.

Then, starting in the tenth century, the Eastern rulers began to resent their Christian visitors. The pilgrims continued to enjoy long periods of cordial relations with the east, but times were changing.

As the eleventh century got under way, pilgrimages to the Holy Land became increasingly popular in Europe. As a result, what had been a healthy tourist industry began to look like an invasion by a foreign culture. This, coupled with a new and official hostility, partly born of religious intolerance, produced a crisis of major proportions. The occasional story of harsh treatment was replaced by reports of the systematic destruction of holy places and the expulsion of Christians resident in the east.

To a Europe steeped in religious devotion and accustomed to endless petty wars, the situation seemed both unacceptable and easily remedied. This was a classic case of two cultures with irreconcilable differences, and for their part the Europeans had the means to handle the situation.

With large numbers of men seeking a military career, undesirable strife holding back progress in Europe and the Holy Land in the hands of a people now seen as openly hostile to Christianity, a military campaign to the east was an idea whose time had come. That would certainly get the surplus of

Pope Urban II
In a sermon delivered at the Council of Claremont calls for
an expedition to liberate the Holy Land.

armed men out of Europe. In addition, it would cut down on regional strife by giving all the Christian principalities of Europe a common enemy.

Pope Gregory VII became an early proponent of the idea. For him it was a way to deal with the European princes' reluctance to give due respect to the Church. An expedition to capture Jerusalem would be an overtly religious enterprise. That would place the Church in a leadership role that could only strengthen its influence over the secular world.

Gregory had a very logical argument for such an expedition. The Church had long promoted visits to holy places as a way the faithful could come closer to salvation. Since Jerusalem was the most holy of holy places, it stood to reason that a visit there would bring the ultimate in spiritual benefit. And actually fighting to free the city from the Infidel would be an even more holy pursuit.

The idea of Christians killing for the Church was something of a problem. For a start, the Ten Commandments forbade killing. Besides, the Christian's obligation to emulate Christ argued against violence. But the groundwork for justifying a military crusade had already been laid. European Christians had been fighting Moors in a more secular context for centuries, and the Moor was an Infidel. In addition, several centuries earlier, St. Augustine of Hippo had apparently put forward the idea of a just war. His views were somewhat distorted by those who wanted to justify their military aspirations, but at least he was available to console potential crusaders.

The papacy had long given its sanction – along with the promise of heavenly reward – to Christians who took up the sword against the Infidel. And in more recent years, the papacy had succeeded in establishing monasticism as a tool of the Church.

At first monasticism might seem to have nothing to do with crusades, but in fact it was one of the most important factors in the development of a crusading spirit. Centuries earlier, Pope Gregory I had wisely recognized the great potential of the monastic concept. He and subsequent popes had carefully fostered it and built it into an institution that was now ready to perform a most important role.

Monks were sworn to do God's work. Making the Holy Land safe for pilgrims would certainly be consistent with God's will. So it was no great leap of logic to see that crusading soldiers would be performing a function not dissimilar to that performed by monks. This removed the stigma of killing and at the same time provided a compelling reason to enlist in the cause. It was a powerful force waiting for the right moment in history.

As the last quarter of the eleventh century got under way, Gregory VII tried to set this force in motion. He began calling for a military expedition to the Holy Land and even offered to lead the troops himself. Unfortunately for him, his ambition was thwarted by a battery of local problems that held his attention until his death in 1085.

Although Gregory never got his expedition off the ground, he had sowed seeds that would soon bear fruit. He had established the need for a crusade

Peter, the Hermit
Preaching the Crusades.

and the logic of his argument was inescapable. All that was needed now was something to ignite the popular imagination.

The Council of Claremont, held near the end of 1095, provided the spark. The new pope, Urban II, agreed that the time for a crusade was at hand. To that end, he delivered a sermon to the council in which he called for an expedition to the east.

Since several versions of the sermon have come down to us, it is impossible to know exactly what the pope called for. Apparently he had in mind a well organized military campaign that would leave Europe in August of the following year. It would proceed to Constantinople, where Alexius, the Byzantine emperor, could assist the expedition on the last leg of its journey to Jerusalem. And there the crusaders would take the Holy City from the Infidel.

It should have worked just that way, but Urban sold the project too well. The people of Europe accepted the call to arms so enthusiastically that they didn't stop to think what they were getting into. They set out almost immediately on a quest that seemed so right they couldn't imagine its failing.

This first attempt at a crusade was an ambivalent enterprise from the outset. It was led by one Peter the Hermit, an itinerant preacher who had no official standing with the Church. Peter was one of those charismatic figures who can easily sway the masses. He was a plain man with an ascetic way of life. Unwashed, wearing simple clothes, carrying no possessions and riding a donkey, he traveled through France and Germany preaching a message that in no way offended Church doctrine. This was an unaffected man of obvious virtue and piety. The people who were privileged to hear him preach must have felt that they had come close to hearing Christ himself.

It was this Peter, a man who straddled the world of the Church and the world of the most common of men, who led the first crusade. Perhaps this fact foreshadowed the fate of the enterprise. By the time he set out for the Holy Land, Peter had more than thirty thousand followers. The group was too large to be a band of pilgrims, and it had too few men at arms to be an effective military force. Its people were disorganized and had no more than a vague notion of what lay ahead of them or what they might accomplish when and if they reached the end of their journey.

Unfortunately, and perhaps inevitably, the "People's" Crusade turned out to be more rabble than army. As they moved through eastern Europe, the mob stole what they needed and killed anyone who provided a convenient target. Alexius managed to move them through his territory with a minimum of damage, but when they finally came into contact with the real enemy, the undisciplined force was virtually wiped out.

Fortunately for the Church, this was not the end of the crusading spirit. While the People's Crusaders were being slaughtered, a much better organized army was on its way east. It contained more people with military experience, and they had taken the time to prepare for a long journey and a serious fight against the Infidel. They were better prepared psychologically as well. The crusaders took a vow and sewed cloth crosses on their clothes as a symbol of their vow. It was a constant reminder of the purpose of their crusade and their obligation to the Church.

This was the first real effort to take the Holy Land from the Infidel, and indeed it is remembered in history as the First Crusade. The army took a year to reach Antioch. They laid siege to the city and finally captured it in June of the following year. The crusaders then proceeded to Jerusalem and took that city on July 15, 1099.

This was the start of a long Christian occupation of the Holy Land. But the occupation was neither quick nor easy.

The early years of the Christians' presence were a time for getting organized. Their adventure was a new experience, and the crusaders had few precedents to guide them. Their first efforts were often awkward, a matter of learning from mistakes and laying ground work for the future.

It is at times like this that legends are born, and the beginning of the Crusades was no exception. This particular setting was to give birth to two organizations, each of which was destined to reach legendary proportions. Together, they virtually dominated the Crusades, but they were slow to claim their place in history.

The first of these organizations already existed in rudimentary form. Since the third century, there had been a Christian presence in Jerusalem dedicated to caring for pilgrims. Some of the Christians who lived there had taken on the responsibility of maintaining a hospital to treat the diseases and injuries to which travelers of the day so easily fell prey.

Over the centuries, the Christian hospital in Jerusalem went through several incarnations, its fortunes waxing and waning according to political changes in the city. By the time of the First Crusade, the tradition of caring for pilgrims was being carried on by two hospitals, one serving women and the other for men. The women's hospital was dedicated to St. Mary Magdalene. The men's hospital, it is said, was dedicated at first to St. John the Almoner but later to St. John the Baptist. This establishment was known as the Hospital of St. John, and the monks who lived and worked there were the Brothers of the Hospital of St. John of Jerusalem.

When the crusaders arrived on the scene, the men's hospital was under the direction of Brother Gerard. He is one of those characters who is known by apocryphal stories because the facts of his life are missing.

Apparently Gerard was a pious man and a capable administrator. His hospital was certainly well established and dedicated to serving any Christian who needed aid. According to the stories, he and his Hospitallers risked their lives to help the crusaders. It is even said that Gerard advised them on how to take the city. Perhaps he did. But whatever the truth of the stories that grew up around them, the Hospitallers were soon receiving large donations from a grateful Christian world.

Peter Gerard
Abbot of the Hospital of St. John at the time of the first Crusade.

Eventually the Hospitallers would become the Templars' chief rivals, but for the time being there was no trace of the military organization they were to become. And the Templars did not yet exist. When the crusaders took Jerusalem, the Hospitallers were a purely charitable organization, and so they would remain as long as Brother Gerard controlled their affairs. It was not until after his time that an unlikely chain of events transformed the Hospitallers and created the Templars.

Godfrey de Bouillon, Duke of Lower Lorraine, was the first of the crusaders to rule Jerusalem. It was a much less glorious position than might be imagined. He found himself the leader of a government that was under manned and under financed. He was surrounded by hostile Moslem princes and had to contend with Christian leaders – both secular and religious – whose one reason for maintaining even a semblance of unity no longer existed. With the Infidel defeated and the Holy Land conquered, it was now every man for himself.

Although the circumstances were less than ideal, Godfrey accepted the responsibility of his office, but he refused to call himself king in the city where he believed only Christ deserved that title. If the historians are right about his leadership and piety, Godfrey might have forged the Holy Land into a powerful and efficiently run nation. Unfortunately, he had little chance to realize his promise. Godfrey died within a year and was succeeded by his brother, Baldwin.

Baldwin did accept the title of King of Jerusalem, but, again, the title was less than it might seem. His was not the only Christian kingdom in the Holy Land. By now the crusaders had divided their newly won territories into small states and were trying to enjoy the fruits of their labor. Thus the new king inherited a tiny kingdom in a disorganized land. Still, as ruler of Jerusalem he was something of a figurehead, and it was up to him to deal with a staggering array of problems.

The crusader states had barely established themselves. Now, lacking manpower and resources, they all faced a struggle merely to survive. Many of the crusaders returned home almost immediately. They considered their mission accomplished as soon as they took Jerusalem. To replace them, new expeditions were mounted. Unfortunately, as soon as the war ended,

Godfrey de Bouillon
The Crusaders proclaim Godfrey de Bouillon the first King of Jerusalem in A.D. 1099.

excitement in Europe died down. The few who volunteered arrived in small numbers, and the Church could raise little money to support them. As a result, the crusaders who remained in the Holy Land were largely left to fend for themselves.

For the moment they could do little to consolidate the territory they had gained. Although they occupied strongholds scattered over the Holy Land, the countryside and the roads were not safe. The principal port of entry for pilgrims was Joppa. It took two days to travel from there to Jerusalem, and the road was so hazardous that contemporary accounts describe it as littered with the bodies of pilgrims and merchants who had fallen victim to bandits, thirst and heat.

Faced with these problems, one of King Baldwin's highest priorities was to rebuild the Holy City. Its population had been decimated in the slaughter that occurred when it was taken. To remedy that situation, Baldwin established incentives to encourage Christians to move in. He also tried to make his little kingdom more attractive to pilgrims. They were a potential source of considerable revenues, and he wanted to encourage as many of them as possible to visit his city.

Here the Hospitallers enter our story again. They played a major role in attracting pilgrims. The Hospital provided medical attention – something for which there was always a need in the Middle Ages – as well as food and money for those who had exhausted their resources by the time they arrived in the Holy Land.

The Hospitallers were promptly rewarded for their service. In 1113, Pope Paschal II gave them a major boost by granting them a charter as a religious order – the Order of the Hospital of St. John of Jerusalem. This new status relieved the Hospital of some of its tax burden and some of the bureaucratic restraints it had previously had to contend with in dealing with the local rulers. This, along with steadily increasing donations, allowed the Hospitallers to begin their growth into a powerful organization.

By 1118, which was to be Baldwin's last year, the crusaders had made considerable gains. The Christians now controlled major portions of Palestine and Syria. More manpower and money were available, and pilgrims were coming to the Holy Land in increasing numbers. But all was not well. The task of providing the pilgrims some measure of protection in their travels had become a serious burden for the crusaders.

During this period, the idea of a police force to keep the roads safe began to crystallize. Precisely when the idea was proposed is not clear. It's the kind of project Baldwin would have welcomed. It fitted well with his plans. But money and manpower were still in short supply, and if Baldwin did want to establish a police force, he may have lacked the resources to get the project started.

History suggests that Hugues de Payens, a knight from Champagne, first proposed the project. He visualized a body of soldiers who would keep the

Godfrey de Bouillon
The first of the Crusaders to rule Jerusalem.

roads open from the coast to the Holy City. These would be men of noble birth who would serve God by keeping His pilgrims safe.

At some point, perhaps during 1118 while Baldwin was still alive, or in 1119 after his death, the police force was actually established. De Payens and a small group of knights – the number usually given is eight – received a mandate to patrol the roads of Jerusalem and escort pilgrims to and from the Holy City.

Now De Payens had to decide what kind of organization his police force would be. The crusaders were already seen as furthering the Church's mission. They were not unlike the clergy in this respect. His knights, however, would be a smaller, more dedicated group within the crusading enterprise. It would be more like a monastic order than the ordinary clergy. This was the spirit that had started the Crusades, and in the Templars it would reach its full potential. The spirit was so compelling that before long someone decided that De Payens' knights should actually *be* monks. And that is what they became.

Since the Templars were to be the first monastic order of knights, they had to make some groundbreaking decisions. In keeping with the role they had assumed, they took the triple monastic vows of chastity, poverty and obedience. They also committed themselves to live under a set of monastic regulations. For the time being, they adopted the Benedictine Rule, which was still considered the standard. Their use of these regulations was unofficial, but it gave them a discipline to follow, and that was a necessary part of the monastic life.

Thus the Poor Knights of Christ came into existence. The king, either Baldwin or his successor Baldwin II, gave them quarters in the Al Aqsar mosque. This building was located to the south of the Dome of the Rock on the mount where King Solomon's Temple once stood. From its lodgings there the Order got its unofficial name, the Knights of the Temple, or more simply, the Templars.

The Templars got off to a slow start. During their first decade their membership grew very gradually. They wore donated clothes and depended on charity for all their other needs as well. But gradually the people of Europe and the Holy Land began to take notice. Contributions increased and the Templars began to see recruits from Europe.

Meanwhile, Jerusalem's other monastic group had not been idle. Brother Gerard died just about the time the Templars were getting started. His successor, Raymond du Puy, realized that times had changed. It was now more important to defend the Holy Land and its visitors than to heal them. Responding to the same conditions that produced the Templars, Raymond began the evolution of his Hospitallers from a charitable order into a fighting force.

By 1125, the Hospitallers had expanded their role to include escorting pilgrims, a decidedly military function. The Hospitallers were also becom-

Joppa

The principal point of entry to the Holy Land, as it appeared to arriving pilgrims.

ing international, with the establishment of hostels in French and Italian ports to see pilgrims safely on their way out of Europe.

Clearly the notion of an order of monastic warriors was an idea whose time had come. But making it a reality would take some work. Both orders expanded their public relations and recruiting efforts, and both quickly realized the benefits of their efforts.

Of the two orders, the Templars – the smaller and younger – were the more in need of support from home. To get that support Hugues de Payens returned to Europe in 1126 to promote his order. For the Templars to be effective, they needed more knights. To support the knights, they needed money. And to legitimize the order, they needed official recognition from the Church.

De Payens hoped to gain all three. He solicited recruits and financial support from the European nobility. Then, armed with a letter from Baldwin II to Bernard, abbot of Clairvaux, he set out to secure a monastic Rule for the order. Being granted their own Rule would constitute official sanction from the Church and would give the Templars a set of regulations tailored to their unique situation.

Bernard was the right man to approach for this purpose. He was one of the most influential figures in the Church. He was universally respected for the soundness of his opinions and his ability to express them, and his approval would virtually insure a favorable response from the papacy

Bernard did give the Templars his support, and Pope Honorius II called a Council to be held at Troyes in 1128 to decide their future. When the Council convened in January of that year, Bernard declined to attend for health reasons, but he had already argued their case with his usual eloquence. The Church's leadership had no doubt that he was firmly behind the Templars, and they could not ignore his reasons for supporting them. Like Bernard, the Council saw the wisdom of a military force operating in the Holy Land under the Church's direct authority. The Templars received the sanction of the Church. Bernard's Rule was approved. And the pope granted the order the right to wear a white mantle as a symbol of purity.

Here we encounter our first enticing hint of a connection between the Templars and the Freemasons. One of the most enigmatic Masonic symbols is the beehive. It is curious, because most Masonic symbols are either architectural or Biblical. The beehive is neither. The Masons use it as a symbol of industry and thus make it fit the image of group of craftsmen working together. But that explanation is less than satisfying. This particular symbol has the air of something that was handed down for generations but whose original meaning has been lost.

Interestingly, St. Bernard is often pictured with a beehive to symbolize his eloquence. Since it was his eloquence that insured the Templars their place in history, we must wonder if the Freemasons were thinking of St. Bernard when they added the beehive to their symbology. If they were, we must then wonder why the Masons would honor him in such a cryptic way if they did not believe that they were the Templars' secret descendants.

There is no proof here. It is at most a suggestion that a small bit of the Masonic ritual contains more than appears on the surface. But we already know that. To see if the beehive and other Masonic curiosities actually mark a trail that leads to the medieval Templars, we must continue our examination of how the Templars grew and how they died.

During the first years of his order's history, Hugues de Payens received considerable donations of money and land. It was obvious, even at the beginning, that a support system would be needed to handle the Templars' assets in Europe. De Payens correctly saw the need and acted promptly. Before returning to the Holy Land, he set up the Templars' first preceptories in Europe. Their function would be to manage the property the Templars were beginning to receive and to recruit and process new members.

At first, the Templars were merely an *ad hoc* organization formed to deal with an immediate problem. They had accepted the standard monastic vows of chastity, poverty and obedience. They had even chosen two men riding a single horse as an emblem of their poverty and humility. Then, suddenly, they were on the move. The Order was bound by a monastic Rule composed by no less a figure than St. Bernard. They had financing, new members and a uniform. Now it was time to carve out a place for themselves in history. But history can be a fickle thing.

It can be argued that even at this early date the Templars' fate was sealed. They had already embarked on a course from which they could scarcely turn back. For the rest of their existence the Order's character was shaped by a blend of monastic and military considerations. On the surface, there might seem to be nothing dangerous about that. But the practical necessities of the day were to have far reaching implications.

The operations of both monastery and army are based on discipline and obedience. To that end, the Templars' highest ranking officer, the Grand Master, was given nearly absolute authority. That authority was conveyed to the members by subordinate officers, who in turn had a great deal of power and little need to explain their actions. In addition to the provisions of the Rule, the leaders could impose special regulations and orders. And in the interest of security, these edicts would be issued on a "need to know" basis and kept secret from the general membership.

While historians know where these provisions were to lead, the Templars knew only that they had found a form of organization that was well suited to a monastic order and an armed force. Since the Templars were both, the structure would serve them well.

When Hugues de Payens returned to the Holy Land in 1130 his order had a firm foundation for future growth. More importantly, it had caught the attention of Europe, a factor that would guarantee a steady flow of finances and recruits. From this point, the Templars grew rapidly.

A few years earlier, the crusaders had fired the imagination of the folks back home. Now, the new military orders were seen as exemplifying the enterprise at its best. Throughout Europe people were eager to be a part of the adventure, and they would pay for the privilege. If they could not join, they would at least give financial support. This spirit was a boon, especially to the Templars, whose founder had established a support organization and thus given them the tools to take full advantage of any money that came their way.

In addition, the Templars soon happened upon another source of wealth. They now had more power than they needed to patrol the roads of Palestine. They had, in fact, become a significant military force. At the same time, most of the crusaders who remained in the Holy Land had settled into a comfortable life and were reluctant to fight.

This provided an unexpected option for the Templars. Intermittent clashes were still occurring between the Christians and the Moslems. With their Christian brothers less and less willing to fight, the Templars had only to offer their services ... for a fee. They seized the opportunity to assume an expanded military role and were well rewarded for their efforts. The Templars' coffers soon overflowed with money collected from their Christian employers and spoils of war grabbed from the Infidel.

Meanwhile, the Templars continued to receive donations of money and land located in various parts of Europe. As their assets grew, managing them became an increasingly important part of the Order's activities. Its preceptories, originally local offices with limited duties, developed into an international network of treasuries. They became very efficient in recruiting members and administering a growing list of properties.

Since the knights' primary function was military, they were ill-equipped to handle the increasingly specialized work necessary to keep their financial empire running smoothly. They solved that problem by enlisting serving brothers – men whose low birth did not qualify them to serve as knights but who could perform administrative and support functions in the organization. These brothers performed domestic duties and kept the Order's records, leaving the knights free to do the work for which they had been trained.

By the time Hugues de Payens died in 1136, he had built his order of humble knights into a powerful military organization, and accidents of history had provided a foundation for even more growth. For their part, the rank and file Templars did not waste the opportunities they received during the early years. Their dedication and labor earned them an enviable reputation. They were universally respected for their courage and integrity and were, in fact, the only Christian force to earn the serious respect of the Moslems.

With these auspicious beginnings, the Templars stood poised for their days of glory. For a while it seemed that each accomplishment was rewarded and every reward paved the way for another accomplishment.

In 1139 Pope Innocent II issued a Bull, *Omne Datum Optimum*, which greatly improved the Templars' position. It allowed them to recruit their own chaplains, who eventually came to be bound by the same obligation as the knights, and to build churches for their own use. In addition, as an arm of the Church, they were exempt from paying tithes and could actually receive tithes from laymen. The avowed purpose of all this was to protect the purity of the knights by further separating them from the profane society. But the Bull effectively made the Templars accountable only to the pope.

The military order was now virtually autonomous, and future popes would expand its privileges further. Exemption from tithes and taxes allowed the Templars to accumulate even more wealth. And their autonomy from local authorities, justified by the fact that they were an international organization, removed the last effective restraints on their conduct. For the rest of their history, the knights could do as they pleased.

As the Templars' power increased, so did their glory. In 1147, on the eve of the Second Crusade, Pope Eugenius III granted them the right to add a red cross, a symbol of martyrdom, to their white mantle. Obviously they had become more than mere heroes to the Christians of western Europe. They were the darlings of an entire continent. But they were not without competition.

By this time, Raymond du Puy had virtually completed his refashioning of the Hospitallers. He had reorganized them as a military order along the same lines at the Templars. In fact, Du Puy used his sister organization as a model for many of the changes he introduced into his own group. The Hospitallers' charitable functions, once the Order's entire reason for existing, were still there but had been reduced to a secondary role. The Hospitallers and the Templars were now cast in the same mold. Both were religious and military orders, bound directly to the Church, largely independent of the secular princes and wealthy enough to make their own way in the world.

In a society characterized by petty squabbling, it was inevitable that tensions would arise between two such organizations. Although they still fought on the same side, the Templars and the Hospitallers had grown into rival organizations. They frequently came into conflict with each other and occasionally came to blows. Their animosity even included the occasional street fight. Perhaps that is more a comment on the times than a reflection on the orders, but it colored their relations until the end.

As the years passed, both orders became more powerful and more involved in political matters. They took active roles in the offensive military actions against the Infidel. And the Christian rulers of the Holy Land became more and more dependent on them for support. Of the two, however, the Templars seemed to have the higher profile; they were always better known.

So they took shrewd advantage of their reputation. Everyone knew that the crusaders' labors earned them heavenly rewards, but in the Middle Ages, gifts to the Church could buy forgiveness, too. Exploiting their special relationship with the Church and their popularity among Europe's nobility, the Templars solicited gifts everywhere. And gifts continued to roll in. The Order's inventory of properties came to include land – still the main measure of wealth – in all the countries of Europe. In fact, their international holdings eventually came to overshadow their military exploits.

The Templars were a well organized, well trained and capable band of soldiers at a time when most crusaders were untrained and barely organized. But their expertise was no longer confined to the battlefield. The properties they owned throughout Europe forced them to develop administrative skills, and this led to their gradually spreading out into other fields.

For a start, storing their steadily increasing wealth required improved security measures. Fortunately, the Templars' work in the east had given them a great deal of experience in building and defending forts. They easily turned their military skills to the task of constructing a network of "temples" throughout Europe. These were massive stone structures, so well designed and solidly built that they were the most secure buildings on the continent.

The Templars' reputation for building in stone became legendary, but they were also known for their ability to move assets. The routine need to finance their military activities required them to transport money from the west, where it was collected, to the Holy Land. This was no real problem, since the Templars could easily assemble a military escort capable of out-fighting anyone foolish enough to try to rob them.

In retrospect, the next step seems inevitable. In an insecure world, a world characterized by violence and treachery, the Templars were uniquely respected for their integrity, strength and skill. It was only natural for princes and nobles to ask them to store valuables. The local temple was the safest place to store anything precious. It was certainly stronger than a small castle, and the Templars were much more capable fighters than a petty nobleman's rag-tag band of retainers.

And when money needed to be transported to pay a debt or ransom, the Templars were the men for the job. In fact, they could usually receive money in one country and pay an equal sum from their coffers in another country without having to transport anything more than a coded set of instructions.

In short order, the Templars became the world's first international bankers. They moved almost effortlessly from storing and transporting valuables to arranging loans for the nobility and royalty. Thus, in only a few decades the Templars assumed the position of financier for the rich and powerful of Europe.

For a time the Templar were indeed the darlings of Christiandom. But as their power and wealth increased, the seeds of their destruction began to take root. They were becoming too powerful and wealthy to hold the love of Europe's Christians. The Templars' piety gave way to pride, and a desire for privilege replaced the spirit that had made them successful. At some point, even the Order's emblem changed. The horse remained, but its two impoverished riders became wings. Thus the symbol of poverty and humility became one of unrestrained power. The winged horse was how the Templars now saw themselves.

But for the time being, their wealth and power enabled them to shape their own destiny. They could make deals – deals that were very much to their advantage – with the most powerful princes and clerics. Their special privileges, especially their exemption from taxes and from obedience to ecclesiastical authority, kept increasing until, much like a winged horse, the Templars broke free of their bonds. What began as a tool of the Church was now a force so powerful that it was virtually independent of all other powers, including the papacy that had created it.

Eventually the Templars even gained the right to make their own treaties. This was obviously intended as a purely practical matter. The political situation in the Holy Land was always fragmented, and the Templars were constantly trying to escape the fetters of having to operate under the authority of the petty kingdoms they served. But this serious expansion of their power added substantially to the criticism they were beginning to receive.

Nor was it only their wealth and power that brought the Templars into disrepute. The problems ran much deeper than that. While most crusaders spent a short time in the Holy Land then went home, the Templars maintained a permanent presence there. It is certain that the Templars and the Moslems became familiar with each other; certainly each developed a soldier's respect for the enemy. But in time the Templars were suspected of making deals with the Infidel. These were not benign trades of the sort that had become routine among the various parties in the east. Instead, the critics said, the Templars had struck clandestine bargains that were contrary to the interests of the Christians. On several occasions the Order was even accused of specific acts of treachery.

It is hard to sort through the record to determine just how many of the accusations against the Templars were justified and how many were a simple product of resentment. Clearly the Templars became arrogant and insolent as their power and wealth increased. Although the record suggests that their founders had a genuine humility, the later leadership lost the ideals the Order once professed. Their wealth generated greed. There is little doubt that at least some of them gave in to various degrees of personal immorality. And there is every reason to believe that the Templars did pursue their own interests to the extent that they occasionally acted against the interests of their allies. But whatever the truth of the accusations, the papacy and the European royalty became increasingly displeased with the Order in the later years of its existence.

The Templars had experienced a spectacular rise. Now history and their own faults would conspire to start their decline. As they gained more and more power, they found themselves with more and more enemies. Worse, they were attracting enemies who had more and more power.

The enmity of powerful figures might not have posed a serious problem for the Templars if they had been able to maintain their base of power in the Holy Land. But, unfortunately for them, their hold on their possessions in the east was about to prove less than secure.

The Downfall

T here was never a time when the Holy Land was wholly and securely in the hands of the crusaders. Christian and Moslem – and the several factions within each camp – shared the land and constantly fought to control it. Battles and skirmishes were commonplace during the entire period of the Crusades, often with the same parcel of real estate changing hands repeatedly.

This state of affairs was complicated by an ethic of expedience. Even the holiest men of that time could rationalize actions that were at odds with the ideals they espoused. Whenever ethics came into conflict with greed, it was usually self interest that won out. Added to this was the feudal mentality, in which each person's main loyalty was to his immediate lord, not to some distant authority who was rarely or never seen.

This was the setting in which the Templars rose to power. Like the other forces in the east, they often placed the interests of the Order above the noble ideals for which they were supposed to be fighting. Even more often, they were accused of doing so. And when the tide of history finally turned against the crusaders, the Templars had to pay for the animosity that had built up against them.

The end was slow in coming. For several decades after the capture of Jerusalem, the Christians were aided by disunity in the Moslem ranks. But in time a leader arose who could unite the Infidel in a holy war against the Christians.

The Moslems' great hero was named Saladin. He had a suitable background, coming as he did from a prominent military family. His father was governor of northern Syria and an uncle served as general of the army. The young Saladin, however, was more interested in religious than in military matters, and he seems to have been guided by a strong moral compass. At the age of fourteen, he entered his uncle's service but soon resigned to protest the corrupt administration he discovered around him.

This was the spirit he displayed as rose in power. Capable and ambitious, Saladin was destined to achieve greatness ... if only he could find the proper springboard.

In 1169, when he was thirty-one, his opportunity finally came. The death of his uncle left him holding the positions of commander of Syrian troops and vizier of Egypt. He now had means as well as motive, and within a few years he was involved in a campaign to unite all the Moslem territories and recapture the Holy Land.

His religious zeal and single-minded devotion to duty made him both an inspiration to the Moslems and a formidable enemy of the Christians. Still, in the fragmented, slow moving world of the medieval east, everything took time. Saladin's goals required the deaths of some of his Moslem enemies as well as weakening the Christian forces. It was a complex undertaking. Intrigue and the building up and tearing down of alliances were often more important than military victories.

Fortunately for his side, Saladin had just the personality he needed to deal with the situation. He put together a campaign that was more a shifting of momentum than a watershed. It took nearly two decades, but in the end the Infidel had his success.

At the Battle of Hattin – July 4, 1187 – Saladin gave the crusaders a devastating defeat from which they could not recover. That victory gave the Moslems the momentum they needed to overrun the Holy Land. Saladin's campaign had been well conceived and well executed. And when the end was in sight, he moved quickly. Within three months he had taken Jerusalem, and the crusaders' hold on the Holy Land was finally broken. Although the Christians managed to keep scattered strongholds, the fall of Jerusalem marked the decisive blow to their cause.

The Templars were especially hard hit. They suffered enormous casualties. Their Grand Master was captured. And Saladin personally ordered their headquarters in Jerusalem dismantled.

While their material loss was awesome, perhaps more important was the blow to their pride. After a spectacular rise to fame and power, the one group that was organized specifically to protect visitors to the Holy Land found itself in serious danger of being expelled from the east, perhaps never to return.

During the years that preceded the fall of Jerusalem there had been some talk about a third crusade. Now the talk became more urgent. Although the city was of limited strategic value, it had always been a focal point for European Christians, and its loss was the spectacular event needed to get the next crusade off the ground.

But something had changed. The Europeans were experienced in sending troops to the east to liberate the Holy Land. The procedure had become almost routine. Now, however, the spirit that inspired the first crusaders had faded. No longer could the western princes count on a religious zeal to overcome the dissension that had always plagued the crusading enterprise. Nor could they enjoy the comfort of attacking an unprepared enemy.

The Third Crusade *began* smoothly enough. Forces were raised and set out for the Holy Land under the leadership of such men as the German Frederick Barbarosa, Philip II Augustus of France and Richard I of England. Unfortunately, the project did not remain uneventful for long. Frederick died before reaching the Holy Land, and Philip and Richard found themselves at loggerheads from the outset.

These were two entirely different men. Philip was very much the politician, outwardly timid and unimpressive. Richard was the general, extremely athletic, volatile and aggressive. The mistrust between them was so strong that it actually bound them together. It was obvious that both had to go on the crusade or both had to stay home. Neither would leave if he knew the other was going to stay behind and scheme against him.

This was the background of the armies that arrived in the Holy Land in the summer of 1191. Philip came first, and when Richard arrived two months later, the French were busily laying siege to Acre.

In a scene that must have been reminiscent of the First Crusade, the two armies brought superior force to bear against an ill prepared enemy. The city's defenders fought hard but couldn't hold; little more than a month after Richard's arrival, they surrendered to the Christians.

A quick victory, however, did not herald a successful campaign. The uneasy alliance between Philip and Richard was made worse by quarreling after the victory at Acre, and their quarreling eventually made a bad situation untenable. Within three weeks, Philip was on his way back to France.

Although citing illness – he was indeed sick, as was Richard – the French king was really disgusted with his adventure in the east. Leaving his army behind to continue the crusade, he was eager to get home to attend to domestic politics, which he much preferred to a distant war. And one of his top priorities was to plot with Richard's brother John against Richard's interests in England.

Richard, a military man at heart, chose to stay in the Holy Land for more fighting. He had set out to recapture Jerusalem, and that's what he was determined to do. During the next year he struggled simultaneously against Saladin at his front and the intrigue that raged behind his back. For a time Richard was successful. In September of 1191 he won a major battle at Arsuf, a town some distance to the south of Acre and just north of the strategic port of Joppa. A few days later he occupied Joppa, but the conquest of Jerusalem, now only a few miles away, was not to be. His attempts to move on the city were frustrated, and his men grew weary. With his supply lines stretched to the breaking point and intrigue threatening his kingdom back home, Richard eventually realized that he would have to settle for a negotiated peace.

Richard I

England's Richard I at the siege of Acre, A.D. 1191.

Now a mix of logistical and political problems led to months of frustration, indecision and vacillation. Saladin knew he had the upper hand and was firm in his demands. During the negotiations, Richard tried to take Jerusalem by force, but he simply could not do it. Finally he abandoned his hopes of ever taking the Holy City and agreed to the terms Saladin had offered.

The treaty was completed on September 2, 1192. Its terms were fair but somewhat disappointing to Richard. The Christians would hold the coast. The Moslems would keep the Holy City. And pilgrims would have free access to the holy places. Clearly this was a compromise, but at least it returned some stability to the area.

In October, with his business in the east as finished as it would ever be, Richard left to attend to matters in England. He continued to play the glorious warrior until the spring of 1199, when he died of a wound suffered in a minor battle. And although he was never able to capture Jerusalem, he at least had the satisfaction of knowing that his great enemy Saladin, exhausted by the rigors of his long campaign against the Christians, had died six years earlier.

For their part, the Templars and Hospitallers had fought hard to help Richard in his attempt to regain the Holy City but, in the end, were reduced to helping establish a treaty that merely guaranteed pilgrims the right to visit it. They must have found the whole affair a devastating disappointment. While the kings returned home to resume their lives in Europe, the military orders stayed in the Holy Land. *That* was their home, and they could no longer keep it safe.

Their inability to take the Holy City outright was symbolic of a subtle change that had occurred over the decades. Perhaps without realizing it, the defenders of the Holy Land had lost their spirit and sense of purpose. True, the crusades had always been partly a matter of military conquest and greed. Its leaders never got along well, and the Templars and Hospitallers were always at odds with each other. Still, they had all embarked on their quest with a sense of adventure and a belief that they were part of something noble and holy. That, more than anything else, attracted such men as Bernard of Clairvaux to a cause that promised to bring them a step closer to God.

But the world had changed in the century since those first idealistic efforts began. The Holy Land was once a mystical place, the source of all that was holy, a land that few people had ever seen. Now all over Europe people could be found who had been there. They could tell of the Holy Land's heat and cold, its dust and freezing rain, the diseases that were common in the countryside and the prostitutes who lived and worked in the cities. And of particular importance in a provincial world dominated by religion, the returning crusaders told of the exotic deities worshiped in the east and of the strange religions that had grown up around them.

The world was opening up. People knew things that they hadn't known before. To a conservative Church that was a matter of great consequence, and for the Templars it would prove to be decisive burden. As long as the Holy Land remained a faraway place, the knights who defended it benefited from a romantic mystique. But as Europe's familiarity with the east increased, the crusaders' human failings became more and more apparent, and public confidence waned.

That was only one of the things the Templars should have been worrying about. As the twelfth century drew to a close, their problems began to multiply. They might still have had time to avoid the tragic end that would ultimately claim them. However, they apparently did not see the danger signs. Their pride, already challenged by their military setbacks, may have kept them from understanding how precarious their situation was, and they allowed themselves to be swept along by events they could have handled better.

Of all the things that were happening to the Templars at this time, perhaps the most important, though they certainly didn't realize it, was the arrival of a new pope. Innocent III came to that office in 1198 and brought with him a burning desire to recapture Jerusalem and to reform the Church.

In the short term, this was a great boon to the Templars, but it set forces in motion that would ultimately contribute to their destruction. To recapture Jerusalem, the pope needed the Templars, but to reform the Church he needed to increase the power of the inquisition. He would realize the first of these ambitions, but only temporarily. The second would bear a bitter fruit long after his death.

The recapture of Jerusalem was no longer the glorious event it had once been. The glamour had worn off, and only the drudgery remained. During the next century the Holy Land continued to be the scene of bloodshed that somehow never came to an end and never resolved any real issues. The Christians gained and lost Jerusalem again. Then, for a time, it seemed that they might prevail. In 1229 Frederick II of Germany negotiated a treaty that once again gave the Christians possession of the Holy City, along with Bethlehem and Nazareth. The treaty called for the return of prisoners, free access to Jerusalem and a peace that would last for ten years. On the whole, it was a promising development.

One disturbing provision of the treaty, though, was that the Dome of the Rock and the former headquarters of the Templars would remain in Moslem hands. This angered the Templars; they wanted their Temple back and had expected to get it. But this setback was of little consequence in the scheme of things. The military orders had gone far beyond their original reasons for existing. Now that the new treaty allowed them to operate freely in the Holy Land once more, they rapidly regained the power and wealth they had lost a generation earlier. Saladin was dead. The Moslems had lost the unity he had given them, and it was again the turn of the Templars and Hospitallers to prosper.

In an era of "might makes right," the two orders of monastic knights had become so powerful that they no longer needed to take instructions from the papacy and the governments they supposedly served. They took on a life of their own, making deals to their own advantage and virtually ignoring a Europe they thought they no longer needed.

While the Templars and Hospitallers increased their power, European support for the crusades continued to wane. Christian Europe came to believe that the Infidel could never be conquered completely. They resigned themselves to the status quo. And the crusaders, like the military orders, lost the last trace of the ideals that had inspired – and once ruled – their affairs. In the end, the Christians in the Holy Land turned against each other. The dissension that had plagued them from the early days of the crusades evolved into unabashed episodes of civil war, and even the Templars and Hospitallers came to blows on the battlefield.

Curiously, the violence of Christian against Christian did not bring business to a halt. In a perverse way, disunity actually helped the military orders. As Europe increasingly turned away from the Holy Land, the Hospitallers and Templars capitalized on the disenchantment. They bought property at low prices and received other property as outright gifts from crusaders who had decided to return home. The orders then strengthened their fortifications in order to protect their increasing political and economic power.

In many ways the middle of the thirteenth century was the best of times for the Templars. It was certainly the height of their power. While Europe tired of seemingly endless struggles with the Infidel, the descendants of Hugues de Payens' poor knights achieved awesome financial power. When Jerusalem fell once more in 1243, they virtually financed a seventh crusade and chose France's Louis IX to lead it. Unfortunately, the effort was ineffective and proved to be the last major attempt to conquer the Holy Land. The crusaders' day in the sun had simply passed.

While the crusaders' best efforts faltered, another great leader arose to unite the Moslems. His name was Baybars, and the critical date was 1260. That year marked the end of a decade of political intrigue and assassinations that disposed of several claimants to the Egyptian throne. Baybars and an emir named Qutuz were the only surviving rivals for Moslem leadership. Then Baybars resolved the problem in a way that was not without precedent. He killed Qutuz and had the army proclaim him Sultan.

At first, the Christians thought they could deal with this new leader of the Moslems, but it quickly became clear that there would be no peace. As soon as he had consolidated his power, Baybars launched a campaign against the Christians. In a dozen years he did irreparable damage to their forces and especially to the Templars. He did not live to see the final victory, but by his death in 1277, he had shifted the balance of power so much that the outcome was inevitable.

During the next few years, the Christians lost ground steadily and could not regain what they had lost. They were driven out of the Holy Land bit by bit until, when Tripoli fell in 1289, only a few scattered possessions remained in their hands. The most notable was the city of Acre, and it was there that the outcome of the crusades would be decided.

The siege of Acre began on April 6, 1291 and it was a fitting end to two centuries of warfare. Both sides fielded large armies. The remaining Templars and Hospitallers were augmented by troops who had retreated to Acre as the last of the Christian strongholds fell. And the Moslems massed a large number of the faithful who were eager to participate in the final battle.

Acre stood with its back to the sea. From there it could easily be re-supplied. The city was well situated to resist a siege, and its defenders knew how much depended on them. They fought bravely, but the Moslems were too strong. After a fierce defense which cost the life of the Templars' Grand Master, Guillaume de Beaujeu, the Christians evacuated the city, and the Moslems finally took Acre on May 18.

After the city's fall, the Templars continued to occupy their castle near Acre. They had no hope of victory. They could not even hold out against the massive army that besieged them. But Templars did not accept defeat easily.

A week later they decided that their honor was preserved. They could now say they had been the last defenders of the Holy Land. The Templars then agreed to abandon the castle and withdraw to Cyprus, but an orderly evacuation could not be accomplished. Tensions were so high that when the Sultan's soldiers entered the castle to supervise the withdrawal, the Templars accused them of looting and raping.

From that point on, events occurred in rapid succession. The Templars killed the entire Moslem party. The Sultan, infuriated by what he saw as treachery, restated his offer to allow the defenders to leave. But as soon as the Moslems had drawn the Templars' commander out of the castle, they slaughtered him and his escort.

On May 28 the castle yielded to a final assault, and the crusades were effectively over. A few castles remained in the hands of the Templars, but they were soon abandoned, and by 1303, the Christian presence in the Holy Land had ceased to exist.

After losing their last stronghold in Palestine, the Templars withdrew to Cyprus. They were led at this time by their newly elected Grand Master, Theobald Gaudin. It was Gaudin who had pulled the Templars out of Acre at the end of that terrible battle. It is said that he personally salvaged the Templars' treasure and took it to Cyprus. If he did, it was a glorious way to begin his term as Grand Master. But his was to be a tragic tenure. Within two years of presiding over his order's final retreat, Theobald was dead.

As the thirteenth century ended, without knowing it the Templars elected their last Grand Master. In 1293, Jacques de Molay took the helm of an organization that almost certainly believed it had a future. But time was running out.

The Order's ranks had been decimated in their last desperate efforts against the Moslems. Their worldwide membership now amounted to about 15,000, of which only 1500 were knights. Still, the Order had suffered severe casualties before, and they had always been able to rebuild their ranks and regain their glory. Even now they dreamed of leading a another campaign to recapture Jerusalem.

The Templars ambitions were much the same as they had always been, and the way they dealt with their situation was much the same, too. De Molay, like Hugues de Payens two centuries earlier, traveled in Europe to promote the Order. He did receive some support. A new century had begun, and he had reason to believe that he might be able to pull off one more revival of the order whose leadership he had inherited.

The idea of a new crusade was not without its supporters. A plan for one more expedition had already been devised. It would probably have been led by Philip IV of France, known as Philip the Fair. This plan involved a proposal that the two military orders, both of which had been seriously weakened during the final battles in the Holy Land, be combined into a single order. This was not a new idea. It had been suggested a half century earlier and occasionally revived since. It had never been attempted because the tension between the two orders made it unlikely that a union could be affected. But times had changed.

In 1305, the new pope was Clement V. He was a Frenchman and strongly influenced by Philip. Now, with the pope in his corner, Philip was in a position to push for a crusade that would be conducted on his terms – terms that included the union of the military orders.

Pope Clement summoned the Grand Masters of both orders to attend him in Poitiers in June of 1306. There they discussed plans for the future. The Hospitallers, owing to either luck or wisdom, did not commit themselves. For their part, the Templars adamantly rejected the proposed union. There is reason to believe that De Molay did not understand the political climate in which he found himself. He seemed to think that the proposed union would be dropped in favor of a new crusade financed and led by the Templars.

Perhaps he was not that naive, but whatever the rationale behind it, his rejection of the proposed union sealed the Templars' fate. With the loss of the Holy Land, their original position in the scheme of things no longer existed. If they were not to lead yet another crusade, their powerful military organization – one that was virtually independent of all civil authority and only nominally subject to the papacy – had no legitimate function. In fact, it was a powerful threat, since it could easily turn against any kingdom in Europe.

The Templars were tolerated in southern and eastern Europe, where military threats from outside still existed. But in the heart of western Europe

France's King Philip IV

things were different. Philip was protected by geography from the Moors to the south and the Tartars in the east. He did not need the Templars. Nor did he like having their power so close to home. They had always been primarily an organization of French knights, and fully a third of their membership now resided in France, where they could easily be drawn into a plot against the crown.

Besides, Philip owed the Templars a great deal of money. He was not alone in this. The European monarchies were an outgrowth of the feudal system. In essence, medieval kings were little more than large landowners, and landowners had always born their own expenses. To their dismay, the kings found that the cost of maintaining their positions, especially the cost of the wars they constantly felt obliged to fight, tended to outpace the revenues they were able to separate from their vassals. Philip was no exception. He was seriously in debt, and his principal creditor was the Order of the Temple. All things considered, it didn't take him long to realize that his life would be much simpler if the Templars were out of the way.

Suddenly it all came down to a simple problem. Philip was trying to forge France into a strong state under his leadership. That would be a major change in the politics of the region, and he felt that both the Templars and the Church stood in his way. He could deal with the new pope, and that made the Church less of a problem. But the Templars refused to cooperate. By 1306, it was clear that the Order would not accept his plan for the next crusade. Nor would they allow him to transform them into a less threatening organization. This left Philip only one option. He would have to eliminate them.

Once he had made up his mind, Philip did not find opportunity lacking. The occasional disaffected Templar was always available to accuse the Order of impropriety. The latest of these, Esquin de Floyran, had recently presented himself to James, King of Aragon and denounced the Templars. James was not much interested in the matter, and De Floyran took his story to Philip.

This provided Philip the *excuse* he needed to move against the Templars, but there was still a technical problem to overcome. The Templars were not under Philip's jurisdiction. They were an international organization answerable only to the papacy. For that reason, the king could not act against them without the pope's consent, and even then they would probably have to be tried by the Church.

At first, Clement was reluctant to act. But by August, 1307 Philip had convinced him to order an inquiry.

Philip now felt that he had a free hand to move against the Temple. Before they could react, he issued orders to arrest every Templar in France. A coordinated series of raids was carried out on the night of Friday, October 13, 1307. Five thousand members of the Order were arrested simultaneously, with only a few managing to escape.

Now that Philip had the Templars in custody, it was urgent for him to act decisively against them. He hoped for a quick and bloodless resolution of the case. His goal was to disband the Order; its individual members were of no consequence to him. So he brought accusations against the Order, not its members. Apparently his plan was to extract quick confessions from enough of the Templars to prove his case. He would present the evidence to the pope, who would dissolve the Order. The king could then confiscate its property. Thus, in one swift action he would be rid of a potential threat to his power, wipe out a major part of his debt and gain a large sum of money in the bargain.

The individual Templars would be little the worse for wear. Following the dissolution of their order, they could repent of their personal sins and be restored to the good graces of the Church.

If that was Philip's plan, it was elegant and simple. But it didn't work. For a start, the pope was reluctant to go along. He did not act as quickly or decisively as Philip expected.

To make matters worse, the Templars offered a much stronger resistance than Philip had expected. Their defense of themselves and their order was a key factor in this drama, because Philip really needed their cooperation to obtain a conviction.

Philip's dilemma hinged on the legal constraints within which he had to operate. The medieval concept of justice was scrupulous, but in a way that is quite foreign to the modern mind. The accused was never convicted without proof of his guilt. But evidence in the modern understanding of the term was not sufficient proof. A confession was required. Confessions, however, were not hard to come by. If the accused did not admit his guilt voluntarily, he could be tortured until he did. And in practice the extent of the torture was limited only by the authorities' determination to obtain a conviction.

Excessive force carried less of a stigma then than it does now. God would grant courage and strength to the innocent, or so it was believed. If the occasional innocent prisoner died under torture, his soul would find its way to heaven, and certainly there was no harm in hastening one of the faithful to his reward.

This is a primitive view of justice, but juris prudence was much less developed then. At the time of the Templar trials, the real enterprise of witch hunting was still in the future. The Spanish Inquisition, led by the infamous Torquemada, did not get under way until 1478, and the last American witch trials at Salem, Massachusetts did not occur until the end of the seventeenth century. At the beginning of the fourteenth century, the Templars had to contend with an even less refined system of justice than did the Jews of Spain or the American "witches."

Still, the medieval mind understood the concept of a forced confession. Any confession made under torture was valid only if it was repeated later in the absence of coercion. Without this confirmation it could not be used as evidence in a legal proceeding. Of course, recanting a confession was not without risk. If the accused recanted, he could be declared a relapsed heretic and burned. But that was no more than a heretic deserved.

On the whole, this was a system that favored the inquisitor, and Philip was determined to have confessions from the Templars. Guillaume de Nogaret, the king's minister, headed the investigation. Although technically the Templars could be examined only by ecclesiastic authorities, De Nogaret had them placed under torture immediately, and several of them confessed during the first few days of the inquisition.

It was now time for shrewd and decisive action. On October 14, the day after the arrests, Nogaret called a meeting of theologians from the University of Paris and explained the case against the Templars. This was only a first step, but a very important one. Philip desperately needed the approval of the academicians. Since he could not count on the proper procedures to accomplish his goal, he found it necessary to exceed his authority and deprive the Templars of their rights.

At the outset, he had to take them by surprise. Otherwise, they might have escaped to other countries where they could expect sympathetic treatment. But now that they were securely in his hands, he had to justify what he had done.

Philip had already received some help from the religious authorities. Guillaume Imbert, otherwise called Guillaume de Paris, the Grand Inquisitor of France, had asked the king to assist the Church in investigating the accusations against the Templars. This gave Philip some justification, but not much. Although Imbert was Grand Inquisitor, and thus the pope's man, he was also the king's personal confessor. Everyone knew that Imbert did Philip's bidding. And the pope, for his part, had only authorized an *investigation*. He had said nothing about arrests.

That was why the opinions of the theologians were so important. And that was why De Nogaret had to consult them immediately. After telling them what he was doing, De Nogaret set about obtaining the necessary confessions. He instructed Guillaume Imbert to draw up a set of questions from information contained in De Floyran's accusations. These questions were promptly put to the prisoners. About two hundred fifty Templars were tortured throughout France, and by October 26 confessions had been extracted from almost all of them, including the Grand Master and other high ranking officers.

On the strength of this first round of confessions, De Nogaret summoned the University theologians again and insisted that they endorse his actions. The academicians approved his interrogation, but stated that only Church officials had the authority to sentence the prisoners.

The case against the Templars was then presented to the pope. At this point, the most important issue was not the guilt or innocence of the Templars but the relationship between the pope and the king. Clement had been one of those compromise candidates chosen because the cardinals were deadlocked. At the time he was Bertrand de Got, archbishop of

Bordeaux, and Philip did everything possible to get him elected. It would be an exaggeration to say that Philip had hand picked Bertrand for the papacy, but it wouldn't be much of an exaggeration.

Bertrand did not have a strong personality and was easily influenced, especially by his friend Philip. Even as pope, he was never part of the Italian Church establishment, and indeed he never moved to Rome, preferring to live in France. He also promoted the interests of the French clergy. Early in his papal administration he appointed ten new Cardinals, nine of them Frenchmen, thus greatly increasing French influence in the sacred college.

No doubt Philip expected the pope to do his bidding, and in most matters he did. But like so many puppets, once he was in office he showed surprising independence. In the matter of the Templars, he refused to put a quick end to the matter, which he could easily have done by acting decisively against the Order.

Clement had other concerns besides his responsibility to the king of France. The Templars were the pope's men. They were a creation of the Church and had served it well for nearly two centuries. Any pope would be reluctant to destroy them, and Clement did not have the heart to go down in history as the one who did it. Instead of honoring the king's wishes, he fired off a letter accusing Philip of acting improperly in conducting an inquisition that could legally be carried out only under papal authority.

It took until November 17 for Philip to prevail upon the pope to reverse his decision and agree to let the inquisition continue. Even so, it was only a partial victory. On November 22, Clement issued a Papal Bull, titled *Pastoralis Praeeminentiae*, ordering the arrest of Templars in all Christian lands. Had everyone obeyed, the issue might have been settled, but most of Europe's rulers saw through the ploy. The Bull found little support outside of France and Italy. In Cyprus, 76 Templars were tried but all were acquitted. In Portugal, the king refused altogether to act against the Order.

From that point on, it was a difficult road for Philip. De Molay and others recanted their confessions. The king was getting much less support than he wanted and was becoming increasingly concerned about public opinion. In an effort to shore up his position, he attempted to portray the Templars as so obviously guilty that they did not even deserve a trial. He, on the other hand, deserved the people's sympathy and support. He was merely a devout Christian who found himself in the position of defending the faith against an evil so insidious that there could be no defense for it. At least, he hoped that no one would insist on hearing a defense.

In early May of 1308 an assembly of the Estates-General held at Tours passed a resolution condemning the Templars. Soon after, on May 29, Philip traveled to Poitiers to meet the pope personally at a Consistory held at the royal palace there. Philip argued that the Templars had adequately confessed their guilt, unequivocally and without coercion. In addition, the king defended himself against the charge that he had acted against them merely to confiscate their property for his own profit.

Now Philip was finally able to get some satisfaction. Although the pope did not immediately rule in the king's favor, he did call a second Consistory for June 14. He agreed to review personally the cases against seventy of the Templars, and on June 27 a carefully selected group of prisoners was turned over to the Church for examination. All of the Templars examined at that time made partial confessions and within another two weeks had repented and were reconciled with the Church.

Now that the pope had seen proof of the Templars' guilt, he could no longer refuse to act against them. On August 12, he issued another Bull, *Faciens Misericordiam*, specifying charges against the Order and calling on the princes of all countries to examine Templars resident in their jurisdictions in anticipation of a Church Council to be held in Vienne on October 10, 1310.

Charges were drawn up, and a Papal Commission was convened on November 12, 1309 to hear anyone who wanted to offer a defense. The Templars were reluctant to attend the proceedings, but at least now they had an opportunity to appear in what amounted to open court. Although the Commission was not authorized to pass judgment, it would give them a chance to state their case and perhaps to do some legal maneuvering of their own.

From November until the following May, the Commission heard from hundreds of Templars, including the Grand Master who renounced his confession and vigorously defended the honor of the Order. During this phase of the inquisition, Philip became increasingly concerned. On the one hand, he had finally prevailed upon the Church to act against the Order, and the members of the Commission were generally sympathetic to his side. On the other hand, the Templars were dragging out the proceedings, recanting their confessions and gaining legal concessions that might possibly lead to their acquittal.

Fortunately for him, a means of bringing the matter to a dramatic and abrupt end were at hand. Relapsed heretics could be burned for their sins. That was a drastic step, but it was preferable to allowing the proceedings to continue and perhaps get completely out of control.

On May 11, 1310 the king singled out fifty-four Templars who had recanted their confessions. He had them sentenced, and they were burned at the stake in Paris as relapsed heretics. More Templars were executed in other towns throughout France, but the burnings in Paris were the most dramatic and devastating. That one incident destroyed the Templars' last chance of acquittal.

The Commission was so shocked that it adjourned for six months. When it tried to convene again in early November it did not have a quorum. By December 17, it was able to get going again, but by this time no one was willing to defy the king. The Commission continued sitting until May 26, when it advised the pope that it could do no more. During those last months it had gone through the motions of gathering evidence, but the final outcome was no longer in doubt.

On October 16, the Commission sent its report to the pope, who passed it on to the Council of Vienne, along with documents assembled from other parts of Europe. It was accompanied by the pope's recommendation that the Council condemn the Templars.

The king made an appearance at the Council to be sure everyone saw things his way, but the gesture was probably unnecessary. By this time the case had already been decided. The Council voted to suppress the Templars.

Legally, the final blow came on March 22, 1312. On that date the pope issued a Bull, *Vox in Excelsis,* ordering the permanent suppression of the Order. Their property was to be confiscated. After the cost of the trials was deducted, the remainder of the property would be turned over to the Hospitallers.

The inquisition had dragged on for five years and was so brutal that more than thirty of the Templars died under torture. A larger number had been burned for heresy, though the exact number was not recorded. And the glory of a once proud order of knights vanished forever.

At this point, the Poor Knights of Christ ceased to exist as an order of warrior monks. That should have been the end of it, but there was one more act in their tragic ordeal.

The leaders of the Temple had been sentenced to spend the rest of their lives in prison. This placed them safely out of public view. They had been stripped of their power and wealth, and there was little they could do to harm their oppressors. Unfortunately, Philip was not satisfied. He was determined to stage a dramatic conclusion that would vindicate his actions.

On March 18, 1314, he paraded the four leaders – De Molay, Geoffroi de Charney, Geoffroi de Gonneville and Hugues de Pairaud – to Notre Dame cathedral, where a platform had been erected for the purpose. There, according to plan, the leaders of the suppressed order of knights would confess their crimes to the citizens of Paris and receive the mercy of king and pope. They had confessed under torture. Now they would do so voluntarily and publicly. The knights would be the admitted villains of the case, while Philip would be remembered as the benevolent monarch who had brought them to justice and subsequently forgiven their sins.

But the events of that day did not go according to plan. When the time came for them to confirm their guilt, De Molay and De Charney renounced their confessions and eloquently proclaimed the innocence of their order. Then they denounced the charges against the Templars and the terrible tortures that had been used to extract confessions from so many of them.

These statements were made more poignant by the appearance of the prisoners. Old and emaciated, bearing the marks of torture and years of imprisonment, they left little doubt who the real victims of the inquisition were.

Now Philip had little choice. The next morning De Molay and De Charney were burned at the stake on the Ile de Palais, almost in the shadow of Notre Dame.

It is often the last in a series of events that is remembered. If the Templars had gone quietly into extinction, Philip might have had some of the vindication he wanted. But as things turned out, the Templars won the last battle of their long history. They were now martyrs and history has come down on their side.

King Philip and Pope Clement had little time to enjoy their Pyrrhic victory. Within a year both were dead. There is no particular reason to believe that they were murdered by the Templars, but one never knows.

The surviving members of the Order – those who had confessed and been forgiven and those who had escaped the inquisition – dispersed. Some were allowed to join the Hospitallers or other monastic orders. They were still monks, and it was fitting that they continue to observe their monastic vows.

It was said that some of the Templars returned to the east where they were taken in by the Saracens. Perhaps that confirmed the charges that they had drifted from the faith and taken on the ways of the Infidel. But many of the men who had a few years earlier belonged to the most powerful organization in Europe – many of these men simply disappeared to live out the rest of their lives in obscurity.

Jacques De Molay
The Templars' last Grand Master is burned at the stake in Paris.

The Charges

The Templars were convicted, but that doesn't mean they were guilty. The political aspects of the story show that much of what happened to the Order had little to do with their guilt or innocence. On the other hand, the fact that they were persecuted does not prove they were innocent.

After all these years, the question of their guilt or innocence may seem meaningless. It is, after all, only a footnote to history. The truth of the matter could not have changed the outcome of the Templars' trial at the time. Certainly it can not be of any consequence now.

To most people, this issue no longer has any substance. It is important to our quest, however, because it bears on the truth that might be contained in the Templar legend of the Freemasons. In the minds of some, if the Templars were guilty of the charges against them, it is even more likely that they were the forerunners of modern Freemasonry. This is a very curious notion, and our next step will be to explore it.

The Templars stood accused of a long list of offenses. Most of them have nothing to do with modern Masons. But among the charges was the claim that the Templars engaged in occult practices. The same charge is often leveled against the Freemasons. The particulars differ, of course, but there is enough similarity to suggest the obvious question. Could both organizations be guilty of the same offense?

Those who believe that Masonic teachings are laced with mysticism and occultism have no trouble believing that they inherited those beliefs from the Templars. But comparing charges with charges is not enough. At most, it might show that the medieval Templars and the modern Freemasons had to deal with the same kind of enemy. Our goal is to discover whether the two organizations are really one. To do that we must look at the facts behind the accusations.

Curiously, the guilt or innocence of either organization, in and of itself, has little bearing on our investigation. Our interest in the issue lies only in what it can tell us about an event that may have occurred in the late Middle Ages. And we must pursue it only because history has left us so few clues to that event.

A superficial examination suggests that the Masons' Templar legend was created in the eighteenth century and has nothing to do with the Craft's history before that date. As we have seen, no evidence of a historic connection between the medieval Templars and the stone masons has come to light. This is not surprising. On the face of it, an order of medieval knights and a group of craftsmen would seem to have little in common.

We must wonder, though, if evidence of an earlier connection *would* have survived. If the fugitive Templars joined the masons, the union would likely have occurred behind closed doors. The Templars had been persecuted and suppressed. True, individual Templars were allowed to join other orders or otherwise retire from their previous calling. But if the Order tried to survive as an organization, it would have had to do so against an express decree of the Church. We should not expect written records of such dealings. Traces of the event – if any traces were left – will likely appear only in the traditions and practices of the two organizations. We must therefore look for things in Freemasonry that would have changed as a result of a union with the Templars. This is where the truth behind the accusations becomes important.

The initial charges against the Templars consisted of a hodgepodge of items. They have the tone that would be expected from an inquisitor who is trying to scrape up every bad thing he can say about a defendant. Curiously, though, the charges came from inside the Order. Esquin de Floyran, whose accusations Philip used as the basis for his persecution, had been a high ranking officer in the Order. He was once the prior of the preceptory at Montfaucon in Perigueux. The man was subsequently re-lieved of that duties. History does not record why, but he apparently had reason to be bitter toward the Templars.

De Floyran made a series of rather general charges that indicated widespread corruption in his former organization. His story was not unlike the rumors that had been circulating for years. It did not stress individual crimes committed by specific members acting on their own initiative. Instead, it was a story of institutionalized wrong doing.

The Templars were supposed to have sworn loyalty to their order above all other institutions and rules of conduct. Any crime they had to commit for the good of the Order was acceptable. In particular, their accusers claimed, they had dealt with the Moslems and betrayed their Christian allies. Initiates were also required to participate in sacrilegious acts and to practice immo-rality, both in the Order's rituals and in their private lives. And, it was said, the Templars routinely murdered any member who betrayed them.

These charges formed a starting point. The king's inquisitors began with them and extracted confessions from the Templars to confirm De Floyran's information and to flesh out his accusations with details of the alleged crimes.

Only a few of the Templars maintained their innocence throughout. The vast majority confessed to some of the charges. Interestingly, though, in almost every case those who confessed did not admit everything. They managed to confess to a few particulars and insist that the rest were unfounded.

Based on the results of the inquisition, Philip had a set of formal charges drawn up. At first, it contained 87 articles. Later, a version containing 127 articles was prepared for submission to the pope. Not all of the additional articles represented new charges; some were just a rewording and editing the original articles. But clearly the indictment included a long list of particulars.

The length of the indictment is not as ominous as it might seem. It included many stock charges that would be brought against anyone accused of heresy. Standard procedure called for the inquisitor to make the list as long as possible, and we can dismiss most of the items as irrelevant. Others, however, are specific enough to require a second look.

One group of charges related to the initiation ritual. Under torture, many of the Templars confessed that new members were required to renounce Christ as a false prophet and spit on the cross. The new member was also required to kiss the initiating brother on the navel or spine. These are euphemisms typical of the Middle Ages. By reading between the lines we can see that the Templars were really being accused of practicing sexual perversion in their rituals.

Another category centered around the accusation that the Order worshiped the devil. They were said to use two idols, a head and a cat. Both are described differently by those who confessed to seeing them. The cat is variously described as being white or black. The head was a woman or a man with long hair and a beard. It was sometimes said to be a skull. Perhaps it was a relic of a former Grand Master; no one seemed to know for sure. And there was a curious item that was never adequately explained. The members wore a cord which had touched the head.

Then there were assertions that the Templars perverted Church practices. The Order's chaplains were accused of making improper changes in the Canon of the Mass. Also, the Grand Master and other officers gave absolution, which they were not authorized to do.

As if these charges weren't enough, the inquisitors threw in another for good measure. They accused the Templars of secret practices.

In those days anything done in secret was automatically suspect. As a matter of historic fact, the Order did hold its ceremonies in secret. Only members were allowed to attend. Still, this charge seems to involve a serious embellishment of the facts. The indictment claimed that everything about the meetings was secret. Members were sworn to observe strict silence on all matters. They could not discuss the initiation ceremonies with anyone, even with other members of the Order. If they did so, or especially if they revealed the Order's secrets to non-members, they would be imprisoned or killed.

Finally, the Templars were accused of practicing vice and sodomy. Not only did they practice sodomy, the charge said, they were not even allowed to decline sexual advances from other members.

Accusations of vice were routine and to be expected in this sort of trial. In the medieval mind, heresy was always linked with sexual aberration. The repressed society of the time found forbidden fruit an irresistible topic for speculation, and a hint of sexual perversion always added spice to any legal proceeding.

Curiously, although this was virtually a *pro forma* charge, it is the one most likely to contain a grain of truth. It is common for all-male or all-female organizations that require celibacy to have occasional problems with sexual impropriety among their members. We may reasonably assume that the Templars were no exception. It is much less likely, however, that vice was practiced on an organizational level. The Templars made considerable effort to enforce celibacy in their ranks. Members were admonished to avoid the company of women. Even looking at a woman too much or kissing a female relative was considered a source of temptation.

Their dress, too, was carefully thought out. Bright colors were forbidden, and knights wore white, even during winter, as a symbol of purity. They were also required to wear lambskin breeches and never take them off. It may well have been pointed out to these soldiers of the Church that Christ was the lamb of God. The symbolism would certainly remind them of their duty if they were ever tempted to remove their breeches to commit iniquity. Further, the members were forbidden to enter the tent of another who had retired for the night. And they were not to bathe together or allow anyone to help them dress or undress.

In view of these extreme measures, it is doubtful that the organization sanctioned sexual acts among its members. Even if they did turn a blind eye to occasional acts of sodomy, it is unlikely that they would make it official by requiring members to accept sexual advances from their comrades. And accepting the idea that they incorporated immoral kisses into their initiation rituals requires a serious leap of the imagination.

Ceremonial kisses are a quite ancient and not uncommon bit of ritual. They are variously used as a greeting and as a sign of respect. There is no reason to believe that the Templars' use of kisses in their initiation ritual, if it occurred at all, was more than that. It is much more likely that the inquisition was willing to misrepresent an innocent practice to make the Templars seem guilty of the standard charge of sodomy.

In any event, the charges of vice, whether true or not, relate specifically to the practices of the medieval Templars and do not shed light on our present inquiry. More important are the charges relating to occult practices. That is where we hope to find the elusive medieval connection.

Critics of Freemasonry have often charged that the fraternity involves itself in demon worship. As we will see, those accusations go back as far as the earliest surviving anti-Masonic documents. Freemasons insist that these charges are unfounded, but their persistence and their existence at such an early point in the Craft's history are a puzzle.

From what we know of the early stone masons, there was nothing about them that would inspire such criticism. Yet the spectre of occultism was being raised even before the craft had completed its transition to a fraternal organization. If that spectre existed earlier – at a time when the craft was completely operative, a time from which few documents survive to describe its activities – that fact alone would constitute enticing evidence that something had changed. Even the suspicion that the stone masons had turned their attention to the occult would indicate that they were no longer the simple group of craftsmen they had once been. And that, again, places accusations made during the Middle Ages at the center of our investigation.

Although the accusations of occultism among the early Freemasons were vague and sketchy, those against the Templars were quite specific and detailed. Initiates were required to trample, spit, or urinate on the cross. Most who confessed to this charge tried to preserve some semblance of personal innocence. They claimed that they had resisted this requirement. Many said that they had spat near – not on – the cross.

This posed no problem for the inquisitors. They were quite willing to let individual members protest their innocence. The guilt or innocence of individuals was not at issue. It was the Order the king wanted to incriminate, and it was against the Order that the charge of heresy was leveled. If the organization forced its members to show contempt for the cross, it had to have a reason, and there was no need to guess what that reason might be. To the medieval mind, it was both obvious and devastating. Repudiating the cross went hand in hand with worshiping the devil.

Thus, the next charge. The Templars as a group were accused of being in league with Baphomet. The head they worshiped was in some confessions said to be an image of that deity. It figured prominently in the initiation and other ceremonies, which at times were attended by virgins or demons appearing in female form.

Although Baphomet has since come to be known as "the god of the witches," the medieval concept of the deity was simpler and more vague. The name itself is a variation of the name of Mohammed (Mahomet), the founder of Islam. Since Islam was the religion of the Infidel, its gods had to be evil. That was all any good Christian needed to know, and most were afraid to learn more.

This primitive notion is reflected by the nature of the confessions the inquisitors were able to extract. Only a dozen Templars admitted seeing an idol, and their descriptions of it bear little resemblance to one another. The Templars did not admit – nor were they accused of – a litany of diabolical rituals. Nor did a list of such rituals need to be proved. This part of the indictment was more basic than that. At heart, it amounts to the accusation that the Order had turned wholesale from the Church and accepted the Infidel's religion.

These charges were the most serious and damning. A military order could be forgiven an obsession with secrecy. Knights who routinely put their lives at risk could be forgiven lapses of personal morality. But dabbling in the occult, that was different. It implied that the Templars were not the pious knights they claimed to be. It suggested that the Order had somehow been perverted. It meant that the Order, not merely its individual members, had turned against the true faith and replaced it with unholy beliefs and practices.

Denying the divinity of Christ, claiming that He was a false prophet and making improper changes in the Mass were specific acts of heresy that, if the Templars really had done such things, separated them from the Christian Church. Considering their long stay in the east, perhaps they had accepted tenets of the Moslem faith. To the European Christians of the day, the religion of the Infidel was a remote and mysterious thing. It was certainly evil and probably involved magic and dealings with demons. If the Templars had dabbled in those matters, that would explain their idolatrous practices. Even the mysterious cord, which the knights were expected to wear next to their skin, was supposed to have some special magical properties.

The strategy behind the inquisition's charges is clear. The good work done by the Templars in earlier days could not be challenged. Instead, they would have to be charged with gradually becoming corrupt during the generations they had spent in foreign lands. There, influenced by constant contact with eastern mysticism and softened by wealth and power, the once honorable knights had given in to temptation.

The latter day Templars, the charges claimed, had strayed from the values of their humble and impoverished predecessors. They had become idolatrous, lecherous and avaricious. They had forgotten that Christ was the comfort and strength of the faithful. And in the end they became as evil as the Infidel the crusaders had been mustered to fight.

Were any of these accusations true? It's hard to say. The truth of the charges, like other things from the period, is elusive, but in this case there is a special reason. True, the history of the Templars is plagued by the illiteracy of the times and the inevitable loss of documents. But that isn't the problem. The Hospitallers, who evolved and fought beside the Templars, left behind a fairly straightforward history.

The difference is that the Templars began as a secret society and continued to practice extreme secrecy throughout their existence. The Order hid its dealings from the world. That was one reason for the Templars' downfall, and it is a major reason that it is so difficult to learn the truth about them.

We may speculate, as people have done for centuries, about the extent to which the charges were founded. That will come later in our quest. But at this point we can draw only a tentative conclusion. Secrecy was at the very heart of the Templars' activities. No doubt it was a necessary safeguard in the early stages of their history. However, it seems that the Templars' cult of secrecy eventually took on a life of its own. It became a thing unto itself.

This, as much as anything else, caused the Order's downfall. It lent credibility to the suspicions, and later to the accusations that the Templars engaged in all manner of evil practices. Their secrecy was so entrenched that, when they were put on trial, it was difficult for them to let the world know the truth about their organization – a truth that might have discredited at least some of the accusations against them.

This is both the strength and the weakness of all secret societies. The secrecy that sustains them and guards them against the prying eyes of outsiders is a sword with two edges. If things get out of hand, it can damage the institution it was intended to protect. And if things go far enough, as with the Templars, it can even deliver a mortal wound.

The York Connection

The Freemasons have a Templar legend. That is a simple fact. But, as we have seen, Masonic legends pose more questions than they answer. In all the higher degrees, there is not one word to *prove* that they evolved in the Middle Ages. Nor does the history of the medieval Templars tell us anything about the gentlemen Masons.

The answer to this question lies in the missing portion of the Craft's history. It is a period from which we can not expect a complete record. Unless more documents surface, and that is very unlikely, we will never have tangible evidence of a connection between the Templars and the stone masons.

Deprived of documentary evidence, we will find that it is very hard to establish a connection between two organizations that no longer exist in their medieval forms. Further investigation will show several enticing parallels between the historic Templars and the rituals of the modern Freemasons. But more than four centuries separate the telling of *this* story and its subject.

To pursue the matter further, we must return to a time when the Templars and the cathedral builders still plied their trades, then we must look for a point of contact. If the two never met each other, they could not have joined forces. But if the histories of the two organizations can be linked in time and space, the possibility of an historic connection becomes at least credible.

Since Freemasonry started in the British Isles, we will look there for the Templars who may have become Masons. Fortunately, this is one of the few pieces of the story that is not elusive. A cursory survey of history reveals that the Poor Knights of Christ did in fact operate in the island.

Hugues de Payens himself founded the preceptory in England. Following a meeting in Normandy with Henry I, de Payens crossed the Channel in 1128 or 1129 and organized Templar operations in London, Essex, Buckinghamshire, Lincolnshire, Hertfordshire and Scotland.

He established the London headquarters to the north of the Thames, at the north end of Chancery Lane, where a ring of modern buildings now hides Lincoln's Inn Fields from the casual passerby. The original building, the Old Temple, stood across the Fields from a spot that would later be occupied by the Old Curiosity Shop.

As the Order grew, the London branch became one of its most important operations. In fact, it was second only to the Paris Temple in terms of size and wealth. With donations of land and money coming in rapidly, the Templars soon outgrew their London Temple and needed a larger facility. To that end they purchased a piece of land stretching from White Friars to the Temple Bar, and from the Strand to the river.

In 1184, they moved their operations to the new quarters, in a place now occupied by the Inns of Court and Chancery. The round church they built there, now called the Temple Church, still stands on that spot. This "New" Temple was consecrated on February 10, 1185 by Patriarch Heraclius of Jerusalem in a ceremony attended by, among others, King Henry II and his court.

The royal presence at this event was more than just a formality. It reflected the bond that had developed between the Templars and the crown. By this time the Order had become bankers to the English kings and the nobility. Templars guarded the royal treasure, which was stored in the Temple as well as in the Tower of London. And on more than one occasion they even guarded the royal person by giving refuge to a king whose safety was in doubt.

The Templars' close relationship with the English kings extended over a long period of time. In a scenario that mirrored the relationship between the Templars and the papacy, several English monarchs bestowed benefits on the Order in return for services rendered. Eventually the Master of the Temple was even granted the right to sit in Parliament. He was the first ecclesiastic baron of the realm.

The English Templars wielded influence beyond their own shores as well. In 1256, an Englishman, Thomas Berard, was elected Grand Master of the Order. He held the office until his death in 1273. This was no mean feat in an organization whose membership was primarily French, and whose leadership was consistently drawn from the continent. The elevation of an Englishman to so high a position shows how important the Order considered its operations in the island. And it is even more impressive in view of the size of the organization's membership in England.

Since Templars resident in England performed chiefly administrative functions, the Order's affairs could be managed by a relatively small contingency. At the time of the persecution, the English operation may have consisted of as few as 250 members. Perhaps that number was suddenly augmented by the few Templars who managed to escape the arrests in France, but it certainly remained small in proportion to the Order's financial resources in the area.

Temple Church
The interior of the Temple Church.

The Temple Church
The Templars' second headquarters in London was opened in A.D. 1185.

In spite of its limited size, the English Temple was extremely well connected. While French Templars languished in prison, their English brothers received protection from the highest authority. King Edward II virtually ignored Pope Clement's order to arrest all Templars throughout Christendom. He went through the motions of referring the matter to his Council but reported that he found the charges incredible and was not inclined to pursue the matter. When Philip insisted that England follow the example of the French inquisition, Edward responded by sending out letters advising several European monarchs to follow *his* example instead.

Edward knew that he could only delay taking action against the Templars, but he played his hand well. First, he justified his reluctance by appealing to English law, which did not allow torture as a means of extracting confessions. Then, when the pope demanded action, the king confiscated the Templars' property but refused to turn it over to the Church. Each of these exchanges took time and did a minimum of harm to the Templars.

The carefully cultivated friendship between the Temple and the Crown was now paying off. During the worst days of the inquisition, the English Templars were allowed time to maneuver. How well they used that time was not recorded, but we may assume that they were far from inactive during the weeks after they learned of the extreme danger their Order faced.

As Christmas of 1307 drew near, Clement insisted on more decisive action from England. The pressure was building, and Edward made another minimal concession. He agreed to make arrests – some 229 Templars were rounded up in London – but the king still would not allow them to be tortured. His country, he claimed, did not even have people who knew how to inflict torture.

The Church supplied the torturers, and Edward finally made the critical concession. He allowed the English Templars to be drawn into the inquisition, but only with severe restrictions. The procedures could not mutilate the prisoners, inflict permanent injury or cause excessive bleeding.

In this way, the English Templars were put to torture, but they admitted little. They confirmed that the Order had a rule of secrecy and that its members made confession only to their own chaplains. But these points were already known and had never been denied. The English Templars seemed to admit that the Order practiced lay absolution, a point that was not conceded elsewhere. Even so, no one could be found who admitted that he had personally granted absolution. And the English members acknowledged that they wore a cord but insisted that this was nothing more than the "Belt of Nazareth," which St. Bernard had recommended to mark off the body's zones of chastity.

Curiously, the English Templars professed their own innocence but would not vouch for the behavior of the Order in other countries. They insisted that they had no personal knowledge of goings-on outside their jurisdiction. This has the sound of a coordinated strategy, no doubt devised

St. Bernard
Patron of the Templars and the possible source of an obscure Masonic symbol, the Beehive.

while the Templars in England still had time to plot their future. They may have considered it the safest way to keep themselves out of the predicament into which their French comrades had slipped. Or they may have wanted to distance themselves from dealings that were practiced on the continent but not in their country.

Whatever their strategy, the English Templars managed to escape the fate of their brothers across the Channel. They were much less persecuted than their counterparts in France and Italy. And this is the key to the possibility of a masonic connection. When the end came for the Templars, they were stripped of privileges and wealth that had taken centuries to accumulate. It did not really matter that they were no longer a band of monastic crusaders. The Holy Land was lost and the crusades were over. Had the Templars not been persecuted, they would have been forced to make major changes anyway. The loss of their status as the darlings of Christendom was the real blow to an organization known for its pride and arrogance. Ever since their official dissolution, rumors have persisted that the Templars simply did not accept such a blow. They continued to operate as an organization, the rumors say, and may well have survived into modern times.

That rumor is not as unlikely as it might seem. Although the Order of the Temple was dissolved, the vast majority of its members survived. Of the Order's 15,000 members, no more than a few hundred died during the inquisition. The rest lived out their lives in a variety of unglamorous roles. History records that most of them dispersed and joined other orders or retired to pursue secular occupations.

There may be no more to the story than this, but the Templars had plenty of reason to want it otherwise. They had been subjected to a persecution that was repulsive even by the violent standards of the day. Many of their number were tortured, some killed. They were stripped of resources they had labored long and hard to earn. And in the end their Grand Master had been unjustly murdered. Perhaps the meek would submit to such treatment, but the Templars were not meek. They were an aggressive caste of warriors who had more than once fought against overwhelming odds and survived. It is not impossible that some of them chose to fight one more battle.

If the Templars did choose to survive as an organization, geography would have been a key factor in the plans they now had to make. Following the persecution, any attempt to preserve their Order in France or Italy would put the members in serious danger of being imprisoned or burned as relapsed heretics. They would stand a much better chance where the long arm of the French king could not reach and where they still had friends and resources.

England was one of those places. The Templars received as much protection as Edward could give them, considering the delicacy of his political situation. And within England it appears that the Templars fared better in the northern parts of the island.

London, the official seat of both the Order and the crown, saw the worst persecution. There, the king had to order arrests and eventually torture, while the pope and the French king constantly pressed him to act more quickly. In the outlying areas, there was less of a sense of urgency. The slow pace of travel and communications helped the Templars in northern England and Scotland. It gave them time to plan and act as decrees and inquisitors moved slowly northward. In northern England, where officials were sympathetic, the Templars were treated with leniency. In Scotland they were scarcely bothered at all.

But getting through an inquisition intact is one thing. Surviving as a fugitive organization is something else. That would require considerable help. If we are to contemplate seriously the theory of a surviving order, we must wonder if they had enough friends and resources to go underground in those outlying areas.

At this point, we discover a most intriguing fact. Although the Templars' headquarters were in London, the bulk of their holdings in the island were clustered in Yorkshire and Lincolnshire. Over the years the Order came into possession of several estates there and established itself as an important corporate member of the community. And at the very center of the area's economy was the ancient city of York.

This was a natural outgrowth of the island's history and economy. The virtues that had made York an important city since Roman times were still in full force. The city was now an important center of commerce and a trading hub for the wool industry that prospered in that part of the island. It was inevitable that the wealthy citizens of the north would donate property to the Templars. Perhaps it was inevitable, too, that the fugitive knights would seek refuge there in their time of need.

In York, Templar history dovetails with a tradition that had existed in the area for centuries. We have seen how operative masonry was reintroduced into England with the aid of the royal house that held court there. That event blossomed into a cultural revival that strongly influenced Anglo-Saxon culture and gave birth to the forces that produced modern Freemasonry.

The birth of Freemasonry is consciously commemorated in the York legend. We already know that the legend was garbled, apparently the result of centuries of oral tradition, before it was finally committed to paper. The key to our investigation is why this story – a story that was old even in the fourteenth century – was dredged up and written down. For some reason it had become important for someone to leave a record of an organization that had previously needed no written history.

The earliest surviving copy of the York legend, the *Regius Poem*, was written around 1390. Although the text carries no date, its content and style point to that time. But scholars have suggested that the *Regius Poem* is not the original. It is probably a copy of a document that was first penned half a century earlier – just before the mid-point of the fourteenth century.

This poses an intriguing possibility. We have seen that Masonic history began with a seventh century nobleman who almost single-handedly created a cultural revival in Northumbria. This revival was preserved by the monks of Jarrow and Wearmouth and later by the architects who built the Gothic cathedrals. It was they who had the education, ability and inclination to carry on the tradition. They were learned monks whose religious leanings and position in society made them the logical ones to keep the nascent "masonic" spirit alive. Apparently they and their descendants did keep it alive without incident for several centuries.

Then, in the first years of the fourteenth century, another group of monks appeared dramatically on the scene. These were the warrior monks of the Order of the Temple. They had served in the Holy Land, where they absorbed elements of eastern culture and developed strong ties to King Solomon's Temple. They were a paradigm of Christian virtue and, if the charges against them were true, they had also delved into the mystical and the occult.

Of course, by the fourteenth century the knights of the Temple had attained an arrogance and corporate wealth that separated them from less wealthy monastic orders. But they were still monks, and their chaplains and serving brothers, especially those who spent their lives in the Order's local temples, would have had much in common with the other monks in their area.

To a monk who had spent his life in the north of England – a monk who spent his days copying manuscripts or carving stone – these Templars whose brothers had fought in Palestine would have been glamorous dinner companions. Even Templars who had not actually served in the east would have marvelous stories to tell. It is certain that these two groups had contact with each other during the nearly two centuries the Templars operated in England. In all probability, they became friends who could count on one another in times of need.

When the warrior monks found themselves persecuted, it was in places such as Cyprus, the low countries and the British Isles that they could turn to their friends for help. In those places, the actions of Philip and Clement were seen as unjust persecution motivated by greed and ambition. The French king and the French pope had fewer friends in those foreign countries than did the Templars.

The record implies that the Templars received aid and comfort in Yorkshire. It does not say whether some of it came from the cultural descendants of Benedict Biscop, but the Northumbrian monks would not likely have refused to help their brothers. It might have been secret help. For a period of time the Templars were, after all, fugitives under threat of torture and execution. Any dealings with them would likely need to be handled with discretion.

Although the Templars were not much persecuted in the northern parts of the island, that situation could easily have changed. King Edward never wanted to act against the Order, but he eventually had to yield to the pope. No one could be sure that the papacy wouldn't make additional demands. During the months that followed the first arrests, the Templars in the north must have feared that a shift in politics or an exercise of Church power would condemn them to prison or death.

Then the final blow came. The Church suppressed the Order, leaving the surviving Templars dispossessed and expected to transfer their allegiance to other monastic orders. In most places the process was straightforward. Any Templar who accepted the judgment of the Church could choose to live out his days in either monastic or secular surroundings. But the north of England presented a different scenario. There, justice had not run its course.

It was in the north that fugitive Templars, separated from their organization and most of its resources, now essentially unemployed and perhaps feeling a need to be inconspicuous, might find a safe haven. In a culture

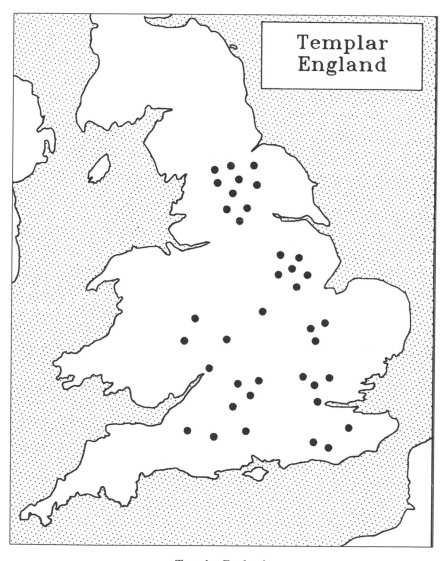

Templar England

The distribution of Templar preceptories in England. Their locations, which are only approximated in this map, indicate the Order's concentration of economic power around the city of York.

whose heritage was more closely tied to the Celtic Church than to the Roman, they could find new lives without accepting the suppression of their Order.

It may have been unemployment more than persecution that caused the Templars to seek a union with their brothers down the road. With their own organization no longer functioning, its members – chaplains and serving brothers as well as knights – would require new employment. Among the stone masons of York, the Templars found not only employment but also a chance to keep some remnant of their Order alive.

The Templars found in the free masons a brotherhood similar to their own. The masons, like the Templars, had an old and honorable heritage, though perhaps they could not remember their origins quite as well as the Templars remembered theirs. Both Templar and mason relied on skill, and both advanced on the basis of meritorious work. The Templars could easily understand the masonic way of life. And the mason could understand the mind of Templar.

It is possible that the Templars as an organization were reborn in York in just this way, melding into an order that at once was similar to theirs yet different, an older group that traced its own origins to the city of York, a group into which the Templars could blend without destroying the culture of either organization.

If the Templars did join the ranks of those working masons, they certainly breathed new life into an old culture. The result might well have been a revitalized spirit of brotherhood. The Templars, especially the illiterate knights among them, would have received a new appreciation for the arts of which the masons had become custodians. The masons, in turn, would have gained a sense of chivalric brotherhood and a new awareness of what had previously been only abstract, theological ties with the Holy Land.

For the better part of two centuries, the Templars had fashioned rough stone into the best and strongest forts in the world. Now they would turn their skills to raising cathedrals. In many ways it was an easy transition, but one they could not have made without a sense of loss.

As the free masons developed over the next few centuries, their rituals would indeed include curious references to Jerusalem and King Solomon's Temple. And there is a tantalizing sense that the masons of later centuries harbored vague memories of time spent in the Holy Land and a longing to return there.

If this is indeed how it happened, the Templars contributed something else to the free masons, something that would have far reaching effects. While the masons had the occasional proprietary secret to protect, the Templars were steeped in secrecy. As soldiers in the field, they concealed their strategy from the enemy. As international financiers and power brokers, they kept their own counsel. As fugitives, they would not likely abandon their cult of secrecy; they would hold more closely to it.

At first, the Templar passion for secrecy might have been accepted, or at least tolerated, by their hosts. After all, the Templars' lives would be at stake if the Church decided to hunt them down. If they continued to operate in defiance of the papal suppression of their Order, the risk of another inquisition into their affairs would be very real indeed. But in time, as the danger subsided and as the two groups influenced each other more and more, toleration of Templar secrecy would naturally become an embracing of it. And thus, Masonic secrecy – *real* Masonic secrecy – was born.

That birth was not announced in the usual way. Its very nature prevented the masons from documenting the change that had occurred in their organization, and at the same time it condemned future historians to search blindly for evidence that never existed. But they may have left a clue to the new direction they had taken. Within a generation or so of the Templars' persecution, a document appeared to attest that free masonry originated in York. It told an old story, but the story had a new feel.

Obviously something happened in the fourteenth century that prompted someone to set the legend down for others to read. Internal evidence suggests that it was written by a monk. It is possible – though impossible to prove – that it was written by one of the Templars' own scribes.

The occasion that prompted the writing of the legend *could* have been something as innocuous as King Richard's call for documents from the guilds. Or it may have been nothing more portentous than a bored monk deciding to preserve a bit of local history. But, on the other hand, it could well be that the legend was written to mark the new beginning of a fraternity that had not yet become a fraternity. It may be that a new sense of brotherhood and mission had been breathed into an old order and inspired that order to reconstruct what it could recall of its own ancient history.

Some Masonic scholars have expressed the belief that the *Regius Poem* was written for a fraternal organization, not for a group of operative craftsmen. That view is hard to support, because the document is so clearly tied to "craft" matters. It could, however, reflect the changes that were beginning to occur in what had suddenly become more than a craft organization.

A Templar influence in medieval operative masonry would certainly explain the Masonic preoccupation with secrecy. It would explain the appearance of the enigmatic York legend, with its feel of an historic story from which something is missing. And it would begin to explain the modern ritual, which hints at a secret so important that it is worth dying to protect.

York Cathedral

Toward a Modern Craft

W e are now in the fourteenth century. For the Freemasons, this century marked the beginning of an interval in their development. The stone masons were busily constructing the Gothic cathedrals of Britain and Europe, and the Poor Knights of Christ no longer existed as a separate body. The forces that brought both groups to this point in history had run their course. The evolution of operative masonry into a social organization was still far away. And the rituals that inspired theories of a Templar connection would not appear in print for another four hundred years.

During the next few centuries the masons of England and Scotland apparently pursued business as usual. They worked on cathedrals and abbeys, and on large secular buildings as well. On the whole business was good and the craft continued to preserve its heritage and its ritual.

There was no real need for change, since free masonry had crystallized into an organization. It was not the organization that exists now. Its members and their modern counterparts would scarcely recognize each other. Nevertheless, the craft existed in a stable form. Its early development was history, and it settled down, as organizations do, to a long period of slow and steady evolution.

The operative craft's basic document, the *Gothic Constitutions*, was re-copied and revised several times during the next few centuries. Its custodians changed and embellished the details of the York legend. New names and events appeared, although the reasons for adding them were not recorded. But the basic story remained the same, and slightly different versions of it were preserved by masonic lodges throughout the country.

In this document can be found the rudimentary foundation for much of the modern ritual's symbolism. Its pages describe masonry as the art of geometry. They make reference to Euclid and the seven Arts and Sciences. And, of particular importance, they provide a code of moral conduct.

The operative masons apparently did little to develop the symbolism that was latent in their craft. They were occupied with raising buildings, not with the subtleties that lay untapped in their organization. The cultural tradition they had inherited from Benedict Biscop may well have survived only as ritual elements whose meaning had already been forgotten.

Anything they had received from the Templars experienced a similar fate. The danger to the suppressed knights passed quickly. With both Philip and Clement dead, few people cared any more. As the persecution was forgotten, the surviving knights and serving brothers settled into the new lives they had chosen for themselves. Those who had joined the descendants of Biscop's stone masons assimilated quickly into that group, and when their generation died out, the "secrets" they had brought from the east evolved into bits and pieces of masonic lore. The Templar tradition's meaning and purpose were increasingly obscured as it was handed down by successive generations of masons. They would naturally reinterpret it in their own terms and thus carry it farther from its origins until it may have become completely unrecognizable for what it was.

We know little of masonic meetings as they existed in the operative period. Scarce documentary evidence has survived to show what earlier rituals were like. But we may consider ourselves fortunate to know as much as we do about the craft in those days. If Templar secrecy had now been added to the illiteracy of the period and the normal attrition of documents, it is remarkable that anything survived.

There are several points of similarity between the current ritual and what we know of its older counterparts, and there are quite a few differences. We have every reason to believe that there was only one level of initiation during the operative period. Since the ceremony served only to accept apprentices into a craft, the ritual didn't need to be complicated. It may have consisted of little more than reading a list of regulations to the apprentice. There was certainly no elaborate system of moral instruction.

To begin with, there is no evidence that the ritual handed down to us by the operative masons included the story of Hiram Abif. Indeed, there is no evidence to show whether the Hiramic legend even existed in their day. If it did, it was not well publicized. But that is not surprising. If the craft did harbor secrets at that time, it is not unreasonable to assume that the *story* of those secrets would have been a secret, too. It may well have been transmitted orally and never committed to paper.

Regardless of when it was invented, the Hiramic legend and its original purpose are on the shadowy side of Masonic history. The legend was either invented or recreated as part of a transition that may have started as early as the fourteenth century and would not be completed until the seventeenth or eighteenth. But it is not clear whether its authors were looking to the past or the future when they wrote the story.

As the building of Gothic cathedrals declined in the sixteenth century, the skilled stone masons who had labored on those massive structures had to look to other horizons. The need for intricate stone work had passed its peak. New styles developed and new materials were introduced. Brick began to replace stone as the substance of great public buildings. Moreover, the changes seemed so permanent that it was unlikely skilled stone carvers would ever again be needed in such large numbers.

This no doubt caused some problems for the individual worker. The contraction of the market would likely mean a scarcity of employment from time to time and place to place. But the decline of cathedral building was a gradual process. It was neither as calamitous nor as sudden as other major events of the medieval world, and the individual free mason must have coped reasonably well with the decline of the Gothic style.

More important, at least in the overall scheme of things, was the effect of the change on the free mason's lodge. When Gothic cathedrals were no longer being built, the lodge lost its reason for existing as a craft organization. At that point, it was faced with the ultimate choice of either going out of business or adapting to new circumstances.

For the organization that had built up around the stone masons, the question of survival was a serious one. The free mason's lodges had earned a position of respect in the community. Their membership must have been relatively small. Even to build a massive cathedral, the need for skilled craftsmen was limited, and the number of free masons in any community would have been small compared with the population as a whole. But this was a proud organization. Along the way it had taken on a life of its own. Like the Templars, it would not accept its own dissolution easily.

Instead of becoming a victim of the operative craft's decline, its lodges chose to use their prestige to evolve into something new and different. With the operative side of their work becoming less important, they stressed the fraternal bond that had long been a part of the masonic enterprise. This made them more of a social organization, and they acted accordingly. By the end of the sixteenth century, they were accepting "gentlemen" who had nothing to do with the building industry to what at first amounted to honorary membership.

The mechanism of this transition was not documented, but we know the climate in which it occurred. As the Gothic era declined, a Renaissance revived the wisdom of the ancients, which had been all but forgotten in the illiterate society of the Middle Ages. From the middle of the fifteenth century, learning spread through Europe at an ever increasing pace. Fostered by advances in printing, learning became more than a cloistered academic pursuit. It was now fashionable for anyone who could afford it to study art and science and literature. The medieval ideal of the armored warrior was replaced by the well-rounded man of letters.

As the sixteenth century established itself, the Protestant Reformation added to the Renaissance by making it acceptable to question Church dogma. The man of letters was increasingly free to think in human terms. He still saw the world as a divine creation, but he could now view the works of man as something distinct and apart from God's plan.

Meanwhile, as the flow of ideas increased, so did the flow of money. Increasing trade gave more and more people the means and leisure to investigate the new learning. What had once been accessible only to the wealthy land owner, the statesman and the Church scholar was now affordable to the merchant and the minor aristocrat. In short, society was becoming Enlightened.

The dark ages gave way to the Renaissance and the Enlightenment precisely when the free masons were less and less needed for construction work. But the masons did have something that was very much in demand. Their lodges held bits of the wisdom they had accumulated over the years from such varied sources as the seventh century monastics, the cathedral builders and the Templars. Thus, the masons were the custodians of something that appealed greatly to gentlemen who were waking up to a new world of knowledge.

We have lost track of the first gentlemen Masons. For the most part we do not even know who they were. Students of such illustrious figures as Francis Bacon (1561–1626) and Christopher Wren (1632–1723) argue that men of that ilk were involved in the birth of "speculative" Freemasonry. To this day, Masonic writers are fond of quoting passages from Shakespeare that *seem* to refer to Masonic themes. It is interesting to speculate about such men as these, though in the end we lack proof that they had any connection with the lodge.

There are any number of figures who may or may not have been involved with operative masonry during the period when the craft became the Craft. Unless new evidence comes to light, we will never be certain about most of them. But if we don't know who transformed Freemasonry into what it is now, we do have some sense of the way the transition occurred.

Just as the operative lodges sprang up when and where they were needed, with little attachment to lodges in other locations, the speculative lodges appear to have evolved where conditions were right. They were widely scattered and showed no indications of being part of a strong national or regional organization.

Operative free masonry had existed all over Europe. But England and Scotland took the lead in its evolution into a fraternal society. This was, of course, the product of a complex set of circumstances. The British operatives were heir to a tradition that had stressed the arts and crafts since the seventh century. British society itself was a melting pot for the several cultures that had each contributed its strengths to the national character. And it was more democratic than most European nations, a factor that proved important – perhaps essential – to the development of modern Freemasonry. If the British masons had inherited esoteric knowledge from the Templars as well, they emerged from the Middle Ages with a culture that was unique among the craft masons of Europe.

Even without the Templars' wisdom, the foundation for a system of moral instruction existed in the operative craft at an early date. Its history, structure and function had given it elements that could be fashioned into an elegant system of moral instruction. From its inception, the craft's connection with religious structures provided a natural link between architecture and religion. The cathedral and the abbey were the physical embodiment of all things spiritual. Jesus had even referred to his own body as a temple, and the Church stressed that analogy. Certainly the comparisons were there. They only needed to be developed and interpreted.

In addition, the very structure of the craft symbolized the quest for knowledge. Master masons were men who had risen through the ranks. They were not born with their skills. Through dedication, hard work and attention to the lessons they were taught – and through the faithful and loyal performance of their duties – ordinary laborers could rise to become highly respected and well paid masters of their craft. This was no small matter in an aristocratic society in which wealth and privilege had traditionally depended more on heredity than on ability.

All of this was tailor-made for the Enlightenment. The operative masons, though not aristocrats, had already earned the respect of the English gentlemen. It was apparently a matter of great pride to be granted honorary membership in their organization. That prestige, added to the knowledge they could offer, was what made it possible for the lodges to survive.

During this period, the modern degree system and the bulk of its symbolism came into being. They were simply a response to the organization's need to survive and its new members' interests in philosophy and science. Whereas the operative masons of a few centuries earlier had largely ignored the symbolic potential of their craft, the gentlemen Masons exploited it.

Considering the spirit of exploration that reached full speed in the seventeenth and eighteenth centuries, it would be surprising if Freemasonry had developed in any other way. It was a classic example of the right tool being available at the right moment in history. As the working stone masons gradually became the minority in their own lodges and more and more speculatives became involved, the gentlemen Masons realized what a wealth of material they had come upon.

This was an exciting time. Like children in a sweet shop, the gentlemen of the Enlightenment explored their discovery with wide-eyed enthusiasm. They had a thousand years of accumulated treasures to choose from. At every turn symbols and legends waited to be developed. And best of all, the restraints that had held back the course of learning during the dark ages were now gone.

When Masonry entered its modern period, it contained substantial Christian elements, as would be expected of a group whose original function was to build Europe's cathedrals. But the Craft now chose a new direction. The end of the seventeenth century marked the end of the divine right of kings. Henceforth, governments would be made by men and fashioned by reason. Science was in its ascendancy. Where religion had once ruled the people's lives, knowledge of the world would take a place in the scheme of things. And philosophy – the wisdom of the ancients – would give people an understanding of their place in the world and their relationship to their God. It was in this context that the Craft would take its rightful place.

Freemasonry had never been a religion. It was always a tradition that embodied a love of art and craft and culture. Now it had become a philosophical society where men of different faiths could come together to explore ideas that had been developed by the Northumbrian monks and the Templars and the writer of the *Gothic Constitutions* and had later been inherited by the thinkers of the Renaissance and the Enlightenment.

As the Craft moved into the future, its symbols would have to reflect its chosen role as a custodian of moral wisdom in the emerging world of science and reason. To that end, its Christian elements were removed or generalized to make them compatible with a variety of religious beliefs. The fraternity would be built on the foundation of a belief in a Supreme Being, but it would not impose any other belief on its members. It would, instead, offer moral lessons that could be taken or left, and understood in the light of each member's faith.

Freemasonry still uses Christian symbols, but in most of the degrees they are explained and interpreted in general terms. While the parochial origins of the fraternity can be seen in the modern ritual, its lessons are now presented as moral, not religious principles.

We have already seen the birth of Masonic secrecy. Now we see the birth of the controversy that has plagued the Craft for three centuries. This unusual blend of religious and moral concepts drew criticism almost immediately. It ran afoul of the common belief that moral principles must be taught in a religious context. Many who witnessed the rise of modern Masonry were alarmed that its teachings did not conform to – and were not expressed through the medium of – their own theological bent.

For the first time, we begin to see documents that show how the man in the street felt about the Craft, and they reveal a remarkable hostility. Somehow, during this period, the Freemasons developed the reputation of being sinister men who met secretly to do evil deeds. There is no evidence of this attitude in earlier years, but now it seems that the community was becoming aware of the lodges' activities, and they didn't like what they saw.

Curiously, the gentlemen Masons' response to this criticism indicates an attitude that is hard to understand. They were distressed not because they were being slandered but because their privacy was being threatened. It was the prying eye, not the sharp tongue, that alarmed them.

And this really is curious. The gentlemen Masons' use of old legends and symbols to express moral values might well have been controversial. Their free thinking might have offended the more traditional of their neighbors.

But what did they have to hide? The whole point of the Enlightenment was to spread knowledge and share it with others. Yet the Freemasons were becoming known as a group that hid its dealings from the world, and their behavior suggests that the reputation was well earned.

Apparently something was afoot. Not only did the community believe that the Freemasons were a secret society. The Masons themselves were concerned with keeping secrets. And for the first time we have some actual documents to show what the commotion was about.

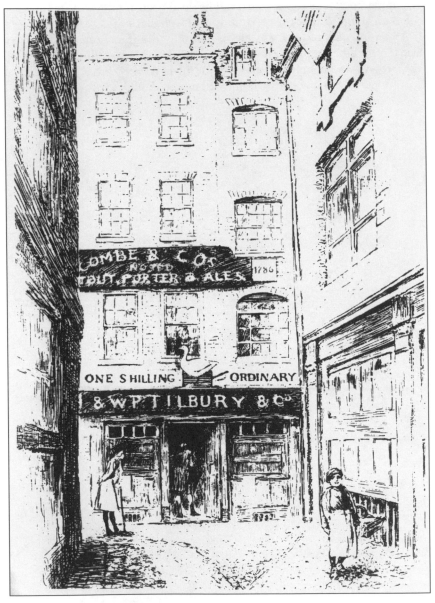

The Goose and Gridiron Alehouse
The first meeting place of Grand Lodge, 24 June 1717. Artist's impression based on a sketch published in 1894 when the building was demolished.

The Paper Trail

We have seen that Freemasonry entered its modern period on June 24, 1717. This is a very specific date, but it marked only one instant in a long and continuous history. By the time the Grand Lodge was formed, the *organization* had existed for centuries and had undergone a number of changes.

Apparently what was new this time was the form the fraternity took. The creation of the Grand Lodge in England gave it an "official" status it had not had before. And there is reason to believe that this development was part – though not the cause – of an increase in public awareness of Freemasonry. A relatively low profile group that had previously caused little commotion was suddenly in the public eye.

In those days, the tavern was a center of social activities, much as the neighborhood pub is in England today. It was a place to take an evening meal, to meet friends and to spend a few hours enjoying drink and conversation.

Masonic lodges chose to meet in an upstairs room at the local tavern, because that was where groups met. They took food and drink during the meeting. That, too, was standard procedure. And at the end of the meeting, the lodge adjourned and the members went their separate ways.

The patrons who congregated in the tavern's public rooms knew about the lodge. It is impossible for an organization to conceal its existence when it holds regular meetings in a public place. But since the meetings were for members only, the general public did not know what occurred behind the closed door of that upstairs room. Nor did they show much curiosity. It was all a low key affair.

Then, when the individual lodges became units of a larger group, they began a process that led to higher visibility in the community. A governing body meant more standardization, more activity and more recognition – by member and non-member alike – that the Freemasons were an *organization*.

During this period, the public's perception of Freemasonry evolved along with the Craft. We see an apparent increase in anti-Masonic writings, which are relatively unknown prior to the formation of the Grand Lodge. And along with the anti-Masonic writings, we see reactions by, or at least on behalf of, the Craft.

Articles and pamphlets attacking the Freemasons began appearing in the early years of the eighteenth century. These attacks were certainly not confined to London. They followed the Masons wherever they went. Our investigation will shortly take us to America, where the colonists first reprinted articles from English newspapers and later produced their own. In time, anti-Masonic sentiment in the Colonies took on a distinctly American character, with shocking results. But that is still a century in the future. For the present we are concerned with the commotion that swirled around the Grand Lodge in London.

As the eighteenth century progressed, the newly reorganized fraternity was increasingly debated in print. It is hard to determine how much of the evidence relates to changing attitudes and how much is the result of a change in the number of surviving documents, but we can clearly see a developing trend.

More and more people came to see the Masons as a secret society. The medieval masons certainly did have secrets, mostly trade secrets. That is undisputed. But those matters were no longer of any practical use to the speculative Mason. Consequently, there was no longer any reason to protect them. Yet the speculatives continued to guard their secrets with a passion.

That might seem a paradox, but what had happened is clear and not at all surprising. If the Masons were not devoting a lot of energy to protecting meaningless and outdated secrets, they must have developed new ones. Obviously the privileged knowledge of the old days had been replaced with fraternal secrets.

The key to understanding Masonic secrecy lies in understanding *why* the speculatives were so serious about keeping their new secrets. And that is a much more complicated thing than we might imagine.

The speculative Masons did have reasons for keeping their new secrets, but those reasons were not merely a product of events *inside* their organization. Masonic secrecy – indeed secrecy of any kind – is never a unilateral thing. Masonic lodges have always existed in the context of the societies in which they operate. They have an impact on those societies and respond to them.

The lodges of the eighteenth century were well aware of the criticism they were receiving. But, like modern day Masons, they were reluctant to respond directly. As a result, we have only clues to the way they reacted.

Our evidence from this period consists of the minutes of lodge meetings, miscellaneous papers that were apparently used within the lodge and newspaper items and pamphlets published for sale to the public. Although documents are now available in larger numbers than in earlier times, it is not easy to sort through them. The original purpose of many is not clear, the authenticity of some has been questioned, and in a few cases the motives of their authors seem deliberately misstated.

An example of this mis-statement comes from 1724. In that year a curious pamphlet appeared in the streets of London. It was titled *The Secret History of the Free-Masons. Being an Accidental Discovery of the Ceremonies made use of in the several Lodges*, but it is more conveniently known as the *Briscoe* pamphlet.

Running just over fifty pages and selling at the time for one shilling, this publication seems straightforward. It contains a fairly accurate text of the *Old Charges*, some commentary and criticism, and a dictionary of purported secret signs used by Freemasons.

Up to that point, nothing is especially novel or interesting. After all, Dr. Anderson had recently published his version of the *Old Charges*. That kind of material had been around for more than three centuries and was doubtless available to anyone who was interested enough to look for it.

A goodly amount of critical material about Freemasonry was also available by this time. But there is something peculiar about this document. Although the pamphlet is apparently hostile to the Craft, some of the author's facts are questionable, and his dictionary of secret signs is a little too fanciful.

More to the point, the author's errors could easily be checked by contemporary readers. For example, he takes Anderson to task for incorrectly stating that wood for King Solomon's Temple was sent from Lebanon to Jerusalem by way of the port of Joppa. In this case, the critic is wrong. Readers could easily confirm the accuracy of Anderson's statement by referring to *II Chronicles* 2:16.

Modern readers might believe that the author of the *Briscoe* pamphlet had simply not done his homework. But there is a much more plausible explanation. Since the errors are so blatant, perhaps they were meant to be spotted. If they were, we must wonder why a critic of Freemasonry would deliberately make errors he knew his readers would notice.

We don't have to look far for the answer. Even at the time, it was suspected that the author of the *Briscoe* pamphlet was actually a friend of the Craft who was trying to discredit a recently published exposé.

The exposé in question, *The Grand Mystery of Free-Masons Discover'd*, was published at the beginning of 1724. Its twelve pages purport to reveal Masonic secrets, and there is every reason to believe that they did.

Unfortunately, we can not be sure precisely what secrets the *Grand Mystery* did reveal. Since few "official" documents from those years have been preserved, there is little with which to compare the early exposés. In fact, *they* are often the standard by which other Masonic matters of the period are judged.

But all is not lost. By comparing these early documents with the modern ritual and with other documents from their own time, we can form a tentative picture of the Masonic rituals of the day. It is far from complete, but it allows us to draw some conclusions. And an examination of *The Grand Mystery* suggests that it was accurate enough to make the Masons of the day very uncomfortable.

Then suddenly after the *Briscoe* pamphlet, the *The Secret History of the Free-Masons* appeared. It, too, claimed to reveal the secrets of the Freemasons, but these secrets were suspect on their own face.

Perhaps the most obvious example is in the pamphlet's claim to reveal the "signs" of a Freemason. *Briscoe*'s dictionary of secret signs runs six and a half pages. It claims to be a list of gestures by which a Mason could communicate secretly when he saw one another in public. A brief excerpt will give the flavor of the whole.

> *Breast.* To clap the right Hand upon the right Breast, is a Signal for a Member to meet him that makes it in St *Paul's* Cathedral at the Time of Morning-Prayer: And to clap the left hand upon the left Breast, signifies you will be in St. *Paul's* Cathedral at the time of Evening-Prayer.

> *Button.* To rub the right Hand down the Coat *Buttons*, is a Sign for a Member to be upon the *Royal-Exchange* at the Beginning of Change Time: And to rub the left Hand down the Coat *Buttons*, signifies he shall be at the *Sun-Tavern* in *Threadneedle-Street*, as soon as Change is over. Also to rub the right Hand down the Wastecoat *Buttons*, signifies he must be at the *Horns Ale-House* in *Gutter-Lane*, at Nine of the Clock the next Morning: And to rub the left Hand down the Wastecoat *Buttons*, signifies that you must be at the same *Ale-House* at Eight of the Clock next Night.

Obviously something is wrong here. Present-day Masons do have recognition signs, but they are very general. Their purpose is simply to identify a man as a Mason, in other words, to weed out impostors. They consist of gestures and statements any Mason should recognize and are not nearly as complex as the list *Briscoe* published.

Undoubtedly the Masons of two and a half centuries ago had recognition signs, too. But it is hard to believe that they needed six and a half pages of them. Remembering such a long list of minutely detailed signals would be nearly impossible, and their utility nearly nonexistent.

Was the author of the *Briscoe* pamphlet the victim of a hoax? Was he trying to perpetrate one on his readers? Or was he merely trying to discredit the Masons? Most likely, his pamphlet was a subtle attempt to discredit the *critics* of the Craft.

With exposés of their ritual beginning to appear, the Masons were becoming concerned. This information was intended for members only. It included the passwords visitors used to gain admission to the lodge, and when *those* secrets were published, the Masons had a problem. Since they didn't know all the visitors who came to their meetings, words and signs were used to verify that everyone present was a member of the Craft. But if the public knew the secrets, impostors could infiltrate the lodge at will.

Contemporary records show that the Freemasons were so concerned about this problem that they debated safeguards to protect the lodges. That's good news for us, because it shows that at least a few of the exposés hit close to home. We may conclude that somewhere in their pages are the real Masonic secrets of the day. And if the Masons were especially worried about *The Grand Mystery*, it may have been the most accurate of the expose's.

In many ways *The Grand Mystery* was a typical exposure. It claimed to proceed from an accidental discovery of the Craft's secrets. It asserted that the secrets "were found in the Custody of a Free-Mason who Dyed suddenly," presumably before he could pass his papers on to another Mason for safekeeping.

The pamphlet consists of a short catechism similar to those presently used in Craft lodges, an oath, a toast, and a short list of recognition signs. Its text is reprinted in Appendix III, but a few comments are appropriate here.

It is interesting that the oath, very brief at 51 words, makes no mention of secrecy. It merely obligates the members to serve God and the king and to assist their brothers.

The toast does imply secrecy, but in a rather curious way. It states in part, "The World no Order knows like this our Noble and Ancient Fraternity: Let them wonder at the Mystery."

The cryptic last sentence suggests an air of secrecy. But by implication it seems to point more to pride in the organization than to a desire to withhold anything important from the general public.

The section titled "Signs to know a True *Mason*" is somewhat more revealing. It lists nine modes of recognition. A few are straightforward. One, for example, has a member "ask what Lodge they were made a Free-Mason at." But others are more clandestine. They include "making a Square *viz.* by setting your Heels together, and the Toes of both Feet straight, at a distance, or by any other Way of Triangle." Others call for repeating specified gestures three times. Anyone familiar with the modern ritual, and its emphasis on the square and the number three, can see that these may once have been official recognition modes. Although they are no longer used for that purpose, they are similar to gestures that still occur during Masonic meetings.

The catechism also reveals the inner workings of the Masonic lodge of the day. It contains references to an obligation of secrecy, including the expression "I Hear [sic] and Conceal." This obviously refers to the penalty of the obligation, of which we will see more later.

The publication of the pamphlet in early 1724 may well have produced alarm among the members of the Craft. Copies of the *Gothic Constitutions* were already available to the public, but *The Grand Mystery* went further. Although we can only speculate about its accuracy, it corresponds very closely in places with modern ritual, confirming our theory that it really did contain "genuine" secrets.

After the pamphlet was in print, the Masons could not prevent the public from seeing it, but it disappeared from the shops very quickly. The remarkable speed with which it sold out suggests that Masons bought up all the copies they could find. But that didn't solve the problem. More copies were rushed into print. At that point the Masons must have realized the futility of trying to keep the pamphlet out of the hands of the public. No matter how many copies they bought, the publisher could print more. Apparently, the only effective action the fraternity could take was to try to discredit both this exposé and others that would likely be published in the future.

The Grand Mystery of Free-Masons Discover'd had been in circulation for slightly less than a year when the *Briscoe* pamphlet appeared. The intervening months allowed plenty of time for concerned Masons to debate their response and concoct a fanciful exposé of their own.

The *Briscoe* pamphlet contained material that had already been published, so it didn't give away any new secrets. But the fantastic claims it made could not be taken seriously.

This was a simple and elegant way for the Freemasons to cast doubt on the other exposés. Readers of *their* exposé would tend to discount the other things they had read about the Masons or, at worst, believe that Masons were prone to playing silly, harmless games. Either way, the fraternity's private affairs would be afforded some measure of protection. The pamphlet would counter some of the more serious criticism of the Craft, and the public's curiosity would be partially satisfied – or at least distracted.

Unfortunately for the Masons, this subterfuge was less than completely successful. Contemporary references to a phony exposé, apparently meaning the *Briscoe* pamphlet, suggest that the public already knew enough about the lodge to tell the difference between real and fictitious Masonic secrets.

It didn't take long for the lodges to recognize the folly of trying to discredit exposés. Examples of this kind of smoke screen were rarely seen again. For the most part, the Craft resigned itself either to ignoring criticism or to publishing books that reveal no genuine secrets while unmasking a few of the critics' errors.

Over the years, exposés continued to appear. They were published sporadically but not infrequently and display varying degrees of accuracy. Some are essentially verbatim copies of actual rituals, often with highly critical commentaries. They contain the passwords and secret handshakes, along with the whole story of Hiram Abif. Others are grossly in error, containing, for whatever reason, descriptions of alleged rituals that would hardly be recognized by members of the Craft.

Coil's Encyclopedia, a leading reference work in the field, lists thirty-nine "exposed" rituals published between 1723 until 1852, and more have come along since then. It seems that revealing Masonic secrets has become a common pastime for those who want to attack the organization, those who want to clarify the record, and occasionally those who want to make a quick profit from exploiting the public's curiosity.

Through all of this, no earth shattering secrets have come to light, and the fraternity has continued to function with no serious impairment. In fact, most Freemasons are unaware that so many exposés have been published over the years. They simply don't know that all the organization's passwords have long been in print and are available to non-members. And when presented with these facts, many Masons seem genuinely shocked.

This is indeed a peculiar situation. And a peculiar picture of the Freemasons is emerging. The evidence we have seen thus far has uncovered no momentous secrets. The Freemasons are custodians of a collection of rituals, legends and passwords. But no really *serious* secrets survived the Middle Ages. Any that did exist gave way to fraternal theatrics which no longer have any practical importance and, in any event, have long been in the public domain. Further, when the Freemasons realize, on sporadic occasions, that their secrets are being revealed, they respond in ways that suggest their primary reaction is a sense of frustration with a problem that seems to have no solution.

In view of all of this, we must wonder about the Masons. We would expect a genuinely secret society to make a serious effort to protect itself. The Templars were accused of killing to protect their secrets. Are we to believe that that the Masons publish phony pamphlets to protect theirs?

If this is all there is to the story, either the Masons do not have any real secrets or they are not very good at protecting them. How secret can a system of secrecy be if it is revealed in books that are available to anyone who is willing to look for them?

But this may be a very inaccurate picture of the fraternity. We have still not explained the legend that tells of Hiram Abif — and of a secret worth killing to protect. That story implies that the Craft does harbor a profound secret. The fact that we haven't found it does not prove that it doesn't exist. And the Freemasons' awkward attempts to protect their secrecy don't prove anything. They might have other, more sinister methods of protecting themselves, methods that have never come to light.

The *Grand Mystery* was published anonymously. Perhaps the Craft simply did not know whom to punish for its publication. Or perhaps the culprit was punished, and his body was never found. If the Masons really do have a secret, their means of protecting it may be as well guarded as the secret itself.

The Penalty of the Obligation

U p to this point, we have said a great deal about secrecy, but we have said little about how the Freemasons enforce their code of secrecy. Obviously, the two go hand in hand. If the Craft has any real secrets, it must have an effective way of protecting them.

Even a brief glance at the fraternity's affairs reveals that it does have a means of protecting itself. From the early days of the modern Craft, the ritual has included what are known in Masonic circles as "the penalties." These are supposedly the consequences of revealing Masonic secrets. Although they form only a small part of the ritual, they are the part the public has heard the most about. They have caused at least as much commotion as the password and the handshake. And they are at least as misunderstood.

Before we go on, we should take a look at the penalties. We will do this not simply because they are controversial. They are. But their importance to our quest lies in what they can tell us about the Masons' attitude toward the secrecy.

One of the most basic concepts of justice is that that the punishment must fit the crime. The petty thief and the murderer do not receive the same punishment. In the same way, the penalties for betraying secrets vary as widely as the range of secrets there are to betray. The child who reveals a secret he learned on the playground does not face the same consequences as the adult who betrays his nation's security to foreign powers.

A sense of fairness dictates that the punishment for betraying a secret correspond to the harm that might be caused by revealing it. Human sensibility recoils from any form of retribution that is too severe to match the offense. On the other hand, any genuine system of secrecy must be enforced by the threat of punishment. The good will and sincerity of those who share a secret is not always enough to ensure that they will keep it.

The Freemasons are certainly not exempt from these simple principles. The presence of a penalty in their early ritual shows that they recognize the need for enforcement. And we would do them an injustice if we believed them incapable of devising a punishment equal to the offense of revealing their secrets. It follows that examining precisely how they enforce their code of secrecy will help us understand what the enforcement is intended to protect.

The penalties described in the ritual are especially harsh. When each new Mason is initiated, he accepts death and dismemberment as the punishment for betraying the secrets with which he has been or will be entrusted. And in doing so, he joins the millions of other Masons who have agreed to the same method of execution since the eighteenth century.

In fact, these penalties are among the oldest features of the ritual. They are even older than the first Grand Lodge. They appear in rudimentary form in a document dated 1696. At that time the punishment for revealing Masonic secrets seems to have been no more complicated than "haveing my tongue cut out under my chin and of being buried, within the flood mark where no man shall know."

This wording, which bears a slight similarity to the modern versions, appears in more than one source, an indication that it was well established by the end of the seventeenth century. It may have been in common use much earlier, but unfortunately we have no way of knowing just how old it really is.

In time, this simple method of dealing with the faithless member evolved into a series of three penalties, one for each of the Craft degrees. They retained the earlier elements of cutting the offender's throat and burying him in an unmarked grave. But such refinements as mutilation and burning were added. It seems that the Freemasons had evolved from what might once have been a practical means of administering justice to a ritualized form of punishment.

The fact that a simple penalty became an elaborate ritual is not surprising. We are already familiar with the Masonic penchant for ritual, and we have seen their skill at reshaping simple things into mysterious and elegant symbols. What is surprising is that the penalties have endured more than three centuries. They have always been a problem for the Craft. Admittedly, they are a major part of the mystique that makes Freemasonry attractive to its members, but they have also proved a serious embarrassment.

As might be expected, critics lost no time exploiting the penalties, which they described as the vile and unconscionable practices of a malevolent order. It's a charge with which Masons have had to contend ceaselessly.

On the face of it, this criticism is quite reasonable. The idea of an organization's killing its own members for revealing privileged information seems out of place in a philosophical and social fraternity. It implies that something quite sinister is going on behind closed doors, a charge the Masons deny fiercely, and we must question why they did not abandon this part of their ritual long ago ... unless it performs a function that makes it indispensable.

For their part, the Freemasons insist that their activities are in no way sinister and that the penalties have never been enforced. But for two and a half centuries they have been unable to extricate themselves from the suspicion that the penalties are just what they appear to be.

To understand how the penalties really function, we must examine them in their historic context. We have seen that they are part of a drama set in the days of King Solomon. They fit their setting well, reminiscent as they are of actual practices from those times, centuries before Freemasonry existed. Their graphic details are attention getting – certainly no accident, since the obligation is meant to be taken seriously. However, the penalties themselves do not have a Biblical origin. In fact, it is unlikely that they date even to the early Middle Ages.

The penalties do not appear in the *Gothic Constitutions*. If they existed at that time, they were not considered suitable to be included in the written history of the craft. It is not until the late seventeenth century we see such wording as,

> if he shall break his Oath ; the Sun in the firmament & all the Company there present, will be witness against him, which will be an occasion of his damnation ; And, that likewise they will be sure to Murder him.

Although the authenticity of passages such as this can be questioned, their parallels to the modern ritual are close enough to make them credible. There is no reason to doubt that punishments of this sort were mentioned in the rituals of the seventeenth century, at least a generation before the formation of the Grand Lodge of England.

Whether the penalties of that day were symbolic or actual is never spelled out. But we may assume that by the time the Hiramic legend was introduced they were purely symbolic. It is inconsistent with the avowed philosophy of the modern organization to impose any sanction worse than expulsion from membership. For that reason, the symbolic penalties appear only in the initiation ritual. They are not written into the books of constitutions as actual methods of punishment. And we have no evidence that the seventeenth century masons were different from their descendants on this point.

But that raises a question. Masonic historians believe that the Hiramic legend did not yet exist in the seventeenth century. If the penalties of that day were symbolic, but if the legend of which they are a part did not yet exist, we must wonder when and where they did originate and what purpose they served.

The oath of that day was administered to the initiate "after a great many Ceremonies, to frighten him." The implication is not that the new member was hazed for the enjoyment of his brothers. Rather, the ceremonies have the appearance of being performed to create a solemn atmosphere and make the initiate regard his oath more seriously.

This is no less than we would expect of the operative stone masons. It was important for them to keep their trade secrets and recognition signs confidential. Their problem was that the young men who joined the craft were not used to being trusted with sensitive information. The masons must have found it necessary to devise a practical way of emphasizing the importance of keeping their secrets. And this is where a strong penalty would be handy. Where a reasoned explanation might not impress a young medieval apprentice, the threat of death would certainly hold his attention. Whether they ever enforced the penalty would be irrelevant. Its real function was to stress the importance of not revealing the craft's proprietary information.

The "operative" penalty, if there was one, was probably no more complicated than a cut throat and burial in an unmarked grave. That is what the earliest Masonic documents stipulate, and it would do the job quite nicely.

Then, when the gentlemen Masons got their hands on the ritual, they embellished the penalties along with the rest of the ceremony. They inflated what must have started as a harsh but simple warning into an elaborate litany of Biblical-sounding punishments.

That started an unending controversy, but ironically it also demonstrated the controversy's basic fallacy. If the penalties were anything other than symbolic, it is unlikely that the Masons would have chosen such exotic methods of exacting punishment. A *real* penalty needs to be practical. It can be dramatic but must not be theatrical. The idea of a modern fraternity littering the countryside with curiously mutilated bodies is hardly credible.

Still, all of this must serve some purpose. As we have seen in other parts of our quest, there is a hint here of more than appears on the surface. The penalties, like the stories of Athelstan and Hiram, are the stuff of legends. And like other Masonic legends, their history is only the beginning of understanding them.

It was during the early modern period that these infamous penalties evolved into their present form. Although they appear in all three Craft degrees, it is obvious that they relate specifically to the Hiramic story of the third degree. They are, quite simply, presented as the punishment Hiram's killers deserved for the crime they had committed.

Perhaps the modern penalties – the ones created by the gentlemen Masons – can be explained as part of the symbolism of that cautionary tale. They fit so neatly into the Hiramic story and further its purposes so well that they appear to be nothing more than an integral part of the story, created especially for the purpose by the eighteenth century authors of the legend.

But we must not forget that the forerunner of the modern penalty predated the Hiramic legend. At least, it predated the inclusion of the Hiramic legend in the Masonic ritual. This proves that the modern version was not, as many Masons believe, cut out of whole cloth. It was at least *based* on something that existed long before Hiram Abif entered the picture.

To an extent we can only speculate about the relationship between the legend and the penalty. It is possible that the legend existed prior to its first known appearance in the ritual. Although written references to it do not appear until the third decade of the eighteenth century, it may have existed in Masonic lore much earlier. Or it may be a modern version of something that was kept secret by the masons of an earlier day.

Interestingly, the penalties of the modern ritual, for all their Biblical flavor, are identical with punishments that were in actual use during the Middle Ages. Although the ritual is set in Biblical times, the nature of the penalties and their historic context suggest that they *refer* to a much later time. Whether they refer to history or legend remains to be seen. But they are apparently either a holdover of actual medieval practice or a legend intended to remind the Craft of its medieval origins.

Here again the spectre of the medieval Templars rises to tease us. The idea of a brotherhood killing its own members for revealing secrets, and using Biblical methods to do it, comes straight out of the trial of the Templars.

We have seen that many of the charges against the Order were at the very least suspect, while some may have been true. Of all the charges leveled against them, the easiest to believe is that they murdered unfaithful members. They must have had military secrets that were worth killing to protect, and severe punishment is sometimes a military necessity. Whether they also had esoteric knowledge that was worth killing to protect is another question and one that is unlikely ever to be settled. But it would be surprising if the Templars did not consider execution a suitable response to any compromise of their security.

Their most likely method of dealing with treachery was precisely what the early ritual stipulated. A few knights would be chosen to approach the traitor. They would kill him quickly and quietly, probably by cutting his throat. Then they would probably dispose of the body where it would never be found, and could never be given a Christian burial.

If we grant that the Templars used methods such as this to enforce their security, we need look no farther for the origin of the Masonic penalties. The stone masons had their own ways of protecting their proprietary secrets, but the Templars' solution was more dramatic and glamorous. When the Templars joined the masons, it was probably included in the initiation ceremony just as other Templar elements were, as something that was consistent with the masonic tradition yet added another dimension to it.

This answers part of our question. If the modern penalties are of Templar origin, we can be confident that the operative masons imported only the ritual, not the actual practice. Once the danger of the inquisition passed, it is unlikely that they would have felt the need to kill their own members for any reason. True, they were now custodians of an esoteric philosophy contributed by the Templars. But that was certainly tempered by the peaceful nature of Biscop's tradition. The fugitive knights no longer belonged to an order of warrior monks and no longer needed the crusaders' warlike spirit. Theirs was now a gentler brotherhood. It may have kept some of the trappings of a military order, but now it was interested in only the spiritual aspects of the crusades.

In any event, a medieval penalty would not have survived to be used in modern times. As the Craft moved into the eighteenth and nineteenth centuries, the spirit of it was retained by gentlemen who loved and respected tradition. When they created the Hiramic legend, it lent itself well to that bit of Biblical symbolism and was adapted and embellished as a part of the story. In fact, the penalty may have suggested the Hiramic legend, and the legend may have been written to give new meaning to an anachronistic punishment whose original purpose had been forgotten.

Since then, the penalties have been no more real than the Hiramic legend. Both have become symbols for something that happened a long time ago, or perhaps never happened at all. Like the square and trowel and other tools that were once used by the stone mason, they are now used only to fashion the symbolic building stone, the initiate who came to the ancient craft to gain fellowship and wisdom.

In their new role as mere symbols, it would seem that the penalties should be harmless. Nevertheless, they continue to cause problems for the fraternity. They are so controversial that several Grand Lodges have considered doing away with them altogether. In 1987 the Grand Lodge of England did change the way it presents the penalties. They are still included in the ritual but are described as being nothing more than "traditional."

Why has it taken three centuries for the Masons to make even this small concession to public opinion? The answer is that the Masons have long faced this dilemma but have never found a satisfactory solution. For all the trouble the penalties cause, they are an essential part of the Craft ritual. From the Masonic point of view, the problem is that everything in the initiation fits together. Its symbolism has been so tightly woven that removing any part of it can distort the rest. Each element influences and clarifies the others, and changing one robs the others of their meaning. Even the "signs" – the gestures by which Masons signify their obligation and by which they can identify themselves to other Freemasons – are graphic descriptions of the various methods used to carry out the penalties.

In their symbolic role, the penalties represent the consequences of evil deeds. After they killed Hiram Abif, the three ruffians – one for each of the three degrees – realized that they deserved to be punished for their crime. They wished gruesome deaths on themselves. And those same deaths are presented to the initiate as the punishment he would deserve if he betrayed his obligation to the Craft. The purpose of all this is to teach him a series of lessons on the importance of duty and honor.

Seen in that light, the penalties really are harmless. Unfortunately for the Masons, they are also too lurid to stay out of the public eye. Even the thought of ritual murder is very much the stuff of rumor and scandal. The mere mention of mutilation and secret burial virtually challenges the casual observer to speculate about their possible use.

Of course, nothing we have seen proves that the Masons *never* killed anyone. Although Freemasonry officially repudiates the penalties as actual means of punishment, its more enthusiastic members might not. Some may misunderstand official policy. Worse, some may feel justified in going beyond its limits to protect what they believe are the interests of their fraternity. All systems are subject to breakdowns. And a system which deliberately makes its basic tenets cryptic is, perhaps, more subject to such failures than others.

This is no trivial concern, because the acts of an individual can cast a long shadow. Though England's Henry II insisted that his "will no one rid me of this turbulent priest" was not a call for action, his knights did murder Thomas Becket. It was their duty as they saw it, but history has judged them *and* their king harshly.

Protestations of innocence do little good when individuals commit crimes on behalf of a cause they may not understand. The Mason who loves his Craft, like the knight who loves his king, may learn too late that the reputation of any group depends more on the things it inspires its members to do than on its official policies and pronouncements.

Early in the nineteenth century, the Masons learned that lesson well. They put themselves through an ordeal that left a permanent mark on the fraternity. It started with an incident that was hotly debated at the time, and although the furor has died down in the intervening decades, the controversy it fueled never completely went away. To this day Masonry labors under the lingering burden of its aftereffects.

No doubt this incident still influences the attitudes of Masons and non-masons who never heard of it. It was the infamous Morgan Affair. And that is what we will consider next.

Captain William Morgan

I n the early years of the nineteenth century, a peculiar series of events occurred. They began with deception and ended in abduction and possibly murder. No one now alive knows exactly what happened. Some of the details were never recorded. Others were recorded too well — in several versions that are inconsistent with each other or with the few known "facts" of the case.

This peculiar series of events was the notorious Morgan Affair. It is now only a footnote to history, but at the time it received a great deal of publicity. It sparked a short lived but dramatic political movement. And it was exploited by people with such strong biases that even at the time the facts became suspect and difficult to sort out.

Even in retrospect, this is a very curious affair. For one thing, it seems out of step with Masonic history. Members of the Craft were accused and convicted of criminal offenses. But that only complicated the matter. Then and now, many people believed that the convictions were just the tip of the iceberg. They claimed that the Masons got away with crimes much more serious than the ones for which they were held accountable. There was a conspiracy, it was said, that reached the highest level of state government and thwarted the investigation.

This was certainly not the first time in history the Freemasons were accused of conspiracy. Because of their secrecy and unusual rituals, they have always been a convenient target for charges of political intrigue. Nor was it the only time they were suspected of killing to protect their order. Rumor has it that they killed Amadeus Mozart for revealing Masonic secrets in his *Magic Flute.* And some say that London's Whitechapel murders were a Masonic scheme to protect the British monarchy. (According to this theory, Jack the Ripper was not a lone serial killer but a group of Masonic assassins bent on ferreting out an illegitimate heir to the throne.) But the case of William Morgan is the most notorious of these episodes and the one that had the greatest impact on the fraternity. Other tales of Masonic murder are rumor. The Morgan Affair is proven mischief. It is definitely known that Freemasons were involved. The only question is how far they went.

We will try to uncover the truth of this affair. But whatever the truth, we will be faced with one inescapable conclusion. The incident shows how the subject of Masonic secrecy has impacted on the popular imagination. In many ways it is the counterpoint to the story of Hiram Abif. Both are cautionary tales. However, while one can be used to justify secrecy, the other warns of its consequences.

The basic facts of the Morgan Affair are as little known as the facts of other similar incidents. It began as a series of inconsequential events in a small town. Few records were kept during its early stages. No reporters maintained a vigil on the developing story. And by the time its importance became apparent, the key events were in the past tense. Then it was too late to document what had happened.

To make things worse, most of those who wrote about the incident were so passionately involved that they could scarcely report anything without letting their prejudices color the story. Still, some details are definitely known, and others may be inferred.

About 1824, one William Morgan moved into the small town of Batavia, New York. He was previously unknown there and had come to the community in a roundabout way. Morgan was born in Culpeper County, Virginia on August 7, 1774. He became a brick mason, working at that craft in Virginia and Kentucky. During the War of 1812, he took out time for a brief military career that included action at the Battle of New Orleans. He served there in General Jackson's army, apparently with the rank of captain, a title he continued to use in later life.

After the war, he returned to Virginia and eventually established his own business in Richmond, where in October of 1819 he married Lucinda Pendleton, the eldest daughter of a Methodist minister. She was sixteen years old; he was forty-five.

The couple soon had a daughter, and in 1821 Morgan moved his family to Toronto. While in Canada he earned his living as a brewer and farmer, but his business was subsequently destroyed by fire, and he moved to New York in 1823. For a short time he worked as a brick mason in Rochester then moved to the town of Batavia, which is located in Genesee County in the western part of the state. His second daughter was born there in 1825.

William Morgan was apparently a shrewd man but lacked education and ambition. Opinions of his personality and character differ. Some said that he was agreeable, drank socially and maintained a good appearance and bearing. Others said that he did not provide well for his family and was often in trouble for failing to pay his debts. He developed a reputation for being lazy and quarrelsome. His honesty was questioned and, so his critics claimed, he tended to drink too much.

Fictitious portrait of William Morgan on left shows how he was depicted by those who opposed his exposé of the Masons; the fictitious portrait on the right is how he was depicted by those who supported it.

Considering how the story ended, the latter version is probably closer to the truth. But when he moved into the small town of Batavia, no one knew what was to come.

As soon as he was settled in, Morgan began to involve himself with the local Masonic community. Representing himself as a Freemason, he often visited lodges in the area. Interestingly, no records have surfaced to prove that he really was a Freemason, and subsequent events suggest that he was an impostor.

It is not hard to understand how he pulled off the deception. Before being admitted to a Masonic lodge, visitors are asked questions to determine if they are indeed members of the Craft. Theoretically, these questions will thwart any impostor who tries to slip into a lodge meeting. In practice, exposés are so common that anyone who is sufficiently devious and determined can learn enough to pass the examination.

It was much the same in Morgan's day. Apparently dues cards had not come into common use, and he was shrewd enough to bluff his way into the local Masonic community with no proof of membership.

In fact, the evidence suggests that he was quite proficient in the details of the Masonic ritual. That knowledge helped him greatly. Not only did it get him admitted to meetings, it also earned him some prominence in Masonic circles. Because of it, he was always in demand in the local lodges, which were glad to have an "expert" in their midst to advise them on procedural matters.

Most likely, Morgan's knowledge of the ritual came from old British exposés and was supplemented by what he saw in the lodges he attended. The more meetings he attended, the more he knew about the Masons. And the more he knew, the more the Masons wanted him in their company. As a result, an impostor who had made a point of acquainting himself with Masonic ritual was now in a position to learn as much as he wanted about matters Masonic.

Surviving records show that Morgan visited at least two lodges, Wells Lodge No. 282 and Olive Branch Lodge No. 215. He may have attended other lodges in New York. Indeed, he may well have conducted the same charade in Virginia and Canada, and possibly even in military lodges while serving in Jackson's army long before he even thought of moving to New York. If so, no records survive to mark his trail. But once he reached Batavia, his movements were documented. During the next few years he continued visiting local lodges and became quite active in their affairs.

It might be worth noting that each Mason is a *member* of his home lodge. When he attends any other lodge, he is termed a *visitor*. But this is only a technical distinction. For all practical purposes, William Morgan enjoyed all the benefits of Masonic membership. And he used those benefits to his advantage. On February 15, 1825 he petitioned to receive the Royal Arch degree from Western Star Chapter No. 33, which met in the nearby town of Le Roy. This degree is open only to people who are already Master Masons, but since everyone believed Morgan was a Mason in good standing, no one objected to his application. It was accepted and he received the degree on May 31.

Morgan's reception in the Chapter indicates that his deception, if deception it was, was still effective. But soon after, his plans started to unravel.

The Masons of Batavia wanted their own Royal Arch chapter. As a member of the Royal Arch and a resident of Batavia, Morgan placed his name on the petition to establish a chapter there. This was purely routine, and in the normal course of events he would have become a charter member of the new Masonic body.

But something had gone seriously wrong. Morgan's name was abruptly scratched off the petition. Interestingly, the document was not re-copied. It was submitted with Morgan's stricken name still on it. No explanation was given.

This in itself proves nothing. It is not unusual for Masonic documents to be processed with items lined out. But it is intriguing to speculate whether this incident has a deeper meaning. Perhaps Morgan had finally been unmasked, and the Masons of the community wanted to leave a permanent record that he was no longer welcome in their company. On the other hand, they might simply have had no time to re-copy the document. In any event, Morgan was not accepted as a member of the new chapter.

About this time, the Knights Templar began work on a new building in Le Roy. As a member of the fraternity and an operative brick mason, Morgan would naturally have been hired to work on the project. He wasn't. This is one more indication that he was now unwelcome among his former brothers.

At this point the plot thickens. It gradually became known that Morgan had decided to publish an exposé of the Masonic ritual. His motives will never be understood completely. He may have decided to expose Freemasonry because of his falling out with the Masonic community. Or they may have spurned him because they became aware of his intentions. It is probable that neither of these is the whole explanation. As is usually the case in human affairs, Morgan's exposé was likely the result of a complex set of circumstances, not a single incident.

Whatever the first stirrings of the matter, events began moving more quickly after Morgan was excluded from the Masonic community. On March 13, 1826 he contracted to publish his exposé with David Miller, a local newspaper man who published the *Republican Advocate* in Batavia.

With few facts available, there is plenty of room to speculate about what these two men hoped to accomplish. At this point Morgan was probably driven by a combination of resentment and the prospect of making money from what he apparently believed would be a bestseller.

Miller may have had similar motives. He had been admitted into the fraternity as an entered apprentice in Albany, N.Y. Then, for twenty years he had not been allowed to receive further degrees. Apparently he, too, had a falling out with the Craft. If so, he might have welcomed Morgan's exposé as a way of getting revenge. And as a printer, he too would have seen the book's potential for financial gain.

There was considerable precedent for the course William Morgan and David Miller had chosen. Many of the early exposés and attacks on Masonry were published by disillusioned members. No doubt some of those individuals acted out of pique. Others were trying to warn the public about an organization they had come to distrust. It is a tradition that continues to this day.

Whatever their motives, Morgan and Miller were now partners in a business scheme. Their next step was to seek financing from two other men, John Davids (Morgan's landlord) and Russell Dyer. This group reached a preliminary agreement and all promised to maintain secrecy. Their plans were formalized by the beginning of August, and Morgan's partners posted a bond of $500,000 to guarantee him a fourth of the profits of his exposé.

That sum seems excessive in view of the fact that several exposés were already in print. Although the partners may have thought they were doing something unique, theirs was just one more in a series of books on the same subject, and historians doubt that Morgan's profits would have been more than a small fraction of the amount of the bond.

This is only one in a series of details that seem irrational. Perhaps the actors on this curious stage were not aware of the availability of Masonic materials. Or perhaps they were merely deluding themselves. Clearly, something was amiss. But in a round of senseless excesses, all the parties involved in this matter acted as if they greatly over estimated the importance of the events that were soon to take place.

Once the stage was set, its central character began to behave strangely. Morgan was less than discreet during the following month. With arrangements for the publication of his exposé nailed down, he made no secret of what he was up to.

No explanation for this behavior has survived. He may have been releasing pent-up frustration. He probably believed that the need for secrecy had past; history suggests that he was not a cautious man. Or he may have had something up his sleeve. It is unlikely – though still possible – that he was activating one more step in a shrewd and complex plan to avoid the consequences of his actions.

Whatever the reason, he apparently did enough bragging about his project to attract the attention of the local Masons. And that really set things in motion.

It is difficult to judge the precise feelings and motives of the Masonic community at this point. Their time was somewhat different from ours. In the nineteenth century, the Age of Enlightenment was coming to an end. It was being replaced in many quarters by a time of narrow views. Religious

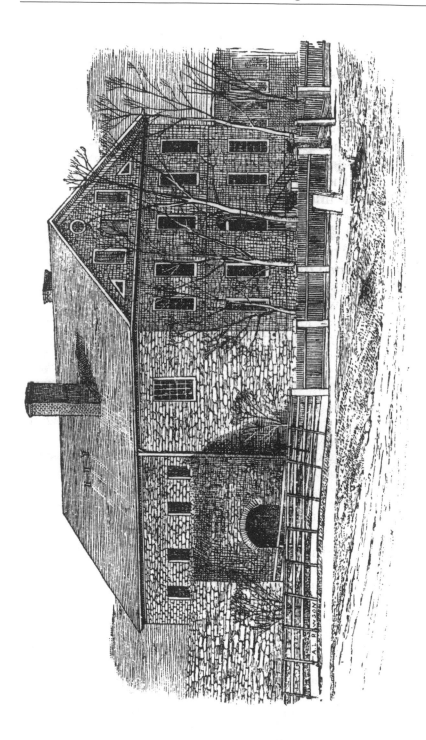

The Jail at Canandaigua

revival was well under way. In New York and elsewhere, strong feelings of nationalism and religious intolerance were becoming the norm. Recent history had included violent clashes – large and small – waged over minor differences in theology. And at that particular moment in western New York the climate was not much different. Everywhere, people entertained their own biases and opinions with the comforting illusion of absolute certainty.

Nor was Freemasonry immune to the prejudices of the time. There was a great deal of anti-Masonic sentiment in the early decades of the nineteenth century. People with exclusive religious views considered Freemasonry a competing religion, or worse, an evil religion in its own right. Those with political leanings saw the organization as a hotbed of conspiracy and intrigue. And the more gullible members of the public were all too eager to believe the worst about a shadowy group of men who met behind closed doors.

Many Masons of the period must have felt seriously threatened by the anti-Masonic sentiment they saw around them. Some may even have believed that an exposé of the Craft would be a crushing, possibly fatal blow to the fraternity. At best, they would have been offended by the prospect of having the Craft's secrets so treacherously revealed. At worst, they would have seen it as a vicious personal attack.

It was in this climate of high emotions and strong feelings that William Morgan wrote his exposé. He apparently delivered the manuscript in two installments, during July and August of 1826. On August 14 he registered his copyright, and everything was set for the book's publication.

By that time any security the project might have had was a thing of the past. The impending publication of Morgan's exposé was public knowledge, and the Masonic community had little time to act if they wanted to prevent it.

The events of the next month suggest a concentrated, perhaps panicked effort by the Masons to thwart Morgan and Miller. In August and early September, the matter was discussed in local newspapers. A notice warned members of the community, especially Masons, to be on their guard against Morgan. It was answered by a letter deploring the commotion that had risen around what was really a trivial incident.

Of these two letters, the first doubtless had the greater impact. Though some in the community had not lost their common sense, things had gone too far to be stopped.

Reportedly, local Masons tried to buy the manuscript to prevent its publication. Morgan was later accused of fraudulently selling them his manuscript and notes after the book had gone to press. Whether he did or not, plans for the book's publication continued.

Miller's print shop caught fire at least once, in August, and perhaps again on September 10. The second incident has been disputed. Miller accused the Freemasons of setting the fire to prevent publication of the exposé. The Freemasons accused him of torching his own business to publicize the book.

When all of this failed, the Masons tried several rounds of legal action, all unsuccessful. The most notable of these were against Morgan himself.

On the morning of September 11, Constable Holloway Hayward arrived from nearby Canandaigua to arrest Morgan. Although the constable was not a Freemason, he was accompanied by a posse of five or six men, all of whom were said to be Masons. This fact might seem trivial, but the details of the posse's mission and the trivial nature of the charges suggest that a serious conspiracy had been set in motion.

The charge was stealing a shirt and necktie from Ebenezer Kingsley, a tavern keeper from whom Morgan had rented a room four months earlier. Curiously, although Kingsley was the injured party, he wasn't the one who pressed charges. The warrant had been obtained by a man named Nicholas Chesebro. Chesebro, it turns out, was Master of the Masonic lodge in Canandaigua and was to play an ongoing and important role as the incident developed.

The posse took Morgan to Canandaigua. There, he was arraigned before a Justice of the Peace, who dropped the charges for lack of evidence.

At that point, Chesebro produced evidence that Morgan had failed to pay a debt in the amount of $2.68. Suspiciously, Morgan did not originally owe the debt to Chesebro. The original creditor had assigned the debt to him. Obviously all of this was arranged ahead of time to be sure the Masons had sufficient grounds to keep Morgan in jail.

Morgan admitted that he owed the debt but did not have enough money with him to pay it on the spot. Consequently, he was held in the local jail overnight.

On the evening of the next day, Chesebro returned with two other Masons, Loton Lawson and Ed Sawyer. Lawson tried to get Morgan released into his custody, but jailer Israel Hall was away, and his wife refused to release Morgan in her husband's absence. Frustrated by this obstacle, the three men made several attempts to resolve the problem. Finally, the jailer's wife allowed them to pay the debt out of their own pockets. At that point, having no further grounds for holding him, she had to release her prisoner.

Chesebro, Lawson and Sawyer then took Morgan to a waiting coach driven by one Hiram Hubbard. The jailer's wife later reported that the four men got Morgan into the carriage only after a struggle and cries of "Help! Murder!"

What happened next is a subject of debate. There is good reason to believe that the Freemasons carried Morgan a distance of one hundred twenty-five miles to Fort Niagara. The troops garrisoned there had pulled out four months earlier, and the fort was now empty except for a caretaker (a Freemason named Edward Giddins) and his wife.

The Masons had chosen the place for its isolation and for the fort's empty powder magazine. Designed for the secure storage of explosives, the magazine had thick stone walls. Its windows were ten feet above floor level.

They served only to ventilate the building, and both the windows and the magazine's only door were reinforced to guard against forced entry – or exit. It was an ideal place for the Masons to hold their prisoner until they could decide what to do with him.

From this point on we have only speculation to guide our investigation. There is no record that William Morgan was ever again seen in Genesee County. The Freemasons were accused of killing him. They denied the charge. They insisted that such an act was inconsistent with the spirit of the Craft, but the criticism did not go away. If the Freemasons had killed a man to preserve their secrets, they had gone too far. In another time and place they might have gotten away with it, but the religious and political sentiment of the time would not allow it. This time, there would be a price to pay.

A Price to Pay

We need not ask why the Masons abducted William Morgan. Obviously they thought they were protecting the Craft's secrets. The more important question is what they did with him once they had him. And the answer to that question quickly became obscured in a frenzy of high emotions and mutual intolerance.

The bulk of the evidence suggests that the Masons tried to persuade Morgan to abort his project and move out of the area. One version of the story has them offering him money and a farm in Canada in return for a promise to go away quietly. There is good reason to believe that Morgan took some money, but that he took it in bad faith. Then, when the Masons realized that they could not rely on him to keep his part of the bargain, they abducted him.

Unfortunately for the Masons, the operation seems to have been hastily organized. Nicholas Chesebro and his assistants originally had Morgan arrested to get him out of Genesee County and into another jurisdiction where his partners could not easily help him. David Miller suspected as much and protested, but Morgan did not yet believe he was in danger and agreed to go with the posse that had come to take him away.

When the first charge was dropped, Chesebro had a second charge ready to press. He was determined to keep Morgan in custody. Once the plan had been put in operation, he did not want to give Morgan an opportunity to return home.

But after Morgan was safely in the Canandaigua jail, it took the Masons nearly twenty-four hours to come back for him. Apparently they needed that much time to decide on their next step, or at least to organize it. The implication is that the Masons were moving quickly and without the benefit of advance planning. This is confirmed by subsequent events. When they returned to carry Morgan off, things did not go smoothly. To begin with, they were surprised to find jailer Hall away and his wife unwilling to take the responsibility of releasing the prisoner in her husband's absence.

Mary Hall's deposition suggests the extent of the Masons' frustration. According to her story, Loton Lawson came to the jail at about seven o'clock and asked to see the prisoner privately. When she told him that it was against the rules, he had a few words with Morgan in her presence. Lawson offered to pay the debt and take Morgan home. For his part, Morgan was in no hurry. He would spend the night in jail and leave the next morning. Perhaps he sensed danger and believed he would be safer leaving the jail during daylight hours. But Lawson insisted, and Morgan finally agreed to go with him.

Lawson then left the jail and spent half an hour trying to find the jailer. After an unsuccessful search of the town, he returned and asked Mary Hall if she would release the prisoner. She did not know the amount of the payment required for his release. Lawson offered to leave five dollars, undoubtedly more than the debt. She still refused. She understood that Morgan was a rogue and that certain parties had an interest in keeping him confined. She would not risk her husband's professional reputation by releasing such a prisoner.

Lawson assured her that the jailer would in no way be blamed. He even offered to post a hundred dollars to indemnify Hall against injury in the matter. That was still not good enough. Money could not pay for the loss of public confidence her husband might suffer. She was simply not going to release the prisoner into the custody of a man she didn't know.

At that point Lawson offered to bring in Col. Edward Sawyer. He was a respected member of the community and could assure Mrs. Hall that everything was in order. Still no good. Mary Hall did not know Sawyer. Besides, since he had no personal interest in the case, it was nothing to do with him.

In desperation, Lawson left the jail and returned with Sawyer anyway. Sawyer talked to the jailer's wife for some time but to no avail.

Lawson and Sawyer were now quite frustrated. They finally offered to locate Nicholas Chesebro. The debt had been assigned to him, after all, and he should decide if the matter was serious enough to justify detaining Morgan for another night.

By a remarkable coincidence, Chesebro was standing in the street a few yards from the jail. He did not want to come in. Nor did he want to see Morgan. But he did agree that Morgan should be released. Since Mary Hall recognized Chesebro and knew his interest in the case, she finally allowed her prisoner to be taken from her custody.

After all that commotion, the release itself was an anticlimax. It's the frantic efforts to get Morgan away from the jail that are the key to this part of the story. They show a combination of frustration and desperation.

Loton Lawson's frustration reveals that things were not going according to plan. His desperation indicates that a plan had indeed been put into action. Had Morgan's release not been tied to a series of other events, Lawson could have waited until the jailer returned to release him.

Lawson's persistence and the lengths to which he was willing to go are more than curious. They confirm that Morgan's release was part of a larger scheme. But it was a scheme that was already beginning to unravel.

The struggle outside the jail reveals still another fault in planning. Either the Masons had miscalculated Morgan's willingness to let them carry him off, or they had backed themselves into a predicament in which they had no choice but to abduct him where witnesses might observe the incident.

All of this suggests quick action with inadequate forethought and explains what probably happened next. Morgan was now being held in a secure building at Fort Niagara. The Masons knew they could not trust him to go away and leave their secrets intact. Whether they came to that conclusion before or after they got him to the magazine is not certain. Perhaps they abducted him in a final attempt to work a deal. But at some point, or so the story goes, they realized the futility of that plan.

The Masons took until September 19 to decide that it was no longer feasible to release their prisoner. He would only return home and add the story of kidnaping and illegal imprisonment to the rest of his exposé. They had gone too far and done too much harm to retreat from their course. Now there was only one way to resolve the problem.

According to this version of the story, for which there is disputed evidence but no proof, the small group of Masons who had been directly involved in holding Morgan in the powder magazine assembled one last time. They drew lots to decide which of them would bring the ordeal to an end. Then most of them went home, knowing only that they had not been chosen to do the deed.

Later that night, two Masons returned to the powder magazine. They took Morgan out onto the river some distance below Niagara Falls or, alternatively, into Lake Ontario. There they weighted his body and lowered him into the water.

It may not have happened this way. Another version of the story has a Mason named John Whitney discussing Morgan's proposed exposé with De Witt Clinton. This meeting supposedly occurred soon after the Masons became aware of their former companion's plans. If it did occur, it proves that the Masons took the matter very seriously indeed. Clinton was one of the most prominent Masons in the state. He was a Past Grand Master and was at that time Governor of New York. This was not the sort of a man who would be consulted about a trivial matter. (Whitney, another prominent Mason, was Master of the Masonic lodge at Rochester and was subsequently accused of playing a leading role in Morgan's abduction and imprisonment.)

After hearing the details of the problem, the governor suggested that the Masons buy Morgan's manuscript and pay him to leave town. Whitney later met with Morgan and offered him the deal. Morgan would be given five hundred dollars to surrender the manuscript and return to

Canada. Additional funds would be used to provide for his wife and daughters until they could join him.

According to this version, Morgan agreed, and the Masons arranged the abduction as the most convenient and least risky way of ensuring that he would keep his end of the bargain. Morgan was taken to Fort Niagara and entrusted to two Canadian Masons, who escorted him to the vicinity of Hamilton, Ontario. There, they paid him the five hundred dollars and secured his promise never to return to New York.

But Morgan's family did not join him in Canada. In 1830, his wife remarried and lived with her new husband until a few years before her death in 1856, which occurred at her daughter's home. If this version of the story is true, Morgan had turned his back not only on his share of the profit from the sales of his book but on his family as well.

We must wonder if Morgan would have abandoned his family in this way. There is some reason to believe that he did not provide well for them. But he carried them with him from Virginia to Canada and back to New York. Although his fortunes changed for the worse in Canada, he showed no signs of wanting to abandon his family then. And if the Masons had given him a farm and money, it seems reasonable that he would have wanted his wife and daughters to join him.

Even at the time, it seemed unlikely that Morgan was staying away voluntarily. Shortly after his abduction, his friends began to suspect that he was in serious trouble if not already dead. They demanded action and got it. On October 4, Miller distributed a circular to publicize Morgan's disappearance and possible murder. At the same time, Governor Clinton issued a proclamation calling on all citizens to help resolve the matter.

On October 26, the governor offered rewards totaling five hundred dollars for information on the whereabouts of Morgan and his abductors. On March 19 of the following year, he raised the rewards to three thousand dollars.

As 1826 drew to a close, criminal investigations were launched to discover what had happened to William Morgan. They gathered clear evidence of wrong doing and presented it to the courts.

In January, 1827, circuit judge Enos Throop tried Chesebro, Lawson, Sawyer, and John Sheldon on charges of abducting Morgan. During proceedings held in Canandaigua, all but Sheldon pled guilty. All were convicted. They received sentences ranging from one month to one year for the crime of kidnaping, which was then a misdemeanor.

These men accepted their sentences but shed no further light on the matter. They insisted that they had done nothing more than assist in getting Morgan into the carriage at the jail. They knew nothing of his fate after the carriage pulled away. Had they told – or been able to tell – the whole story, the incident might have ended there. But the most serious questions had not been answered, and many in the community were determined to know more.

For its part, the legal system had not finished with the case. Trials continued until 1831. Fifty-four Masons were indicted on various charges. Some died or fled the state before their trials came up. Others were acquitted. But ten were convicted of abducting Morgan or of illegally detaining David Miller in a separate incident. Testimony placed Eli Bruce, sheriff of Niagara county, in the carriage that abducted Morgan. Bruce went to jail for twenty-eight months, and John Whitney served fifteen months for his involvement. Others received sentences of as little as one month, all for convictions relating to Morgan's abduction and imprisonment.

Obviously the law was convinced that Morgan had been kidnaped. But was he murdered? To answer that question, a body – either dead or alive – was needed.

A body did surface, but it did more to complicate the case than to resolve it. An unidentified man washed ashore at Lake Ontario, about forty miles down river of Fort Niagara, on October 7, 1827. He wore clothes different from those Morgan was known to have. This was not a serious issue, considering the time that had elapsed since his disappearance. But this man had hair where Morgan was bald. And he had a beard. When last seen Morgan was clean shaven.

A coroner's jury decided that the body was not William Morgan. It was buried and might well have been dismissed as one of the several bodies given up by the Niagara River each year. But the case was not allowed to rest there. The people who had rallied to Morgan's cause refused to accept the verdict.

Thurlow Weed, an editor from Rochester, joined David Miller and Lucinda Morgan in demanding that the body be disinterred and re-examined. A second inquest was held and, partly on the strength of Mrs. Morgan's identification, decided that the remains of William Morgan had at last been found.

This verdict was even more controversial than the first. Weed was accused of having the body altered to resemble Morgan. The physical evidence was somewhat contradictory and varied from the evidence presented in the first inquest. But for the moment the body was William Morgan.

Then another complication arose. One Sara Munroe arrived from Canada to see if the body might be her husband, who had recently disappeared while boating on Lake Ontario. She gave a detailed description of her husband and his clothes, some of which she had made with her own hands. This identification, along with corroborating testimony and medical and dental evidence, led a third inquest to conclude that the now famous body was that of Timothy Munroe.

At this point the battle lines firmed up. The Freemasons and their supporters were satisfied that the body yielded up by the river was not William Morgan. Those who believed Morgan dead insisted that the body was his and that justice had not been done. In fact, it had probably been miscarried by influential Masons determined to conceal the truth.

The details of William Morgan's fate were never established beyond a reasonable doubt. Rumors spread rapidly. Some related the particulars of Morgan's death. Others told how he was seen alive and well in various parts of the United States or Canada. Several men confessed to the crime, though most of the confessions were promptly discredited. Some were patently inconsistent with the known facts. Others at least had credibility, but none was found to be a true account of Morgan's death.

Nor were the lack of an undisputed body and a proven killer the whole of the story. The trail was confused even more by the belief, still held by many, that Morgan was an accomplished confidence trickster.

It is just possible that he devised a plan to victimize both his partners and the Masons. His curious actions prior to the publication of his exposé could have been carefully calculated to set his friends and enemies against each other. If so, his plan succeeded exactly as he envisioned it.

Perhaps he well and truly disappeared, a con man with a pocket full of money, leaving behind the confusion and false trails for which a master of *that* craft always strives. What better end to his plan than to leave people believing he was dead, pointing fingers at one another instead of trying to track him down and bring him to justice.

William Morgan may have made a final appearance before leaving the stage of history. In 1827 the ship *Constance* ran aground on a coral reef off Cuba. Survivors were picked up by the Schooner *Star* and put ashore on Grand Cayman Island. Among them was one William Morgan. *This* William Morgan remained in the islands, married a local woman, had nine children and died in 1864 at the age of 89.

Of all the stories that Morgan survived and lived out his life far away from the Freemasons of Batavia, this one may have the ring of truth. Still, at the end of the day it proves nothing. There is no serious evidence that the two William Morgans were the same.

At this late date, there is little chance of learning what really happened to this peculiar man. The facts have been examined and re-examined with little success. They are, purely and simply, inconclusive.

Whatever the truth of the Morgan Affair, Freemasonry was to suffer from its aftermath for years to come. The whole story might well have gone unnoticed or barely noticed. Morgan was neither prominent nor famous, and his disappearance left no proof that he had done anything other than leave the country, perhaps under duress but more or less voluntarily. So far as it went, this was a minor and local incident.

But Morgan's disappearance was only part of the picture. Miller's newspaper office had burned under suspicious circumstances. That was apparently arson committed by Masons to protect their secrets. In addition, many of those assigned to investigate and prosecute the case were Freemasons. When the wheels of justice turned at their usual slow speed, the obvious conclusion was that justice was being thwarted by a Masonic conspiracy.

This view was intensified by the religious spirit of the time and by a general distrust of secret societies. Several church denominations opposed any organization that required its members to take an oath, especially an oath of secrecy. Now their ministers jumped at the opportunity to preach eloquent sermons against the Masons.

Anti-Masonic sentiment did not begin with the Morgan Affair. The suspicion of the Craft we have already seen in eighteenth century England came to America as soon as Masonic lodges began springing up in the colonies. It manifested itself from time to time and in various ways. Much of the opposition to Freemasonry was religious, some was political. But as a rule it was expressed with much sincerity and little effect. The critics of the lodge were simply unable to attract much support. As a result, during most of the young country's history, suspicion of Freemasonry lay relatively dormant. Then, in 1827, it was revived with a vengeance.

For anyone who did not already know, Morgan's exposé, which was published in December of 1826, revealed that Masons took a solemn oath of secrecy. That secrecy – it said so plainly in the ritual – was enforced under no less a penalty than death. Morgan had revealed the Masons' secrets. Now he was missing and probably dead. It seemed that the Freemasons had condemned themselves with their own words.

Suddenly, the penalties of the ritual had come off the page and entered the world of everyday life. If the Masons actually did kill their own to protect their secrets, perhaps the other charges against them were true as well. Vague stories took on sharp definition, as people everywhere took a new look at old accusations. Non-masons now believed that Freemasonry really could be a false religion. It might indeed be a shadowy organization of highly placed individuals who engaged in political intrigue.

As the publicity over the Morgan Affair increased, more and more information came to light. The public became aware of how many prominent men belonged to this strange organization. At that time, Freemasonry was mostly urban, its members mostly affluent. They included many politicians and business leaders – precisely the sort of people who could make a cabal work. At every turn, the facts seemed to confirm the rumors.

Now that they had an audience, the critics of Freemasonry had a field day. They portrayed Freemasonry as a sinister organization. More than sinister, it was dangerous. Its rules contradicted the principles on which the republic had been founded. If left alone, it would destroy the very fabric of society. Consequently, it had to be expunged before it did irreparable harm.

In the years following Morgan's disappearance, an upsurge of anti-Masonic activity, both religious and political, swept the country. The political movement lasted until 1840, but its effects lasted longer. The religious element never died out.

Nor did it take long for the critics to act. Only a month after William Morgan disappeared, Rev. David C. Bernard of the Baptist church of Warsaw, New York renounced his membership in the Masonic lodge and began a personal campaign against the Craft that was to last forty years.

Masons across the state followed his lead. Incensed by what they believed was the fraternity's betrayal of their faith in it, they resigned their membership. Many publicly renounced Freemasonry. Some went farther and took strong action against an organization to which they had once sworn loyalty.

In 1828, Rev. Bernard and David Miller were among forty-one former Masons who organized the Anti-Masonic Society in Le Roy, New York. Thurlow Weed quickly lent his support to the Society and helped move it toward political action.

On July 4, 1828, a Convention of Seceding Masons met at Le Roy to draft a Declaration of Independence from Freemasonry. Patterned after the Declaration of 1776, it reviewed the principles on which the United States was founded and asserted that Freemasonry's "principles and operations are calculated to subvert and destroy the great and important principles of the commonwealth."

Although the Seceding Masons did not name him, they cited the fate of William Morgan and proceeded to enumerate the Craft's offenses against church and state. They concluded by calling upon their fellow citizens to help them expose the evils of Freemasonry.

The Seceding Masons also confirmed the accuracy of Morgan's exposé and an exposé of the Royal Arch degree that had just been published by Elder Barnard, a Baptist minister from Chautaugua County. The Convention's proceedings were published and distributed widely in several states, giving both added credibility and timely publicity to the anti-Masonic movement.

And a movement was indeed under way. In the wake of Morgan's disappearance and the apparent cover-up that followed it, the public demanded action. The political arm of the movement revived the spectre of Freemasonry as a vehicle for political conspiracy. Obviously a disproportionate number of politicians were Freemasons. If they really were organized in an evil conspiracy to wield political power, they were certainly operating contrary to all religious and democratic principles. That was something that could not be tolerated by decent, God-fearing Americans.

This sentiment never reached truly national proportions. The movement began in New York and New England and spread unevenly into the south and midwest, but it was always strongest in the northeast. There, it drew its strength from the rural areas and directed its hostility toward the urban centers of power and wealth.

Town meetings throughout the northeast resolved that Freemasons were unfit to hold public office. Masonic candidates were defeated at the polls. The more extreme critics even called for legislation to prevent Freemasons from running for public office.

Soon political candidates were coming forth to run on a plank of doing away with Freemasonry. The Anti-Masonic Society became the Anti-Masonic Party. It ran candidates for public office and actively campaigned against any candidate who was a Freemason. As a political force, it was destined to have a short life. After all, it was riding a wave of popularity in a trend that had never been able to sustain much momentum. But in its prime, this single-minded party received support from such notable figures as John Quincy Adams, Martin Van Buren and William Seward.

In 1832, the Anti-Masonic Party even ran a candidate for the United States Presidency. He didn't win, but his campaign gave valuable publicity to the movement. Although its attempts to elect national candidates were not successful, the party did score victories at the state level. Most notably, it got William Seward and Millard Fillmore elected to the New York Legislature and Joseph Ritner elected Governor of Pennsylvania.

By 1838 the political movement had run its course, and little more was heard of it. But during its decade, the party and the more general anti-Masonic sentiment had done serious damage to the Craft. As we have seen, many Masons resigned their memberships. While the resulting loss of numbers was important, it was not the whole of the damage. Although records can not confirm the fact, it is certain that many who kept their membership became inactive, withholding their support from an organization that was suddenly an embarrassment to them.

Without support, the lodges could not survive. In just a few years the Craft suffered devastating losses. The Masonic community in New York decreased from four hundred eighty lodges to fewer than fifty. Freemasonry in Vermont became virtually extinct, while Connecticut, Massachusetts and New Hampshire lost half their lodges.

The Craft was less seriously affected in other states. Perhaps social differences were not as strongly felt in the south and west. Or perhaps people in those outlying areas saw the controversy as a matter of local interest that did not affect them. Nevertheless it did affect Masons everywhere. It took a generation after the decline of the Anti-Masonic Party for Freemasonry to recover the bulk of its losses. And its reputation was permanently tarnished.

Although the Party lasted barely a decade, many of its people had found a permanent home. Once they had a real enemy, they continued their crusade long after the popular appeal of the movement faded. Casual supporters might come and go, but the truly dedicated kept the faith. They would not let the spirit of their movement die.

Thurlow Weed was a prime example. He became editor of one of the anti-Masonic publications that arose in the wake of the Morgan Affair. His relationship with the Anti-Masonic Party was always stormy, and when the party faltered, he went on alone. He continued his campaign against the Craft for the rest of his life.

On his death bed, Weed fired his last shot against the fraternity. He claimed that in 1860 John Whitney told him the truth about the murder. According to this story, Whitney was one of the Masons who rowed Morgan out into the river, bound him with chains and threw him in. Told so long after the fact, this account had little effect on public sentiment. Still, it shows the tenacity of the hostility that spectre of Masonic secrecy can generate.

We have seen what the early critics of the Craft were like. Some thought the organization merely silly. Others feared political intrigue or heresy at the hands of this "secret" society. But their fears were always shadowy and unsupported. The disappearance of William Morgan changed the equation. Now, at long last, evidence had surfaced to demonstrate the lengths to which the order would go to protect itself. To make things worse, in a nation that prided itself on freedom of speech and an unbridled press, a secret society had tried to suppress a book, and failing that had killed its author. At least, so the critics believed and argued.

In retrospect, it is hard to believe that the citizens of a small nineteenth century town would kill anyone for revealing Masonic secrets. Exposés were readily available in New York. They had been available for more than a century in England. Obviously, a new exposé could add little to the secrets that had already been revealed. Anyone who knew Masonic history would have realized this. But how much did the Masons of Batavia know?

Even now many active Masons, indeed many of the fraternity's leaders, know little about the literature that surrounds the Craft. In a small community, at a time when communications were much less efficient than they are today, perhaps the prospect of a book exposing Masonic secrets seemed more important than it really was.

If members of the lodge did kill William Morgan, it was an example of misplaced loyalty and a perversion of Masonic secrecy. It was a throwback to the darkest days of the Templars, when justice was held in the hands of those who had the power to torture and kill. But power has never been completely unrestrained. There is always a price to pay. In the middle ages, even the king could not act with impunity. And if Morgan was killed by people determined to protect the fraternity, they came close to destroying it instead.

The few who knew the truth about the Morgan Affair are now dead. The documents that survived them are confusing. They are laden with contradictions, bias and self-serving statements. Nevertheless, more than a century later, the controversy refuses to die. Anyone who is still interested in the subject can find ample evidence to prove that Morgan was murdered ... or that he was not.

In the final analysis the truth of this matter, like the truths of so many historic events, has become less and less significant as the years pass. More important than the literal truth of the incident is what it symbolizes. The story of William Morgan has become a Masonic legend in its own right. It is truly a cautionary tale. In that role, it has a lesson of importance to communicate to Masons as well as to their critics. And that lesson has to do with the consequences of misguided actions.

In 1882 a monument to the memory of William Morgan was erected in Batavia. It was financed by contributions from twenty-six states. The monument still stands, forty feet high. It bears an inscription that reads in part, "He was abducted From near this spot in the year 1826 by Free Masons And Murdered for revealing the Secrets of their Order."

Monument to Morgan, at Batavia, N.Y.

The Mason Word

The pieces have finally fallen together. We now have a clear picture of an organization that evolved from obscure origins in the Middle Ages into an international fraternity. We have seen how its procedures were formalized into rituals that teach moral lessons, and its medieval cult of secrecy was fashioned into a new secrecy that, curiously, seems to have no practical use.

Nevertheless, that secrecy has become almost an obsession with many Freemasons, as it has with some of the fraternity's critics. As a result, the fraternity finds itself dealing with the same kind of two-edged sword the Templars created centuries ago. Their commitment to a secrecy that is incomprehensible to the public has generated suspicion and resentment. People who never heard of William Morgan are perfectly willing to believe that the Masons kill to protect their secrets. And to prove that charge, they point to the penalties spelled out in the ritual itself.

But did the Freemasons ever have secrets that were worth killing to protect? The Masons say they did not. Some of their critics insist they did and perhaps still do.

So far our investigation has skirted this issue. We know how the Craft's cult of secrecy developed and how its secrets were woven into a ritual complete with gruesome penalties whose misuse can lead to actual murder. But we have not ruled out the possibility that the fraternity really is dedicated to keeping something from the world. To find out if that possibility exists, we must look at the Masons' greatest secret.

This is the notorious "Mason Word." Speculation from outside has it that the word is a deep secret and that it is guarded jealously by the fraternity. The Craft denies that the word is as momentous as the world thinks it is, but they can not deny that it is at the center of their cult of secrecy. At the very least it can be seen as a metaphor for the whole of Masonic secrecy. It is the one thing that Freemasons swear to protect and keep from outsiders at all cost.

And it is the climax and focal point of the initiation ritual. As a result, most Masons treat the word as if it were something of utmost importance. If Freemasonry does have a *real* secret, it will be found here.

We can easily believe that the Mason Word conceals a secret. The version in use today is so obscure, the Freemasons themselves do not know its meaning. Either the original meaning was lost over time, or perhaps it was never there. Some scholars believe that word was never intended to be understood. They say it isn't a word at all but a collection of syllables specifically created to fit into the scheme of Masonic symbolism.

These comments apply primarily to the "modern" Mason Word, which is somewhat different from the one used three centuries ago. And it may be very different from the word used in the Middle Ages, if there was one at that time.

Much speculation has been directed to whether the masons had a special password in the operative days. The records from that period are so sketchy that such a thing, if it did exist, would not likely have been documented. So we may never know to what extent the modern word had its origins in medieval times.

In the days of operative masonry, a password would have been of some utility. In the absence of union cards, the Master architect needed a convenient way to tell trained masons from unskilled workers. Since some masons traveled long distances to work sites, and since large numbers of people worked on a single project, sorting out the applicants could not have been an easy task. A mode of recognition would be a very convenient and logical development for the craft. But a password used to identify a man as a trained mason is neither an urgent secret nor a bit of esoteric knowledge. It is a matter of convenience. If a worker were hired as a skilled mason and later proved to be an impostor, he would soon be found out and discharged.

Once again we see a hint that there is more to the ritual than meets the eye. And, once again, the Templars provide a more satisfying explanation. When they built their force in the Holy Land, the military needs of the crusader came face to face with the intrigue for which the east is justly famous. Treachery was routine, and alliances shifted faster than the sands of the desert. We know that the Templars responded well to the challenge. They developed an efficient intelligence network, learned important lessons from friend and enemy alike and eventually became masters even of the Infidel's game. In that setting passwords and secret modes of recognition were not merely useful, they were literally a matter of life or death.

Interestingly, the esoteric knowledge the Templars are supposed to have brought back from the Holy Land might also explain the modern Craft's association of passwords with moral lessons. The operative masons needed passwords only as a mode of recognition to keep impostors from gaining employment. The Templars must have considered them an integral part of their Order. A word of recognition was one of the tools the Templar used to do God's will.

As knights in those days were illiterate, the written word would have been useless to them. They needed specialized words – words that would not likely be spoken by coincidence – or simple designs that could be scratched in the dirt and quickly erased. Something that held a special significance for the knights would be easier to remember. And a password that evoked the Templar's mission would add to the mystique the Order developed over the years.

The scenario is simple and elegant. The Templars became free masons, hoping that they could salvage something of their own culture. They found in the masons an organization that, like their order, had a password and used secrecy to protect its specialized knowledge. It would have been a simple thing for the Templars to become a part of – and contribute to – the culture of the medieval masons. If that is indeed the way it happened, the words and emblems of modern Freemasonry may very well have evolved from a union that is now only vaguely remembered.

However it came about, the Mason Word gained additional significance as masonry moved into its speculative phase. As we have seen, when *that* transition occurred, things that formerly had practical significance became teaching tools.

By this time, such proprietary secrets as the method of constructing a right angle, once a key element of the stone mason's craft, had lost their utility. The secrets of the old craft had either died out – because they were no longer needed – or been translated into symbolic elements in the ritual of the emerging social organization. Just as the penalties are regarded by the modern Craft as symbolic elements, the secrets they once protected had by this time become symbolic as well. They could be used to teach moral lessons, and henceforth that would be their reason for existing.

If the secrets and penalties contained some of the exotic, mystical knowledge the Templars brought back from the Holy Land, so much the better. As Freemasonry embraced the philosophical impulse that now animated it, the memory of a romantic order of Christian knights from Jerusalem and their esoteric knowledge was quite appropriate. It appealed to the romantic and enlightened minds of the time and meshed perfectly with the organization's developing body of symbolism.

What we know of the Mason Word's early development is consistent with this interpretation. The earliest known references to it appear in the seventeenth century, and it seems to have been used in Scotland before it was in England.

By this time we begin to see indications that Masonic lodges were the custodians of esoteric knowledge. There are references to "the Mason Word and everything contained in it." The implication is clearly that it was more than simply a word, that it contained something else, probably something that was not obvious upon seeing or hearing the word itself. And references to secrecy seem to imply that it had become more than just a practical means of recognizing other Masons.

The seventeenth and eighteenth century references to Masonic secrecy are cryptic. They suggest that the Freemasons had something unique to protect but do not reveal much about the nature of the Craft's secrets during that period. Still, in the light of what the Craft was soon to become, it is fair to assume that those secrets were already becoming associated with Masonic legends.

This confirms that the word was not simply a thing that stood on its own. Nor was it *simply* a password by which a man could identify himself as a Mason and thus gain admission to a lodge meeting.

It would be nice if we knew what the word was. Unfortunately, at this point we are embarrassed by a surplus of evidence. The documents of the day represent several different words as *the* Mason Word. We must conclude that either the documents are in error or the Masons had several words. These are two distinct possibilities, and we can not dismiss either of them out of hand.

Many of the old documents are suspect. Some are exposés that may have been based on faulty information. Others are scraps of paper whose source and intent are unknown. It is quite possible that more than one of them contain bogus words, words that were never used by the Masons and might well have been planted by Masons trying to obscure the facts.

On the other hand, prior to the formation of the Grand Lodge the speculative Masons were still a fragmented fraternity. As independent groups, they may not all have used the same word. The various lodges may well have capitalized on the "old" masonic secrets by inserting their own symbolic passwords in place of obsolete words for which they no longer saw any need.

Some of the words we see at this time were taken from the Old Testament and survive in the modern ritual. They do have the feel of symbols that were used to serve a fraternal order, not a working craft. But if they were once the central word of a speculative lodge, they have now been demoted to the status of ordinary passwords in the first and second degrees. Others no longer appear anywhere in the Craft. If they ever were Masonic words, they have since fallen victim to the evolution of the ritual.

Since most of them have no direct connection with the Hiramic legend, we can understand their disappearance. They may well have been central words that were later replaced when the story of Hiram was elevated to its present status. This makes the circumstances around the creation of the Hiramic legend even more critical to an understanding of the one Mason Word that did survive. And as we investigate that word, we will return again and again to the legend to see how they fit together.

Early documents contain several obsolete variations of the modern Mason Word. They appear to be phonetic corruptions of a common ancestor. We don't know whether this was the *original* word, but it is the only one that comes to us in more than one version. That tells us two things. First, there was once a single word, which was garbled in oral transmission over a period of time. And second, the word is quite old. Several distinct versions were in existence in the late seventeenth and early eighteenth centuries. This indicates that the process of garbling had been under way for some time and places the original word some decades, or even centuries earlier.

One of these versions, *Machbenah*, appears in *Masonry Dissected*. Some scholars believe that it was concocted to have the sound of a Hebrew word. That makes sense if the intention was to lend Biblical weight to it. But the word might be more easily explained as being of Scottish origin and preserving the sound of the Scots language.

Another early document, *The Whole Institutions of Free-Masons Opened*, gives three sets of words. Each set apparently consisted of a password and a counter sign. The first "word" was *Jachin* and *Boaz*. Its counter sign was a gesture. The third was *Gibboram*, answered by *Esimberel*. This pair is curious and does not appear to have been in common use. But the second word, *Magboe* and *Boe*, is obviously a two part version of *Machbenah*. As the word of that day was probably communicated by whispering, as it is today, we can easily believe that it could be misheard and misspoken until one of these became the other.

Two more versions are *Mahabyn* and *Maughbin*. They compare very closely to *Machbenah* and *Magboe Boe*. Obviously these four words are related to a common ancestor and confirm that the old Mason Word was garbled over a period of time.

Since they all come from seventeenth and eighteenth century documents, these variations show what the Mason Word had become. They also give us clues to the changes it experienced during the years it was passed down orally. By comparing the variant spellings, we may guess how the original was pronounced.

Here an especially peculiar version comes to our aid. Quoted as *matchpin*, it bears no clear relationship to other versions of the Mason Word. It is obviously a sound-alike. The most plausible conclusion is that an English speaking initiate, unfamiliar with the Scottish dialect, mis-heard one of the more Scottish-sounding versions as two English words with which he was familiar.

We need not try to mimic an old Scottish accent. Even professional linguists can only approximate the way people spoke centuries ago, and the Scots always had more than one accent. For our purposes, it is enough to read the words aloud as if they were in modern English. If we read each of the four words aloud and follow it with the English words, "match pin," we will develop a feel for the way the original must have been pronounced. And we can see that there is less difference in the way the four words sound than there is in the way they are spelled.

Now that we know how to say the old Mason Word, we can turn our attention to its meaning. But that will be a much harder nut to crack. The meanings assigned to it at the time show more than a little confusion. In the early documents it is said to have such unrelated meanings as "the Builder is smitten" and "Marrow in the Bone." Sometimes no meaning is offered.

Obviously the word's original meaning had been lost by this time, and the Masons were struggling to explain something they no longer understood. By the nineteenth century, they had given up trying to explain the word altogether and merely communicated it to the initiate.

Recovering the word's meaning after all these years will require a bit of detective work. The first step is to exploit our theory that it is of Scottish, not English origin. This is suggested not only by its sound but also by the existence of the patently English *matchpin*, which demonstrates that in the seventeenth century the word was foreign to the English ear.

It is not at all surprising that the word shows Scottish influence. Freemasonry was born in Northumbria, just south of the border, and the key events of its history were played out in the north. According to legend, more than a few Templars fled to Scotland to avoid persecution. There, they may well have joined the masons of Kilwinning Abbey and the cathedrals of Edinburgh and Glasgow, just as their comrades may have done at York.

As the Craft entered its modern period, the gentlemen of Edinburgh took to it as they did to the more general rebirth of ideas of which Freemasonry was a part. The Scottish branch of the fraternity proudly carried on the heritage of Kilwinning. They provided a creative impulse at the precise moment the modern ritual evolved. It is easy to believe that they created the Mason Word, if not the entire third degree. And they would naturally have done it in their own language.

In addition, at the time of the Templars' persecution, the people of northern England and southeastern Scotland spoke the same language. It was the "Inglis" brought to Northumbria by the Angles. During the fifteenth century that language began to diverge into two distinct tongues. South of the border, it was increasingly influenced by southern dialects, while the Lowland Scots kept Northumbrian Inglis for their own.

By the time the gentlemen Masons began penning the early Craft's documents, Scots had taken on a distinctive character. Still heavily laced with Old English, it recalls the language spoken by the earliest free masons. If the Mason Word has a meaning, it is only fitting that it come from the language that was once spoken by Biscop and his masons and by the gentlemen of the north who may have inherited the Templars' secrets.

Unfortunately, we have little hope of finding what we're looking for merely by searching the Scots language. There are just too many possibilities, especially since we don't know precisely what the original word was.

The many variations of the Mason Word that have come down to us lead in several directions. One of them suggests that the word might have been derived from *mach*, or its variants *macht* or *maught*. They mean "might" or "strength." That could refer to the mighty warrior monks or to the strength of the building stone. But the same word denotes mental ability. In that sense it might refer to Hiram Abif's wisdom.

Mach (or *mauch*) can also mean "maggot," a possible reference to Hiram Abif's burial. The ritual does in fact go out of its way to describe the decomposed state of his body when it was found.

Another version of the old Mason Word could have come from *magg*, which means "to carry off clandestinely," precisely what the ruffians did to the Grand Master's body. But *magg* also refers to the payment due a servant. Could this be the wages of a master mason?

Mack means "to make," "shape" or "fashion." That's what the masons did to stone, and what their spiritual descendants do to the initiate.

The old catechisms sometimes say the word means "marrow in the bone," a meaning born out by the Scots words *mauch* (or *maucht* or *maich*), meaning "marrow," and *ben*, "in" or "inside." But *ben* (or *bin*) can also mean "mountain." The ritual tells us that early masonic meetings were held on the highest hills or in the lowest valleys. It can also mean "key." The old catechisms commonly speak of the "key to your lodge." Or it can mean "to bind." Each initiate is bound by the cable tow (a long rope) when he enters the lodge for his initiation.

A similar Scots word, *binn*, refers to the reaper that brings in the harvest. Could this have been the Grim Reaper who took Hiram away? If we want to stretch the point, *bensie* means "to strike vigorously," possibly a reference to the blow that killed the Grand Master.

A word we have seen before, *bin*, also refers to a species of salmon. That has nothing to do with Freemasonry, but given enough time a scholar somewhere can undoubtedly make it fit the legend.

We could continue with this word search, but the point is obvious. An examination of the language will not take us where we want to go. We quickly discover that we are operating under too many handicaps to have any hope of success.

For one thing, the variant spellings of many Scots words reminds us that for a long time it was an oral language used in a largely illiterate society. A word could be pronounced any number of ways, and without standardized spelling each pronunciation could result in a different spelling. Trying to trace words in such a maze can get us hopelessly lost.

In addition, there are too many parallels between Scots words and passages in the old Masonic documents. Obviously someone got here before us. Many of the cryptic passages in the old catechisms and expose's are undoubtedly attempts by the gentlemen Masons – or perhaps even by their ancestors – to do the same thing we are trying to do. Explanations like "marrow in the bone" and "the builder is smitten" may be nothing more than a seventeenth century Mason's best guess at which Scots word the Mason Word evolved from. And we are farther from its origin than he was.

If we hope to accomplish anything with this exercise, we must pause and try to find another clue. That's the only way we can narrow down the excessive list of meanings we have to choose from.

A survey of the early catechisms reveals repeated references to something that at first glance seems unrelated to our quest. But on closer examination, it cuts right to the heart of the matter. In the 1696 catechism from Edinburgh we see,

> . . . they will say I see you have been in the Kitchine but I know not if you have been in the hall, Ans[wer] I have been in the hall as weel as in the kitchine.

Kitchens and halls have little to do with Freemasonry. Further research, however, reveals that this passage had something to do with the new Mason's progress through the degrees. *A Mason's Examination*, published in 1723, tells us that a Mason was in the kitchen *before* he was in the hall. The same catechism explains these peculiar terms as a way to tell a man's Masonic rank.

> To know an entered Apprentice, you must ask him whether he has been in the Kitchen, and he'll answer, Yes.

> To know an entered Fellow, you must ask, whether he has been in the Hall, and he'll say, Yes.

The Grand Whimsey, from 1730, gives us a little more insight into the meaning of this curious exchange.

> Q. Have you been in the Kitchen?
>   N.B. You shall know an Enter'd
>   Apprentice by this Question.
> A. Yes, I have.
> Q. Did you ever dine in the Hall?
> A. Yes, I did.

There is some difference between merely being in a hall and dining there. Apparently our attention is being directed to the difference between the servant – who worked in the kitchen preparing a meal, and who would take his own supper there – and the aristocrat, who would be served his meal in the dining room. This clearly symbolizes the Apprentice, who was a lowly member of the craft, and the Fellowcraft, who had advanced to a higher rank. (At this point we should remember that early Masonry had only two degrees, making the Fellow the higher of the two grades.)

Why do we single this bit out from all the other curious passages in the old documents? What sets it apart is that it goes to the very heart of the Craft's symbolism. Everything in Masonic teachings revolves around the reward for a Mason's work. Whenever a lodge adjourns, its Master symbolically calls the Craft "from labor to refreshment." This conjures up an image of a team of masons who have finished their work for the day and can stop to enjoy food and drink. Many modern lodges act out that bit of symbolism by actually adjourning to a dining room and serving refreshments after their meetings.

The Mason Word itself is a symbol of labor's reward. According to the ritual it is the one thing that allows a worker to earn the wages of a Master Mason. It is the thing the Grand Master promised to give to all worthy masons when the temple was completed – that is, when the labor was finished. In the Masonic allegory this is, of course, a symbol of the eternal reward for a well spent life.

Here we see the heart of all the Masonic lessons. Hiram gave his life to protect a word, but it was not simply a word. It was the key to salvation, the key to the ultimate reward for a lifetime of labor. Only those found worthy may have it, and then only when their work is finished.

Freemasonry's central secret, the Mason Word, *must* be related to that reward. It would be a disservice to the legend writers to think that they would create so elaborate and complex a ritual, one so fully laced with symbol and allegory, then at the critical moment – at the very climax of the three degrees – top it off with a word that did less than focus everyone's attention on the one thing it has all been about.

This is where the kitchen and the hall enter our search. When they are properly understood, they draw our attention to the very heart of the Craft's lessons.

The kitchen is where the feast is prepared, the hall is where it is eaten. The catechism implies that dining in the hall is a reward for working in the kitchen. The Entered Apprentice labors in the kitchen, symbolically of course, and his reward is to be made a Fellow. He receives this reward only if he is found worthy, only if he has labored well. But if he does receive it, he may leave the kitchen and henceforth dine in the hall, taking all his meals with others who have been found worthy of the same reward.

Modern Masonic catechisms always refer to the ritual. Their questions and answers are about things that actually occur in the lodge. These are things that Masons would know, because they have seen them happen. Unless the old catechisms were very different, we must conclude that their references to the kitchen and the hall reflected actual practices of the day.

In operative times, it is likely that the young apprentices' duties included preparing supper for the craft. After serving their betters, they probably had to eat at a separate table as well. But how does that relate to the modern Craft?

Some of the medieval practices may well have survived into the early modern period. While lodges still met in taverns, they took food and drink as a regular part of their meetings. The tavern's serving girls would bring platters and pitchers to the upstairs meeting room, but then the door would be closed and the members would hold their meeting in private.

With only their own present, the Masons would have to fend for themselves. It was undoubtedly the apprentices who served the food and poured wine for toasts, and then probably retired to a separate table to eat their own supper. That is the stuff of modern fraternities, and we must not doubt that the gentlemen Masons chose to benefit from the labor of their young initiates.

If they had the use of two rooms, the Masons could literally advance an apprentice from one room to another when they found him worthy to become a Fellow of their Craft. If they had only one room, the move would have to be symbolic. Perhaps it was illustrated only by chalk marks drawn on the floor to represent a separate room and a doorway. But the spirit of the lesson – that's the important thing – would still be there. The apprentice had labored. He had been found worthy, and now he would receive his reward.

When the lodges stopped meeting in taverns, they lost the benefit of that bit of symbolism, and references to the kitchen and the hall dropped out of the catechisms. It may be just as well. They had served their purpose. As the Craft evolved, it needed new catechisms to reflect its changing procedures.

Interestingly, a remnant of that old practice may still survive. Modern lodges have a preparation room. The initiate is left there to change into the costume he will wear during his initiation and to reflect on what he has gotten himself into. Then he is ushered into the meeting room, where he is advanced to the next level of Masonic membership. He has been found worthy. He will receive his reward. But he probably doesn't realize that the act of stepping through the door was once a matter of great symbolic importance.

Today's Mason must wait for the climax of the Hiramic legend to experience that bit of symbolism. It is always the initiate who plays the role of Hiram. As the ritual nears its conclusion, he has been killed and his body carried off and buried. Then King Solomon and King Hiram find the body and raise it from the ground. At that moment the Mason Word is whispered into the initiate's ear, and he begins his life as a full fledged Master Mason.

The symbolism is clear. The act of advancing the Fellowcraft to the status of Master Mason symbolizes Hiram Abif's resurrection. The Grand Master has come to the end of his labor. He has been found worthy, and he now passes from the kitchen of life to the heavenly hall where he will receive his eternal reward.

Since the Mason Word is communicated at that moment, it must "contain" something that once focused the new Mason's attention on his own transition from labor to refreshment. That is, after all, the essence of Masonic teaching and the one lesson all the initiate's work has prepared him to receive.

With this perspective we can now return to the Scots language and the maze of sound-alikes in which we hope to discover the real meaning of the Mason Word. Of all the words we have seen, and some we have not bothered to look at, only a few have anything to do with a transition. And of those, one pair stands out.

The verb *mack* means "to make" and denotes a going or coming. A person would "make" his way from one place to another.

As a noun, *ben* means "an inner room." As an adverb or preposition, it refers to moving from one room into another, or moving toward the speaker. The sense of this word is that the place a person is about to enter is better or more important than the place he is leaving. It often implies being admitted with a special feeling of honor or friendship. For example, *to come ben* denotes being advanced or receiving an honor.

If we combine *mack* and *ben*, at long last we see what the original Mason Word must have been. It was a phrase which, like most Masonic symbols, operated on two levels. It was a straightforward invitation to advance to a higher level of membership. Yet at the same time it was a profound statement about the reward that waits at the end of a well spent life.

This pair of words expressed the idea of moving from one room into another. It meant going to a better place. And it implied a sense of acceptance and honor – of being found worthy. Whispered into the initiate's ear, the Scottish phrase "*mack ben*" was a recognition of his labor and an invitation to come into a better place and receive his reward. He was being told, "Well done, good and faithful servant . . . enter thou into the joy of thy lord."

These words invited the seventeenth century apprentice to go from the kitchen into the hall. Their modern counterpart welcomes the modern Mason to the fraternity. And they may some day usher the weary traveler to his eternal reward.

The Lost Word

W e now understand the meaning of the Mason Word and the way it functioned in the ritual the gentlemen Masons inherited from the medieval craft. But why are we told that the word was lost when Hiram Abif died?

The drama of death and resurrection is a fairly straightforward story. It assures the initiate that a lifetime of conscientious labor will bring him eternal reward. The working tools symbolically show him the virtues that contribute to a well spent life. And the degrees as a whole show him the nature of knowledge and the method he must use to obtain it. From there, each Mason may look to his own religion for guidance in his path to salvation.

There is nothing in all this that has been lost. Yet at the most critical part of the ritual, the part where its most important lesson is unveiled, we are told that the word *was* lost. More than that, we are told it so dramatically and with such emphasis that we must take it as one of the Craft's most important symbols. If it does not fit into the Masons' system of morality, we must turn again to their shadowy history to discover what it does mean.

In a very real sense, the Freemasons did lose their word. By the seventeenth and eighteenth centuries it had disintegrated into a number of sound-alikes. We have seen four different versions in the old catechisms. No doubt the lodges across the country had several more that have vanished over the years. And the catechisms' attempts to explain the word show that they had lost its meaning as well as its correct spelling.

We can imagine the challenge those gentlemen Masons faced. Following the formation of the Grand Lodge, they tried to standardize the Craft's procedures. In fact, they may have founded the Grand Lodge specifically *because* they saw that the ritual needed to be standardized.

But recognizing a need is one thing. Getting the job done is quite another. They seem to have done pretty well with the ritual itself. The early documents suggest that it was well on the way to a standard form early on. However, that was the easy part. They merely needed to assemble the rituals used in the various lodges, keep any elements that were common to all – or at least most – of them, then pick and choose from any "non-standard" bits that had crept in over the years.

In that way, the early Masons could reconstruct a ritual most of the lodges would accept, and it would be a fairly authentic version of what the ritual had been years earlier. But the Mason Word was not so easy. They could guess at its original pronunciation, just as we have done. But they had no idea what it meant. Simply put, they had lost the meaning of the Mason Word and didn't know when they might find it again.

In addition, the Masons had apparently lost track of *how* their word was originally used. They were aware that it had served a purpose, but over the years that purpose had been forgotten. However the word might once have functioned, by the seventeenth and early eighteenth centuries the Masons knew only that it "contained" something. This suggests that it was not simply a word with a dictionary definition. Either it was something more than a word or it was a word that was used as a focal point for something very esoteric.

Meanwhile, the Craft was developing into a social and philosophical fraternity. A few decades after the formation of the Grand Lodge, it had evolved into a something that today's Freemasons would recognize, more or less, as the same organization to which they belong. Its teachings were fairly well developed, and the Mason Word had taken its place among the symbols of the Craft.

We may assume that the word served partly as a dues card, just as it had in the Middle Ages. There is evidence that members and visitors were admitted to the lodge on the strength of knowing it and perhaps a few other items from a catechism. This is the practice in modern lodges, and some similar procedure must have been used in those days.

It is interesting that a man had to know the word before he was allowed to enter the lodge. This says something about the Masons' attitude toward their inner workings. Clearly they felt that what went on in their meetings was not for the public to know. Restricting lodge attendance to "members only" insured that the public would not learn what Masons knew. But it also underscores the symbolic function the Mason Word had assumed. Since it "contained" something, and since it served as a password to protect some other bit of knowledge from the public, the word was obviously not important in and of itself.

This is the key to understanding the Mason Word. Whatever it was in the middle ages, by the seventeenth century it performed a symbolic function. It served to point the way to – and give access to – something else. And that something was a bit of esoteric knowledge that was for Masons only.

Unfortunately, by this time the Craft – a product of the Enlightenment whose members valued and sought knowledge – did not know its own origins. It had legends that told how it might have started – one of them was contained in the *old constitutions* – but its history was too shadowy for comfort. In addition, it had a cryptic word as a constant reminder of how much the Masons had forgotten. They had no choice but to retain the word as the focal point of their ritual. Obviously that's where it belonged, and they respected tradition too much to throw out something they realized was very important. But not knowing its meaning or how to use it must have really vexed them.

This was the state of the Craft when the Hiramic legend came into existence. And it is probably why the legend was created. The intellectuals of the Enlightenment were attracted to the old organization because they saw in it a framework that would lend itself well to their study of science and philosophy. They adapted old symbols to new methods of teaching. And bits of all-but-forgotten history became elements in a complex system of allegories and legends.

While these gentlemen of the Enlightenment were trying to learn as much as they could about the world around them, they may have found their greatest challenge in their own fraternity. That ever present Mason Word virtually dared them to discover its meaning ... and its origin and its history and the reason it had been forgotten.

Freemasonry was well equipped for the job. Its ranks included some of the best minds in England – as well as the best minds in the other countries to which the Craft was rapidly spreading – and those minds were already directed toward seeking knowledge.

To find the answers they wanted, they must have explored their old documents and the annals of British history, just as we have done, and they may have drawn the same conclusions. But like us, they couldn't prove what they had learned to anyone who didn't want to believe it. There were too many missing pieces, and it was a story that required too much speculation to be presented as unvarnished history. In short, it was more legend than history.

But obviously the Masons did learn something about their history, something which they didn't know before and which they considered a new and important aspect of their heritage. Proof of that lies in the fact that they had to create a new legend to tell the story of what they had learned.

That was when – and why – the legend of Hiram Abif appeared. It told the old Masonic story of death and resurrection, of labor and reward. And at its end, the old Mason Word was whispered into Hiram's ear to welcome him to his eternal reward, and to welcome the initiate to the Craft. All of that had been part of the ritual for generations.

But the story of Hiram Abif told something else as well. Still using allegory and symbol, it told of an ancient history that was intimately tied up with a quest for salvation. It told of a word whose meaning was lost, and it told of a quest to rediscover what had been lost.

This explains how the Hiramic legend can be an afterthought tacked onto an existing ritual, and at the same time go to the very heart of Masonic teachings. It was never a part of the old degrees, but it tells a story that tries to explain them and the ancient organization that created them.

None of this is fantasy, nor is it theology. It is what the gentlemen Masons had come to understand about their own history. They told it through the cryptic medium of their ritual because, after all, Masonic affairs were not for the public to know. But in telling it, they did something else as well.

When the gentlemen Masons decided to use the ritual to tell their own story, they set the last stone in the wall of Masonic secrecy. A legend is only a legend, but the Masonic ritual is a legend turned to a purpose. As such, it functions in a different way. Its curious blend of forgotten history, myth and moral instruction does more than tell a story. It actually blurs the distinction between what the Craft is and how it functions.

This is a difficult point to understand and may seem trivial, but it resulted in a new secrecy. The practical secrets of the old craft were gone. Their remnants survived only as the tokens and emblems of the gentlemen Masons, who found the old craft's air of secrecy both appealing and useful. Then, when the Masons created the Hiramic legend and the story of the lost word to tell the Craft's forgotten history, they revived the old Templar secrecy and made it an imperative.

The story gave the fraternity an unusual mystique and added an elegant touch to the symbolism of the degrees. But it also told each new member that he must "ever conceal and never reveal" what he learned in the lodge. And that is precisely what the Masons have done ever since.

We began our quest by observing that few people understand Masonic secrecy. We have now arrived at the thing they fail to understand.

When the craft became the Craft, and when its secrets lost their intrinsic value, there was no longer anything to conceal. Masonic secrets continue to be secrets simply because that is how they function in the ritual. There is nothing in them – no information or truth or wisdom – that would benefit either the eavesdropper or the critic. Nor is there anything in them that would hurt the fraternity if it were revealed to the public, as all the secrets have been for centuries.

Nevertheless, each Mason is required to take a solemn oath, backed up by a gruesome punishment, that he will protect what have become the best guarded and worst kept secrets in history. And like his predecessor of a few centuries ago, he has no idea what the secrets mean, because his organization has once again forgotten its own history.

Form and Function

To understand why the Masons continue to guard the Craft's secrets with a zeal that seems all out of proportion with their importance, we must take one more look at the way the modern organization functions. That's one of the things the gentlemen Masons changed, and in doing so they altered the concept of Masonic secrecy forever.

Here, the Morgan Affair points the way. That incident, more than anything else, proved that large numbers of people are quite willing to believe that the Freemasons commit murder to protect their secrets. But the public's perception is only one side of the coin. More importantly, the Masons themselves take the charge seriously enough to respond to it. A century and a half after the fact, Masonic writers still pay attention to the case. They usually conclude that the charge of murder was absurd, but not until they have offered a detailed argument to dispute the evidence. Both sides of this controversy, in other words, treat it as a credible issue – as something that *could* have happened.

What is it about an organization that makes ritual murder even a possibility? What, indeed, since the history of Freemasonry reveals that when the Craft entered its modern phase, its secrets had evolved into nothing more sinister than a system of moral instruction.

The free masons' trade secrets were for the most part simple exercises in geometry. They may have been impressive to illiterate peasants during the middle ages, but today's children learn most of them in school. Now that the traditional crafts are dying out, there is more need to preserve and document the old craftsmen's skills and techniques than to conceal them.

The Templars' secrets, too, have lost the urgency they once had. Matters of life and death in the fourteenth century have become historic curiosities, more in need of being documented than of being hidden from a world that no longer remembers or cares.

Obviously by the eighteenth century, maintaining secrecy was no longer essential to the well being of either Freemasonry or its individual members. It was a matter of neither professional nor political expedience.

This is underscored by the fact that all the secrets in the modern ritual have been revealed repeatedly without serious harm to the fraternity or anyone else. And it is reinforced by the obvious fact that those who reveal the secrets don't understand what they are revealing.

The writers of modern exposés portray handshakes and passwords as the be all and end all of Masonic secrecy. These traditional modes of recognition, they claim, are the way members of this secret society identify themselves to their fellows. But in a world where Masonic jewelry is bought in shops on main street and worn openly, and where dues cards are issued yearly, a code word or secret handshake no longer has much utility.

Still, exposés play up the superficial, while they fail to explain why some elements of the lodge's procedures do remain secret after all these years. Clearly *why* is the important question, but the exposé writers apparently don't know the answer.

Fortunately for them, they don't need to know. Masonic "secrets" never lose their hold on the popular imagination, and the purveyor of the sensational can make money simply by exploiting what he finds on the surface.

But although the exposé writer exploits this situation, he didn't create it without help. In no small part the Masons share responsibility. It was their own lore that glamorized passwords and handshakes until they took on a life of their own.

No wonder the subject is so complex and enigmatic. Masons are fond of saying that theirs "is not a secret society; it is a society with secrets." They believe this statement solves the problem, but in fact it makes things worse.

Though well meaning, this distinction sets a dangerous trap. It calls attention to words and gestures that are all too easily mistaken for the essence of a cult of secrecy. The Masons themselves *imply* that their secrecy consists of passwords and handshakes. And that in turn encourages everyone – member and non-member alike – to focus on the superficial and neglect what lies just below the surface.

In reality, Masonic secrecy is much more than a single word or slightly irregular handshake. It is an integral part of the history and symbolism that make Freemasonry unique among fraternal organizations. It all fits together, and no one can understand the secrets without seeing the larger picture.

At one level Freemasonry is just like other fraternal clubs. Some members join for fellowship. Some engage in politics, running for office so they can have a hand in setting policy. Others become experts on procedural matters and serve as elder statesmen. But the fraternity operates on a much deeper level as well.

This is because of that peculiar thing which happened in the eighteenth century. And when we understand that we will understand what Masonic secrecy is all about.

When the gentlemen Masons took over the stone masons' lodges, they used the remnants of a thousand years of history to assemble a body of symbolism. But in doing so, they created a paradox. As they put the pieces of their new ritual together, the distinction between what Freemasonry *is* and what it *does* fell by the wayside.

Unfortunately for the student of Masonic history, it is not easy to reconstruct what those gentlemen Masons were doing. When the modern degrees were written, the situation was already vague enough, because the original purposes and meanings of so many things had been lost. Then it got worse.

Since those degrees were written, language and customs have changed. And from time to time the rituals have been edited, often by people who didn't understand the original point of the words they were changing. In addition, errors in transmitting the rituals through the years left bits and pieces of the Masonic work disjointed and fragmentary.

Some parts of the ritual are hard to understand simply because we are so far separated from the culture that created them. The degrees often employ outdated words and refer to practices and objects that are no longer in use. Other parts have been stripped of the context that gave them meaning. But with our understanding of the degrees' history, we can now reconstruct enough to understand what the gentlemen Masons were trying to accomplish.

The basic thing to remember is that Freemasonry teaches its lessons by means of a series of allegories. In this respect, it is heir to a very ancient method of instruction.

The western world as a whole was profoundly influenced by the ancient practice of communicating through parables and allegories. The Bible uses them extensively, and fairy tales and myths use the same method to express the values of the cultures that created them.

Modern Freemasonry, evolving as it did during the Renaissance and Enlightenment, was especially influenced by this tradition. The rediscovery of old myths, cultures and literature gave people access to previously forgotten ideas and encouraged them to use forms of expression that were long lost and only recently found again.

The gentlemen Masons took full advantage of this by clothing their lessons in symbols. And the result is that the elements of the ritual are not complete in themselves. They always point to other things. And the new member must go beyond the symbols he is shown to understand their hidden meaning.

This is no accident. The gentlemen Masons purposely constructed lessons that would require thought and study to understand. There was, after all, more to understand than there had been in earlier times. And there was more interest in learning; a spirit of inquiry was replacing the uncritical faith of the Middle Ages.

The medieval emphasis on faith was necessary because of the condition of the society in which it developed. Literacy and learning had disappeared everywhere, and the curiosity that learning inspires had vanished, too. Medieval peasants could neither read nor write. Aristocrats were so uneducated that they could not hope to understand the complex issues of morality and religion. Even Church scholars, the only remaining custodians of learning, relied more on the established dogma that was given to them than on inquiry.

Then, suddenly, all of that changed. Learning returned to the western world. Now both the means and the inclination to learn existed. The relationship between man and God, the relationship between man and man, the place of the natural world in the scheme of things ... all of these could be investigated and understood.

But not all learning was the same. The chemist and the theologian *had* to use different methods. The subjects they studied were so different that the same approach could not possibly be used to investigate everything. So the chemist used the flask and beaker, while the theologian and the philosopher relied on allegory and parable.

The fact that the writers of the Masonic ritual availed themselves of allegories shows that they understood this fact very well. Their use of the ancient method of teaching was far from arbitrary. It was the best method for presenting moral lessons. By their very nature, moral truths are based on things that are intangible. It is almost impossible to teach them without using symbols to make them easier to grasp.

The rich fabric of Masonic symbols made the use of allegories the most logical, and perhaps the *only* way of teaching them. Symbols were virtually a necessary tool for presenting complex and abstract ideas to people whose background often did not prepare them to deal with such things. Unfortunately, they also made it difficult to state in precise terms what Masonry is and how it functions.

This is where the exposé writers have always gone wrong. In an allegorical method of instruction, handshakes and passwords simply can not be the real secrets. They *must* be symbols of something else.

People who have read what the exposés say about handshakes and passwords can attest that they know little more after reading them than they knew before. And that is because these "secrets" are simply not important in themselves.

But if they are not the point, if the remnants of the recognition signs and trade secrets of the operative masons and the military secrets of the medieval Templars are not the point of modern Masonic secrecy, then what is?

The essence of Masonic secrecy lies in what it represents, and understanding that is the hard part. Even a cursory look at the ritual reveals symbol after symbol. In fact, it is easy to believe that everything in the initiation stands for something else. And just when the initiate thinks he's beginning to understand what's being shown to him, he is told that he must place his own interpretation on the lessons.

At that point, the new Mason may feel that he has fallen into a quagmire of symbolism from which he has has no hope of escaping. There are too many symbols and no one to explain them to him.

But that, too, is part of the system. This emphasis on personal interpretation has its roots in the transition that created modern Masonry.

In its early days, the craft's initiation ceremony consisted of little more than a code of ethics and a history lesson. Then, when the gentlemen Masons took control, they moved the organization into an area that had previously been the exclusive province of the clergy. They transformed the ritual into a study in philosophy and religion. It became a complex lesson teaching people how to conduct their lives and how to approach their Creator.

The gentlemen Masons were able to deal with these subjects because of a new openness, a new spirit of inquiry. The Reformation had fragmented the power of the religious establishment. The Renaissance had allowed laymen to ask questions previously reserved for the theologian. And finally the Enlightenment provided a secular basis for moral inquiry.

The Masons – armed as they were with the symbolism of King Solomon's Temple and the Gothic cathedrals, which combined the rock-hard stuff of the world with the ethereal substance of the divine – were leaders in this new inquiry. It was in this setting that Freemasonry developed its unique character. It drew from its own history, reshaping the old ritual and traditions in light of the new spirit of inquiry. Simple lessons about the history of architecture and the Christian principles stone masons were expected to uphold were replaced with the most general and abstract of moral symbols. That was necessary to open the Craft to men of all faiths, which in turn was necessary to bring it in line with the new perspective of the Enlightenment.

And this is where the gentlemen Masons blurred the line between form and function in their ritual. When they rewrote the ritual, they made it an allegory of the quest for knowledge, and they chose man's quest for knowledge to symbolize what they were doing. Thus *the symbol came to represent itself.*

Anyone who examines the ritual carefully can see how this works. When the initiate enters the lodge for the first time, he is asked what he wants. He answers that he is searching for light (in other words, for knowledge). And that is what he is given. The rest of his initiation is a symbolic portrayal of a quest for knowledge.

But throughout the degrees, the distinction between the symbol and the thing it represents is blurred. The initiate seeks knowledge by playing the role of an initiate who is seeking knowledge.

This is like a play within a play or a movie within a movie. It's like an actor playing the part of an actor. The initiate pretends to be the person he really is; he pretends to be an initiate who's trying to understand what he's gotten himself into.

And this merging of form and function begins even before a Mason becomes a Mason. One of the least known features of Freemasonry is that prospective members are not invited to join. In fact, Masons are admonished not to discuss membership in the fraternity with any outsider who has not first inquired about the subject.

This may appear to be the ultimate in secrecy. In fact, it is at once more mundane and more sublime than it seems. On the practical level, this policy protects non-members from arm twisting by overly enthusiastic Masons. But on another level it is one of the Craft's most important bits of symbolism.

One of the ritual's main lessons is that knowledge does not fall into our laps. We must make an effort to search for it. This is the *real* reason invitations to membership are not offered. Anyone who wants to become a Mason must take the first step. And as soon as he does that, he has received his first Masonic lesson — that knowledge, like membership in the Craft, is something he must actively seek.

Thus requiring a prospective member to seek membership is a way of teaching the first of the Craft's lessons. Even before becoming a member, the initiate finds himself acting out the Craft's symbolism.

Nor does this process stop when the new member finishes the first stage of his initiation. It continues through all the degrees. It forms a never ending bond between what the Craft does and what it is.

But this still does not explain why anything in the ritual should be secret. Here again the curious observer may feel that something else is afoot, that something is missing. And the ritual itself admits as much. It tells of something that was lost. Perhaps it will someday be rediscovered. Perhaps not. But in the meantime, Freemasonry remains the custodian of the story of the thing that was lost. And that is the thing that must be kept a closely guarded secret.

This is the paradigm of a story that tells itself. And we must not forget that in this case we are talking about the story of Hiram Abif. We have already seen that the Hiramic legend somehow tells the story of the Craft's forgotten history. Now we realize that somehow it refers to itself.

This may seem confusing in the extreme, but it is really quite simple. When the gentlemen Masons reconstructed their history, they decided to present it in the same way the Craft presents its other lessons. They made their history an allegory — the allegory of Hiram Abif — and added it to the rest of the ritual.

As a result, when the new Mason goes through the initiation, he not only acts out the moral lessons he is learning, he also acts out the history of his fraternity.

Freemasonry is indeed the custodian of a ritual that embodies vague memories of something lost. This lesson is laid on top of the fraternity's basic symbols but underlies its moral lessons. It falls somewhere between the two and describes events and secrets that were once very real.

True, much of the story has been forgotten and garbled over the years. It was changed by those who did not know the story's original meaning and purpose. It was changed so much that in places only bits and pieces of it remain. But they do survive in the story of Hiram Abif. This story is not just a lesson in morality. It is not just a cautionary tale. It is a history lesson as well.

In this lesson we see the very essence of the fraternity reflected in its own procedures. The initiate is led step by step through three degrees. He is told that they will teach him moral lessons. Then he is warned that there is a deeper meaning but is left to discover it for himself.

This is clearly the method of people steeped in secrecy. It reflects the methods of the operative craft, whose apprentices learned by doing. They received knowledge only when it was time for them to have it.

The method also reflects the obsessions of the Templars, who were determined to keep their secrets from prying eyes. It is a way of presenting knowledge to those who deserve it, of giving it to them when they are ready to receive it, and of keeping it from those who are not able to use it properly.

Knowing what we do of the fraternity's history, we can see that this is a very Masonic attitude. The very nature of the ritual is to dole out knowledge in stages. The "entered apprentice" is shown a set of working tools and told how to use them – not really but symbolically. In the next stage of his initiation, he is a "fellowcraft" and is shown another set of tools. And so it goes. Nothing is offered to the new Mason until he has been given a foundation on which it can rest.

This subtlety in presenting the Masonic degrees may not be apparent to the casual observer, but it is the most carefully constructed aspect of the ritual. It forces the initiate to act out the process of gaining knowledge. The system of revealing symbols a few at a time gives them an almost tangible expression. As the Mason moves from one degree to the next, he does not know what he will learn next, though he soon discovers that pursuing his quest diligently will lead him to some bit of knowledge that is worth having.

But no matter how far he progresses, no matter how many degrees he takes, he is given to understand that there is one more bit of knowledge to discover. Whatever that is, it is something that is never quite spelled out in the degrees. In the end, he is left to find it for himself, if he can.

Symbol and Secret

N
ow we return once more to the very center of Masonic secrecy, the legend of Hiram Abif. If there is any real secrecy in the Craft's mix of form and function, it will be found here.

Since the paper trail indicates that secrets – including a puzzling Mason Word – existed before the Hiramic legend, we must conclude that the legend was based on those secrets. In other words, the legend was created to explain something that was already in the craft's history when it began to take its modern form.

If this is true, neither the legend nor Masonic secrecy can be understood without the other. They are so intertwined that they must be considered part and parcel of the same thing.

The legend is clearly a vehicle for presenting moral lessons. But we have seen that Freemasonry operates simultaneously on a number of levels. What at first appears to be a matter of procedure turns out to be an exercise in symbolism. A seemingly accidental arrangement of degrees is a profound statement about the nature of knowledge. Everything seems to have a dual nature, and in this complex mixture of form and function, the legend of Hiram Abif may carry more than one meaning.

This is complicated by the fact that the ritual is really a puzzle, and one that is very hard to solve. Since parts of it have been lost over the years, it is no longer possible for us to see the whole picture. But even that fact has been incorporated into the symbolism.

By the eighteenth century, when the modern ritual was written, the Masons were aware that they had lost much of their history. They could no longer tell their own story in its entirety. So they told what they could and included the loss of the rest as part of the story.

In the Masonic degrees, knowledge is always represented as fragmentary, but this is not just a comment about the nature of knowledge. It is another statement about Freemasonry itself. It is the voice of the old masons reaching across the centuries, telling us what really happened to them.

Everything about the Masonic ritual gives the impression that it came to us from the distant past. Even the story of the lost word has a haunting air of reality. It is easy to believe that it involves a true bit of history – not the story of the metal worker Hiram, of course, but something from the history of the old craft, something whose original significance has since been forgotten. If so, the early history of the organization must contain some event that was used as the basis for the story.

When we look into Masonic history, we find an unbroken thread that goes back to the seventh century. It began when a little remembered Northumbrian monk brought stone masons to England to build religious buildings. Along with masonry, he revived the arts and crafts and a general love of knowledge. The tradition he started then wound its way through the centuries, held in the custody of the Northumbrian monks, the stone masons, perhaps the Templars, and finally the enlightened scholars of the eighteenth century until it became the basis of modern Freemasonry.

Somewhere in that maze of historical events we will find the real Hiram. He will certainly have a different name, and the facts of his life will not be exactly as the legend describes them, but we will recognize him when we see him.

The first reference we have to the Hiramic legend occurs about 1730, shortly after the Craft's documents begin speaking of a "third" degree. No records survive to show precisely when and where it was created. Probably there never were any records. This is the sort of thing that is done behind the scenes. Scholars believe the legend was introduced into Freemasonry by French Masons. But whatever its origin, we can be certain that its first appearance marked the introduction of something quite significant in Freemasonry, since it was a departure from the traditional view of the Craft.

It is easy to explain the old, established legends and symbols that deal with the stone masons. The evolution of Freemasonry from the operative craft brought with it the use of architect's tools as objects of symbolism. The stone masons' appreciation of their own history survived in the form of references to Greek styles of architecture. And it was only natural for the medieval masons to trace their heritage to King Solomon's Temple, the Biblical equivalent of a great European cathedral.

And the *Regius Poem*'s references to the seven Arts and Sciences can be traced to the tradition started by Benedict Biscop. His love of the arts and crafts (and of learning in general) survived in the monastic and educational traditions of the Middle Ages. The seven Arts and Sciences became the basis of medieval education, and Biscop's work certainly established them as part of the Masonic tradition.

The Hiramic legend, on the other hand, does not quite fit. We still do not understand why the Masons chose a relatively obscure figure from the Bible to embody the story of their history and their need for secrecy. Nor do we have an explanation for their embellishment of the original (i.e., Biblical) version of the story. The gentlemen Masons seem to have gone to a great deal of trouble when much simpler options were available to them.

We must wonder, then, why this particular legend fitted their needs better than the other legends and myths they could have chosen. And we must ask why they preferred Hiram to all the other characters they might have used.

Historians always face a dilemma when they try to answer this sort of question. Confronted with only fragments of the past, they have to fill in the missing pieces if they want a complete picture of history. But they must guard against too much speculation, because they are seeking a true picture of the past, not a fairy tale.

In this respect, the legend of Hiram Abif does give us few pieces to work with. But since we know so little about how it was created, we will concentrate on its content.

The story tells of the death of a Grand Master, a lost word, a substitute for the lost word and a curious need for secrecy. This is hardly a tale of normal life in the Middle Ages. To the extent that it isn't just a moral allegory, it must be something more clandestine than the day to day workings of the stone masons.

The likelihood that the legend was created − or at least influenced − by French Masons suggests another possibility. The story of Hiram calls to mind a bit of French history that contains the very elements of loss and secrecy we can't find in the stone masons' past.

The French Masons certainly knew the story of the Templars. It was a dramatic part of their national history. And by the eighteenth century, the English Freemasons had doubtless forgotten much of any Templar connection they might once have had. Quite possibly this explains how the French came to tell a story that we would expect to hear from the English.

At this point the question is not whether Masonry has a Templar connection. It clearly does. The presence of Templar degrees in the York and Scottish Rites establishes that much. The question is the *nature* of the connection. We must ask when the legend first entered the Craft, and whether the French Masons created the story or revised an old story that had been forgotten or badly preserved by their English brothers.

The Templar degrees are often traced to Andrew Michael Ramsay, known in Masonic circles as Chevalier Ramsay. As the Orator of the Grand Lodge of France, he delivered a lecture that apparently launched Masonic interest in the Templars. He first gave the lecture in 1736 and later delivered a revised version in several Masonic lodges across France. In it, he claimed that speculative Masonry did not evolve from the medieval stone masons. Instead, Ramsay said, its history went back to the crusaders. He did not mention the Templars. It was the Knights of St. John to whom he gave credit for starting what was to become Freemasonry. But he had proposed an idea that would quickly find a home.

The idea that the Craft had chivalric origins appealed to the French aristocracy, who were heavily represented in that country's lodges. Within a few years, Templar degrees began appearing to flesh out the theory, and so called Chivalric Masonry has prospered ever since.

Although there is no proof that Ramsay took an active role in creating these degrees, he is generally cited as starting the movement. But did he invent the idea, or did he borrow it from an existing tradition?

The Templars may not have survived to become part of the Masonic tradition. But if they did, we have reason to believe that it happened in northern England and Scotland. Ramsay was a Scotsman, educated in Edinburgh and initiated into the Craft in Westminster. It was British Masonry that he knew best. He may have found something in it that led him to preach the chivalric origins of the Craft. And where better to preach that idea than in the country where the Templars were martyred and where the notion of the Order's survival would be most welcome?

We know that some elements of the legend existed in the older ritual, which contains references to King Solomon's Temple and penalties not unlike the modern ones. And the Hiramic legend itself predated Ramsay's oration by at least a few years.

Perhaps the history of that legend – or of something that came before it – goes back much farther. But if it does, how far back *does* it go, and what was it like originally?

The Hiramic legend of the eighteenth century seems to capitalize on the operative masons' recognition word. It's central element is the Word known only by the master builder, but clearly the story is about more than that.

This suggests that a new legend was introduced into an organization that was well suited to receive it. And although there is no evidence to the effect, it is quite possible that Hiram entered the operative masons' esoteric material long before the third degree was thought of. So the new Hiramic legend may be a reconstruction of a garbled legend that had been preserved by the operative craft, perhaps in a much cruder form, for centuries.

A glance at the particulars of the Hiramic legend shows close parallels to the persecution of the Templars. Hiram was killed as the result of a conspiracy. The action was taken by three men who had previously been associated with him. They confronted him, one at a time, and when the third accosted him, the conspiracy reached its climax and the Grand Master was killed.

This is, in brief summary, the same story as the fall of the Templars. They were first accused by Esquin de Floyran, who had been a high ranking Templar. Later, the Order was confronted by King Philip of France, who had had close connections with the Templars and with Jacques de Molay himself. And finally Pope Clement, once their benefactor, took action against them. It was this third affront that proved fatal. It led to the destruction of the Order and the death of its Grand Master.

All three of the Templars' accusers had once been the Order's friends. And although history suggests that each acted independently in many respects, the Templars must have felt that they were victims of a grand conspiracy.

The Hiramic legend also makes it clear that the Grand Master's organization continued to exist and function, though it was diminished by the loss of its leader and the Word that only he knew. This is a story of lost glory and quite possibly a clue to the real fate of the medieval Templars.

At last we begin to understand some of the curious features of ritual. On the surface, its central legend is the allegory it appears to be. But just below the surface, in the shadow world of forgotten history and esoteric rites, it serves equally well as a veiled description of the fall of the Templars. The similarities are so strong that it is hard to believe the legend writers were unaware of them.

The eighteenth century was a time when gentlemen Masons were actively creating degrees suitable for the organization into which Freemasonry was evolving. They operated in that unique moment when the Craft's history had laid the foundation for a modern fraternity, but its facade was still unfinished; it was still capable of being changed and shaped according to its members' will.

The new degrees, as we would expect, looked forward to what the organization was becoming. But they also looked back at the Craft's history.

In particular, the French Masons of the eighteenth century embraced the notion that Freemasonry had descended from the Templars. They welcomed the new degrees that told the story as a Masonic story. And, thus, the Templar legend of the Freemasons became so firmly established that it became a permanent part of the organization. While other degrees came and went, the Chivalric degrees remained.

Interestingly, the English Freemasons accepted the Templar degrees, too. This suggests that the Templar theory was consistent with what they knew of their organization. Perhaps they accepted the Chivalric degrees because they recalled a tradition that tied their organization to the Templars, and because they knew that their third degree already told the same story.

But if the legend of Hiram Abif really is a veiled retelling of Templar history, we still have to discover what the central part of the story means. Hiram could very well represent the Templars' Grand Master, and the three ruffians might be their accusers. But what is the meaning of the lost word? Is this merely an unrelated element from an already existing Masonic legend? Could it be a clumsy attempt to incorporate the operative Mason Word in order to make the new legend more acceptable to the descendants of the stone masons? Or does it symbolize something that came directly from the medieval Order's history?

It is unlikely that the lost word is a stray bit of material which was thrust into the ritual at the last moment. This word is so central to the Hiramic legend that it must have been a part of the story from the beginning. If not *the* central part of the legend, it is at the very least one of its most important elements. In fact, if the word were left out of the story, the legend would have little substance. It is as if the legend were created not to commemorate the fall of the Templars, which in any event is a well documented bit of history, but to keep alive the story of the lost word itself.

It is easy to understand how the word functions as part of an allegory. Masonic writers have spent much effort discussing it on that level. They see it as part of the story of death and resurrection. And it clearly is that. But understanding it on another level, as part of a thinly disguised history, is more difficult. And not the least of the difficulty is an apparent contradiction in the story.

According to the Masonic ritual, when King Solomon and King Hiram learned that Hiram Abif was dead, they agreed on a substitute word to be used until such time as the lost word might be recovered. But this is very peculiar. In fact, it's downright impossible.

If Hiram alone knew the word, the two kings could never expect to find it again. It would have died with the Grand Master. On the other hand, if anyone else knew the word, there would have been no need for a substitute. The original word couldn't really be lost if someone in the craft still knew it.

If the word is merely a symbol, this contradiction can easily be over-looked. Symbols are meant to point the way to something, and they need not be perfectly logical. But if the word was once a real piece of history, we must must not dismiss the contradiction too quickly.

The context of the story suggests that the lost word is not a word in the ordinary sense. What can be lost and recovered is not a collection of whispered syllables but something tangible. More than that, it would have to be something important, something of significant value, a treasure that would be worth trying to find. And this is where we come closest to the Templars.

A persistent bit of Templar history insists that they owned and preserved just such a treasure. When they were driven out of the Holy Land, they supposedly rescued it and carried it off with them.

They had certainly come to have a great deal of money, which they kept safe in their castles. But their real treasure, it is said, was something of a spiritual nature. History is vague on this point because the treasure, if it ever existed, did not come to light among the properties that were divided up after the Order's suppression.

If there were a treasure, it would go a long way toward explaining the lost word of the third degree. Clearly the lost word represents something of spiritual significance. That is obvious from the fact that it is woven into a story of death and resurrection. But it is also something that is concealed from the outside world; although it is known to exist, only those who are worthy may have access to it.

To the medieval mind, a tangible treasure of spiritual significance would most likely have been a relic. The Middle Ages was a time of relics. A bone from the body of a saint, or failing that something he had owned or touched or used could serve as a holy symbol. Relics were revered and used in religious services. They bestowed God's blessing and the power needed to do His will. Churches displayed them and placed them in their altars. Wealthy individuals sought to own them. Even the crusader army had its own relic – a bit of wood thought to be a piece of the true cross. The crusaders carried it into battle before them, and when the Infidel captured it, the crusaders went to great lengths to regain it.

The Templars might well have acquired a major relic of their own in the Holy Land. In fact, given the popularity of relics, it would be surprising if such a prominent group did not have one to use as a focal point for their mission. Indeed, although history only flirts with the question, tradition has it that the Templars managed to lay their hands on the ultimate relic, the burial shroud of Christ.

To the medieval Christian, the body of Christ would have been the ultimate relic, the most holy object possible. But the central tenet of Christian belief was that Jesus had risen from the dead, and thus His body no longer existed in this world. The truth of the religion itself was based on that assertion.

In the absence of the body of Jesus, the cloth that had touched it at the moment of His resurrection would be the ultimate relic. It certainly contained traces of the Savior's own blood, and blood has always been one of the most powerful religious symbols. The shroud held the only physical traces of the Savior that still remained in the world. And it bore the image of the Savior as proof of its own authenticity.

Until the Savior returned, the shroud would be a substitute for Him. It would be a thing to revere, a reminder of the Word of God incarnate and the rewards He would grant to those who were found worthy on the day of judgment.

A shroud does exist, but like the Templars and the Freemasons, its early history is legendary and elusive. Shortly after the crucifixion it is supposed to have traveled northward to Edessa, a city in what is now Turkey, where it disappeared for nearly a thousand years. By the middle of the tenth century it was housed in Constantinople. With the sack of that city in 1204 the shroud was lost once more and did not resurface for another century and a half. When it was seen again, it was in the hands of the De Charny family of Burgundy.

This family may have been related to the Geoffroi de Charney who died at the side of the Templars' last Grand Master. The De Charny's gave several of their sons to the crusades, but family ties from that period are hard to sort out.

They did have the shroud, though. That is a fact. It was in their possession until 1453. In that year Marguerite de Charny, who had no heirs and felt that she could no longer safeguard the sacred relic, sold it to the House of Savoy. They kept it for a while at their estate at Chambery in southeastern France then moved it to the Italian town of Turin, where it remains today.

Historians argue about where the shroud was between 1204 and the 1350's. The burial cloth of Christ, if that's what it was, could have been destroyed at any time during the turmoil of the Crusades. If it was, the De Charny shroud would have to be a forgery. But if there were two shrouds, did the Templars have the real or the fake? There are so many gaps and vagaries in the historical record that we can only speculate on any of a dozen questions about the shroud.

Fortunately, most of these questions do not bear on our investigation. The authenticity of the shroud is not an issue here. We are only concerned with whether the Templars had it during those years. If they did, they almost certainly accepted it as authentic.

Some historians believe that the Templars did have the shroud and that it explains the mysterious head they were accused of worshiping. The head was sometimes described as the head of a man with long hair and a beard. It might well have been a figure painted or carved in the likeness of the image on the shroud. The accusers claimed that the mysterious cord the Templars wore had touched the head. Perhaps it had been wrapped around the figure in imitation of the crown of thorns then given to the initiate as a reminder of the ultimate sacrifice he might have to make as a soldier of Christ.

If the Templars had the shroud, it would have to play a role in their rituals. They would not have been able to resist its lure. Yet, curiously, their confessions during the trial suggest that many Templars were unaware of the head. Others admitted knowing about it but insisted that they did not understand its significance.

But this is easy to understand. We have seen that the Order was secretive and hierarchical. Information was routinely transmitted only to those who needed to have it. If the Templars did have the shroud and chose to keep it a secret, only the highest ranking officers would know the whole story. Only those who proved they were worthy (and here we see shades of the Masonic ritual) would be given access to the most sacred relic, which had the power to show humble knights the way to a heaven where they would receive a proper reward for their labors.

The shroud would certainly be a thing to guard jealously. The Infidels might well destroy it if it fell into their hands, just as the Christians destroyed objects of pagan worship. The Templars might not even have trusted other Christians to know about their treasure. It was not unknown for relics to be stolen. An object so close to being a key to salvation, something at the very center of the faith, would have been a prize to be coveted and protected.

But did the Templars really think they had a right to hold such a relic as their exclusive property? They did have more than their share of arrogance. Perhaps some of that arrogance arose from the knowledge that they possessed the most sacred relic of all. Certainly they would have considered themselves well qualified to keep it. And their reasoning would have been sound. They were a religious order. That would seem to be the first qualification. Besides, thanks to the events set in motion by Pope Gregory the Great, the Templars had risen so far above the constraints of worldly politics that they were almost in direct contact with Christ Himself. Only the pope stood between the Templars and the Savior. That certainly gave them a right to the shroud, and in order to protect it the Templars had the strongest forts and best trained soldiers in the world. Even kings entrusted their valuables to the Templars. Who better to protect the greatest treasure of all?

Among the Templars, their Grand Master would bear the ultimate responsibility of protecting the shroud. When they were driven from the Holy Land, that duty fell to Theobald Gaudin. With the aid of De Molay and De Charney, so the story goes, he personally carried the shroud to the Order's temporary haven in Crete. Upon De Molay's election as Grand Master, its continued safety then rested on his shoulders.

Soon after, the end came for the Templars. But the shroud was not found. If the Templars ever had it, it was now well hidden – De Charney may have managed to smuggle it to members of his family for safekeeping – or perhaps it was already lost and beyond the power of the Order's surviving members to recover.

The sense of loss was surely overwhelming. Whatever future historians might say, the Templars believed they had been unjustly deprived of the wealth and power they had labored to achieve. Now their treasure was gone, too. Those who understood its true significance would have been crushed by the tragedy of their fate.

The more practical of the surviving Templars must have known that their Order had been broken forever. It could never hope to regain its wealth and power. But their treasure – their prized relic – might someday be recovered.

As their persecution began, the Templars undoubtedly lacked the means of recovering the shroud. Perhaps they, or at least their English contingency, did not even know what had happened to it. Destined to be a band of fugitives for some time to come, they had more immediate concerns. The recovery of their treasure would have to wait until they had regrouped and become strong again.

In the meantime, the central element of their ritual was gone. They needed something to replace it. And they needed something to keep their lost relic alive in their memories. Perhaps the legend of a lost word was created to keep the Templars mindful of their loss and to hold a central place in their ritual until they could once again possess the shroud.

Here at last we have something tangible, something that was lost and might be found again. It was a spiritual thing that was associated with the reward for a life well spent – in Masonic terms, the master's wages.

This could well be the first example of the Masonic blend of form and function. Until the relic could be found again, a legend would take its place as the Templars' most important ritual object. And the legend would tell its own story – the story of why a substitute had to take the place of an important token. The shroud was a substitute for the Savior who had left the world. Now, the legend would be a substitute for the lost shroud. And the lost word would be a ritualistic symbol of the substitute.

How much of this entered Masonic lore in the fourteenth century and how much was added centuries later – from the perspective of the Enlightenment – is impossible to tell. Most likely a rudimentary form of the story was handed down from the Middle Ages, while its modern version did not develop until much later. It may be, however, that the gentlemen Masons created the whole of the story with nothing more than their unexplained word and a desire to know its origins.

Either way, we now have an explanation for the Freemasons' central secret and the reason it has come down to the modern fraternity accompanied by an inordinate emphasis on secrecy. But we must still understand why the legend writers chose Hiram Abif as the main character in their drama.

When the modern version of the legend was written, it called for a Grand Master who would die to protect the special knowledge he held in trust for his brothers. The legend writers chose King Solomon's Temple for its symbolism and perhaps for its association with both the Templars and the stone masons. The fact that the Bible told the story of the building of the Temple gave it an added touch of authority. But who would be the Grand Master?

King Solomon might be a good choice, but his life was too well documented. Everyone knew that he didn't die for the craft. And there was another reason the Grand Master could not be a king. The historic Templars' main enemy was a king. The legend builders needed a Biblical character who was less than regal but still important enough to be portrayed as the director of workmen at the temple. The only such character mentioned in the Biblical account is Hiram. He was not in fact the chief architect of the temple, but that could easily be changed with a little dramatic license.

The legend of a lost word, then, took its place in the ritual of an organization that was doubly secret. It had once been a society of knights who valued secrecy. Perhaps they valued it too much for their own good.

Then they were driven into hiding as fugitives. Now even more concerned with protecting what was left of their order, they were determined not to leave behind any evidence that could be used against them. And another level of secrecy was added to the first.

By the time the modern Craft evolved, that need for secrecy had faded away. Only the tradition of it remained, but traditions have a powerful appeal. They often survive long after they have lost their utility.

Templar secrecy apparently functioned in just that way. When it was no longer needed, its custodians found an excuse for keeping it anyway.

The gentlemen Masons knew very well that the Templars stood accused of possessing occult knowledge. But this accusation can have two interpretations. King and pope charged the Order with committing sacrileges based on demon worship. A more charitable view has the Templars building a culture that blended orthodox Christian beliefs with knowledge they found in the Holy Land, and perhaps with their belief that they were the custodians of the burial shroud of Christ.

The more charitable version was the one that appealed to the Freemasons of the eighteenth century. In it we have a romantic group of men who sought and discovered a body of philosophical and religious knowledge. Even better, the trappings of their quest included an air of secrecy and exclusiveness. It was just the thing for an age that romanticized knights in shining armor and the quest for exotic knowledge. And it was just the thing for an organization that was evolving into a prestigious social club but still carried in its ritual the remnants of operative secrecy and an elitist tradition.

These two traditions – the Templar and the Masonic – blended quite well. Not only did they share bits of philosophy and procedure, they even shared some of the same experiences. The criticism the Freemasons had already encountered must have made them quite sympathetic to the story of an elite group that was persecuted by less enlightened forces. Even if there had never been an historic connection, the Freemasons could well have imagined themselves the spiritual descendants of the medieval Templars. Certainly that is how they portrayed their fraternity in the legends they wrote for themselves.

As a result of their efforts, the modern Freemason inherited a legend and a substitute word. That word is the most secret of all his secrets, in spite of the fact that those early Masons forgot its meaning.

Actually, it is his deepest secret specifically *because* they forgot its meaning.

What It All Means

O ur journey has been long and in places has offered a surprise or two. Now we have reached its end, and it's time to take stock of where we have been and what it all means.

For centuries people have tried to discover the beginnings of Masonry. Much of their work has been futile because they were looking for an ancient organization that evolved into the modern fraternity. But Freemasonry has never been a single organization. It has always been a tradition.

If we are to understand it at all, we must understand it on its own terms. We must concern ourselves with the spirit of Biscop Benedict. We must look at the moral and artistic values of the medieval stone masons. And we must focus on the idealism that was preached – but not always practiced – by the Templars.

And so it is with their secrecy. What often passes for secrecy among the Masons is in fact obscurity. From its earliest days, the Craft was heir to forgotten history, vague memories and garbled rituals. The first masons had their reasons for keeping secrets. They understood them and why they were important. But when the need for a practice is gone, the form sometimes remains. Organizations that emphasize tradition and ceremony are especially prone to retaining formalities after their original reason is long forgotten.

Few Masons devote much time to studying their own history, how their ritual evolved or the meaning that lies below the surface. They value the fraternity's tradition and antiquity but take them at face value. They are taught the symbolism of the building stone, but few are curious enough to wonder what lies beneath the stone. As a result, even the Craft's most active members are at a loss to explain its origins or its original purpose.

This is not unique to Freemasonry. Members of most organizations would be hard pressed to recite the history of their group or to give the rationale for its procedures. But when secrecy and mystique are added to a lack of knowledge, a potential for abuse is born.

The gentlemen Masons of the eighteenth century must have been aware of this potential. They knew that their fraternity was changing and that much of its history had already been forgotten. More would be forgotten in the future. That is the curse of a secretive organization, and there was nothing they could do to prevent it. But they could leave a warning behind. Perhaps that is what they had in mind when they added the Templar legend to the ritual.

In a sense, it no longer matters whether Freemasonry's Templar connection dates to the Middle Ages or the eighteenth century. Nor does it matter whether the Hiramic legend was a product of the Northumbrian monks or the Enlightenment. In our century, the Templars' contribution to Freemasonry lies in the lessons that can be learned from the degrees which are based on their history.

The historic Templars changed over the years. Their humility changed to arrogance. Their poverty evolved into wealth and greed. And their chastity became excess.

In the beginning their humility was characterized by the image of knights so poor that they had to share a single horse. This imagery is retained by modern Freemasonry, whose members are not allowed to carry money into the lodge room on the night they are initiated. But humility is hard for the members of a rich and powerful organization to retain. The Templars eventually saw themselves not as two knights sharing a horse but as the high flying Pegasus. It was a subtle shift, as shown by the small artistic change needed to go from one image to the other. But sometimes a small change can have dramatic consequences.

In the end, the Templars put the interests of their Order above all other considerations. They neglected the higher cause they had once embraced, although that cause was their avowed purpose and their very reason for existing.

Because they valued their order so highly, they were often accused of treachery to the cause they were supposed to serve. Many of the accusations were untrue, but the arrogance that prompted them was real. And so was the tragedy that inevitably flowed from it.

After two centuries of fighting for their country and their church, of shedding their blood for a cause they cherished, the Templars were persecuted by the very institutions they had served so loyally and so long. They were imprisoned, tortured and killed not because of any real acts of treachery, but because they had become a threat.

This is the legend the Masons have so carefully preserved. They present it to each new member, but it is so veiled in allegory and symbolism that few understand it.

Here the ritual enters our story for the last time. One of the characteristics of an allegory is that it does not provide answers. It is, after all, only a vehicle for communicating symbols. And symbols merely direct our attention in the right direction. The rest is left to us.

The individual Mason is free to interpret the lodge's lessons as he will. The ritual invites him to do so. Once he has been shown the Craft's legends and given its secrets, he may conclude that the lessons are intended either to separate or to unite, that the fraternity's passwords and secret signs are designed to exclude the enemy or to welcome the friend.

One way leads him to believe he is under an obligation to keep secrets he doesn't understand. It gives him a preoccupation with his organization's critics. And it makes him lose sight of the very lessons to which he should be paying the greatest attention.

The other way leads him to believe that the penalties are only symbols, and the secrets are there to point the way to moral lessons. It makes him understand that, although parts of the ritual are considered secret, the lessons that underlie them should be shared rather than concealed.

The difference between these two approaches is more than academic. It can have far reaching effects. This is the real cautionary tale of Freemasonry. And it is both a lesson and a warning.

Modern Freemasons, like their nineteenth century counterparts from Batavia, hold the spirit and reputation of their fraternity in their hands. They will act the part of Hiram or the part of the ruffians, depending on the way they interpret their ritual.

Had the Freemasons of that small town known the damage they would inflict on their fraternity, they might well have wished the penalties on themselves rather than proceed with the conspiracy they had set in motion. Unfortunately, they paid more attention to the Craft's secrets than to its lessons. The result, regardless of William Morgan's fate, was a needless tragedy. The Craft suffered for decades because a handful of its members became obsessed with what they thought were secrets.

But the lesson the Templars left the Craft was never a secret. It is a warning against folly that issues from arrogance and distrust.

Both the preoccupation some Masons have with secrecy and the obsessive attacks of its critics are based on a common point of view. That point of view binds the Mason and his critic together in a bond that is stronger than the Masonic bond of fellowship. It promotes intolerance and exclusiveness. And it contradicts the benevolent spirit Masonry has taught since its beginnings.

Freemasonry was born in the emptiness that was left by the fall of the Roman Empire. The earliest ancestor of the Craft, a Northumbrian monk of the seventh century, recognized the wisdom that could be imported from foreign countries. His accomplishments, if not his name, were remembered in the *Regius Poem*, and the whole of Masonic symbolism and secrecy unfolded from his quest for knowledge.

Freemasonry has survived the centuries partly because of the spirit it inherited from the Northumbrian monks. Their disposition was very different from that of the Romans they succeeded.

In the Romans' view, anyone who was not one of their own was a barbarian. They expected to have enemies and treated the world accordingly.

When the Roman legions conquered new territory, they passed judgment on the people who had resisted them. Those who were considered harmless – those who had neither the power nor the malice to be a threat to the mighty Roman Empire – were given their freedom and allowed to return home to serve as loyal citizens of an expanded empire.

Those who might someday cause trouble did not fare as well. They were "numbered among the enemy." The historian who reads those simple words does not need to guess the fate of those poor souls. The unfortunate ones who were numbered among the enemy were sold into slavery or put to death, not because they were enemies of Rome, but because they someday might be enemies.

The Roman Empire never ran out of enemies. And in the end, when the Empire finally collapsed, only its enemies were left.

Epilogue

This book began with the observation that not everyone would believe its conclusions. Nor should everyone believe them.

There was never anything about Freemasonry that was intended to lead everyone to the same conclusion. So there is no reason an investigation of the Craft should lead to a single conclusion.

The fraternity's history and procedures have always been obscure, as much to its own members as to outsiders. And that obscurity is one of the most ancient parts of its make-up.

It never was fully understood. Even the fourteenth century monk who wrote the *Regius Poem* had lost track of its origins. In other words, at the very dawn of the organization's written history, it already had a prehistory that had been forgotten by its own members.

In their turn, the speculative Masons of the seventeenth and eighteenth centuries had to deal with an even more uncertain history. By the time they inherited the organization and took charge of its evolution into a modern fraternity, the heritage of the medieval masons had been obscured by the effects of time and changing cultures. Even then, the old masonic secrets had become quaint and curious relics. They came into the modern era as garbled bits and pieces whose meaning and significance were lost.

The new gentlemen Masons, driven as they were by a spirit of exploration and a quest for knowledge, tried to rebuild the old secrets and use them as a vehicle for moral instruction. But they could only speculate about the original purpose of the legends they had inherited.

In our quest for the origins of Masonic secrecy, we have reconstructed the course of events that produced the modern Craft and made it what it is today. We have presented facts about this enigmatic fraternity. We have explored theories that can be neither proved nor disproved. And we have tried throughout to keep straight the difference between the two.

THE DEATH OF THE GRAND MASTER HIRAM ABIF
As portrayed in the Masonic ritual.

But the distinctions and arguments we have seen make little difference. There are so many missing parts in this story, it is unlikely that the whole of it will ever be known. And in the absence of a neat set of facts and a tidy conclusion, the readers of this book must draw their own conclusions.

In the final analysis we are left only with a fraternity that evokes strong emotions. Even its basic nature is fated to remain a subject of debate. Freemasonry exists in a shadowy world of lost documents, of legends that deliberately redefine the past, of avid critics and equally avid defenders.

This is a world in which arguments are accepted or rejected as a matter of preference. Facts are less important than beliefs. And beliefs, in turn, are defined by loyalty to one side or the other. In this world, there is more than enough truth to go around, and few people use more of it than they need to prove their case.

When all is said and done, the one thing that can not be avoided is the secrecy. Freemasonry would not be Freemasonry without it. But these things take on a life of their own. They become separated from their origins, and the reason they exist is forgotten.

Therein lies a danger. When an organization no longer understands the "why" of its procedures, its members' actions, even if performed loyally and in good faith, can be very destructive indeed.

We have now come to the end of our quest. We have told our cautionary tale, and our readers will make of it what they will. At this point, there is only one more piece to add to the puzzle.

The central element of our story was the death of the Grand Master Hiram Abif as it is portrayed in the Masonic ritual. This image, more than any other, illustrates Masonic secrecy because it lies at the heart of the fraternity's cult of secrecy.

It is also an event that never happened. It was added to the ritual as a symbol of what the organization had once been. It was an attempt to recapture what was lost. The ritual itself tells us as much.

But at its core the ritual also contains a word of warning. The ruffians murdered their master not for the wages they hoped to receive but for a word. And as things turned out, that word, in and of itself, had no value. When it was lost, it was easily replaced by another. Simply put, it was for a word with no meaning that the ruffians sacrificed their lives.

Perhaps this is the ultimate cautionary tale of the Masonic ritual. If we pay too much attention to the form of a thing and fail to understand its substance, we are doomed to go astray.

The Masons of the Enlightenment built into their legends the admonition that we must always strive to understand what lies below the surface. But that lesson, like the Craft's other lessons, is not an easy one.

Unfortunately, most of the people who deal with modern Freemasonry – members and critics alike – see only the form. They are satisfied with what they find on the surface and fail to see the meaning that lies beneath it all.

Thus a system that was carefully constructed to create light too often produces darkness. And what was meant to bring people together is too often used to keep them apart.

Telling a man something – anything – then warning him that it is a secret is the best way to separate him from the people around him. It forces him to chose between hiding his knowledge from others and betraying those who gave it to him. And either course is divisive.

This book has unveiled many of the fraternity's secrets, but that was not its purpose. Its purpose, like the purpose of the Masonic degrees, was to tell a story that explains something.

Anyone who has stayed with us to the end of our quest should have a better understanding of the origin of the Freemasons' secrets, what is and is not secret, and why. And in the end, it is probably better to understand a thing than to be mystified by it.

List of Appendices

Appendix I

The *Regius Poem*
A Poem of Moral Duties

The *Regius Poem*, otherwise known as the *Regius Manuscript* or the *Halliwell Manuscript*, has found a place in history as Masonry's oldest document. The poem itself is undated, but its language and style place it in the late fourteenth or early fifteenth century, and within that period 1390 is generally regarded as its most likely date.

Its origin, too, is unknown. The only surviving copy belongs to the British Museum. That manuscript identifies neither the author nor the reason it was written.

The *Regius Poem* may have a working document used by the medieval stone masons, but some scholars think its character doesn't fit that scenario. The text has a fraternal and religious tone that suggests it was not merely an operative document. Although it may have been drawn from earlier craft documents – or at least from an earlier tradition – some believe this curious document represents the first stirrings of the modern fraternity.

The original was written in Middle English. The version reprinted here is a modern English translation published by the Masonic Service Association.

The Regius Poem
Modern Translation

Here begin the constitutions of the art
of Geometry according to Euclid.

Whoever will both well read and look
He may find written in old book
Of great lords and also ladies,
That had many children together, certainly;
And had no income to keep them with,
Neither in town nor field nor enclosed wood;
A council together they could them take.
To ordain for these children's sake,
How they might best lead their life

Without great disease, care and strife;
And most for the multitude that was coming
Of their children after their ending.
They sent them after great clerks,
To teach them then good works;

And pray we them, for our Lord's sake.
To our children some work to make,
That they might get their living thereby,
Both well and honestly full securely.
In that time, through good geometry,
This honest craft of good masonry

Was ordained and made in this manner,
Counterfeited of these clerks together;
At these lord's prayers they counterfeited
   geometry,
And gave it the name of masonry,
For most honest craft of all.
These lords' children thereto did fall.
To learn of him the craft of geometry.
The which he made full curiously:

Through fathers' prayers and mothers' also,
This honest craft he put them to.
He that learned best, and was of honesty,
And passed his fellows in curiosity,
If in that craft he did him pass,
He should have more worship than the less.
This great clerk's name was called Euclid,
His name it spread full wonder wide.
Yet this great clerk ordained he
To him that was higher in this degree,
That he should teach the simplest of wit
In that honest craft to be perfect;
And so each one shall teach the other,
And love together as sister and brother.
Furthermore yet that ordained he,
Master called so should he be;
So that he were most worshipped,
Then should he be so called:
But mason should never one another call,
Within the craft amongst them all,
Neither subject nor servant, my dear brother,
Though he be not so perfect as is another;
Each shall call other fellows by friendship.
Because they come of ladies' birth.
On this manner, through good wit of geometry,
Began first the craft of masonry:
The clerk Euclid on this wise it found,
This craft of geometry in Egypt land.

In Egypt he taught it full wide,
In divers lands on every side;
Many years afterwards, I understand,
Ere that the craft came into this land.
This craft came into England, as I you say,
In time of good King Athelstane's day;
He made them both hall and even bower,
And high temples of great honour,
To disport him in both day and night,
And to worship his God with all his might.
This good lord loved this craft full well,
And purposed to strengthen it every part,
For divers faults that in the craft he found;
He sent about into the land.

After all the masons of the craft,
To come to him full even straight,
For to amend these defaults all
By good counsel, if it might fall.
An assembly then could let make
Of divers lords in their state,
Dukes, earls, and barons also,
Knights, squires and many more,
And the great burgesses of that city,
They were there all in their degree;
There were there each one always,
To ordain for these masons' estate,
There they sought by their wit,
How they might govern it:

Fifteen articles they there sought,
And fifteen points there they wrought.

    Here begins the first article.

The first article of this geometry:-
The master mason must be full securely
Both steadfast, trusty and true,
It shall him never then rue:
And pay thy fellows after the cost,
As victuals goeth then, well thou knowest;
And pay them truly, upon thy faith,
What they may deserve;
And to their hire take no more,
But what that they may serve for;
And spare neither for love nor dread,

Of neither parties to take no bribe;
Of lord nor fellow, whoever he be,
Of them thou take no manner of fee;
And as a judge stand upright,
And then thou dost to both good right;
And truly do this wheresoever thou goest,
Thy worship, thy profit, it shall be most.

    Second article.

The second article of good masonry,
As you must it here hear specially,
That every master, that is a mason,
Must be at the general congregation,
So that he it reasonably be told
Where that the assembly shall be held;

And to that assembly he must needs go,
Unless he have a reasonable excuse,
Or unless he be disobedient to that craft
Or with falsehood is overtaken,

Or else sickness hath him so strong,
That he may not come them among;
That is an excuse good and able,
To that assembly without fable.

Third article.

The third article forsooth it is,
That the master takes to no 'prentice,
Unless he have good assurance to dwell
Seven years with him, as I you tell,
His craft to learn, that is profitable;

Within less he may not be able
To lords' profit, nor to his own
As you may know by good reason.

Fourth article.

The fourth article this must be,
That the master him well besee,
That he no bondman 'prentice make,
Nor for no covetousness do him take;
For the lord that he is bound to,
May fetch the 'prentice wheresoever he go.
If in the lodge he were taken,
Much disease it might there make,
And such case it might befall,
That it might grieve some or all.

For all the masons that be there
Will stand together all together.
If such one in that craft should dwell,
Of divers diseases you might tell:
For more ease then, and of honesty,
Take a 'prentice of higher degree,
By old time written I find
That the 'prentice should be of gentle kind;
And so sometime, great lords' blood
Took this geometry that is full good.

Fifth article.

The fifth article is very good,
So that the 'prentice be of lawful blood;
The master shall not, for no advantage,

Make no 'prentice that is deformed;
It is to mean, as you may hear,
That he have his limbs whole all together;
To the craft it were great shame,
To make a halt man and a lame,
For an imperfect man of such blood

Should do the craft but little good.
Thus you may know every one,
The craft would have a mighty man;
A maimed man he hath no might,
You must it know long ere night.

Sixth article,

The sixth article you must not miss.

That the master do the lord no prejudice,
To take the lord for his 'prentice,
As much as his fellows do, in all wise.
For in that craft they be full perfect,
So is not he, you must see it.
Also it were against good reason,
To take his hire as his fellows do.
This same article in this case,
Judgeth his 'prentice to take less
Than his fellows, that be full perfect.
In divers matters, know require it,
The master may his 'prentice so inform,
That his hire may increase full soon,

And ere his term come to an end,
His hire may full well amend.

Seventh article,

The seventh article that is now here,
Full well will tell you all together,
That no master for favour nor dread,
Shall no thief neither clothe nor feed.
Thieves he shall harbour never one,
Nor him that hath killed a man,
Nor the same that hath a feeble name,
Lest it would turn the craft to shame.

Eighth article,

The eighth article sheweth you so,
That the master may it well do.
If that he have any man of craft,
And he be not so perfect as he ought,
He may him change soon anon,
And take for him a more perfect man.
Such a man through recklessness,
Might do the craft scant worship.

Ninth article.

The ninth article sheweth full well,

That the master be both wise and strong;
That he no work undertake,
Unless he can both it end and make;
And that it be to the lords' profit also,
And to his craft, wheresoever he go;
And that the ground be well taken,
That it neither flaw nor crack.

Tenth article,

The tenth article is for to know,
Among the craft, to high and low,
There shall no master supplant another,
But be together as sister and brother,
In this curious craft, all and some,
That belongeth to a master mason.
Nor shall he not supplant no other man,
That hath taken a work him upon,
In pain thereof that is so strong,
That weigheth no less than ten pounds,
But if that he be guilty found,
That took first the work on hand;
For no man in masonry
Shall not supplant other securely,
But if that it be so wrought,
That in turn the work to nought;
Then may a mason that work crave,
To the lords' profit for it to save
In such a case if it do fall,
There shall no mason meddle withal.
Forsooth he that beginneth the ground,
If he be a mason good and sound,
He hath it securely in his mind

To bring the work to full good end.

Eleventh article,

The eleventh article I tell thee,
That he is both fair and free
For he teacheth, by his might,
That no mason should work by night,
But if it be in practising of wit,
If that could amend it.

Twelfth article,

The twelfth article is of high honesty
To every mason wheresoever he be,
He shall not his fellows' work deprave,
If that he will his honesty save;
With honest works he it commend,

By the wit that did God did thee send;
But it amend by all that thou may,
Between you both without doubt.

Thirteenth article.

The thirteenth article, so God me save,
Is if that the master a 'prentice have,
Entirely then that he him teach,
And measurable points that he him tell,
That he the craft ably may know,
Wheresoever he go under the sun.

Fourteenth article,

The fourteenth article by good reason,
Sheweth the master how he shall do;
He shall no 'prentice to him take,
Unless divers cares he have to make,
That he may within his term,
Of him divers points may learn,

Fifteenth article,

The fifteenth article maketh an end,
For to the master he is a friend;
To teach him so, that for no man,
No false maintenance he take him upon,
Nor maintain his fellows in their sin,
For no good that he might win;
Nor no false oath suffer him to make,
For dread of their souls' sake,
Lest it would turn the craft to shame,
And himself to very much blame.

Plural constitutions.

At this assembly were points ordained more,
Of great lords and masters also,
That who will know this craft and come to
      estate,
He must love well God and holy church
      always,
And his master also that he is with,
Whersoever he go in field or enclosed wood,
And thy fellows thou love also,
For that thy craft will that thou do.

Second point.

The second point as I you say,
That the mason work upon the work day,
As truly as he can or may,

To deserve his hire for the holy-day,
And truly to labour on his deed,
Well deserve to have his reward.

Third point.

The third point must be severely,
With the 'prentice know it well,
His master's counsel he keep and close,
And his fellows by his good purpose;
The privities of the chamber tell he no man,
Nor in the lodge whatsoever they do;
Whatsoever thou hearest or seest them do,
Tell it no man whersoever you go;
The counsel of hall, and even of bower,

Keep it well to great honour,
Lest it would turn thyself to blame,
And bring the craft into great shame.

Fourth point.

The fourth point teacheth us also,
That no man to his craft be false;
Error he shall maintain none
Against the craft, but let it go;
Nor no prejudice he shall not do
To his master, nor his fellow also;
And though the 'prentice be under awe,
Yet he would have the same law.

Fifth point.

The fifth point is without doubt,
That when the mason taketh his pay
Of the master, ordained to him,
Full meekly taken so must it be;
Yet must the master by good reason,
Warn him lawfully before noon,
If he will not occupy him no more,
As he hath done there before;
Against this order he may not strive,
If he think well for to thrive.

Sixth point.

The sixth point is full given to know,
Both to high and even to low,

For such case it might befall;
Among the masons some or all,
Through envy or deadly hate,
Oft ariseth full great debate.

Then ought the mason if that he may,
Put them both under a day;
But loveday yet shall they make none,
Till that the work-day be clean gone;
Upon the holy-day you must well take
Leisure enough loveday to make,
Lest that it would the work-day
Hinder their work for such a fray;
To such end then that you them draw.

That they stand well in God's law.

Seventh point.

The seventh point he may well mean,
Of well long life that God us lend,
As it descrieth well openly,
Thou shalt not by thy master's wife lie,
Nor by thy fellows', in no manner wise,
Lest the craft would thee despise;
Nor by the fellows' concubine,
No more thou wouldst he did by thine.
The pain thereof let it be sure,
That he be 'prentice full seven year,
If he forfeit in any of them
So chastised then must he be;
Full much care might there begin,
For such a foul deadly sin.

Eighth point.

The eighth point, he may be sure,
If thou hast taken any cure,
Under thy master thou be true,
For that point thou shalt never rue;
A true mediator thou must needs be
To thy master, and thy fellows free;
Do truly all that thou might,
To both parties, and that is good right.

Ninth point.

The ninth point we shall him call,
That he be steward of our hall,
If that you be in chamber together,
Each one serve other with mild cheer;
Gentle fellows, you must it know,
For to be stewards all in turn,
Week after week without doubt,
Stewards to be so all in turn about,
Amiably to serve each one other,

As though they were sister and brother;
There shall never one another cost

Free himself to no advantage,
But every man shall be equally free

In that cost, so must it be;
Look that thou pay well every man always,
That thou hast bought any victuals eaten,
That no craving be made to thee,
Nor to thy fellows in no degree,
To man or to woman, whoever he be,
Pay them well and truly, for that will we;
Thereof on thy fellow true record thou take,
For that good pay as thou dost make,
Lest it would thy fellow shame,
And bring thyself into great blame.
Yet good accounts he must make
Of such goods as he hath taken,

Of thy fellows' goods that thou hast spent,
Where and how and to what end;
Such accounts thou must come to,
When thy fellows wish that thou do.

Tenth point.

The tenth point presenteth well good life,
To live without care and strife,
For if the mason live amiss,
And in his work be false I know,

And through such a false excuse
May slander his fellows without reason,
Through false slander of such fame

May make the craft acquire blame.
If he do the craft such villainy,
Do him no favour then securely,
Nor maintain not him in wicked life,
Lest it would turn to care and strife;
But yet him you shall not delay,
Unless that you shall him constrain,
For to appear wheresoever you will,
Where that you will, loud, or still;
To the next assembly you shall him call,
To appear before his fellows all,
And unless he will before them appear,

The craft he must need forswear;
He shall then be punished after the law
That was founded by old day.

Eleventh point.

The eleventh point is of good discretion.

As you must know by good reason;
A mason, if he this craft well know,
That seeth his fellow hew on a stone,
And is in point to spoil that stone,
Amend it soon if that thou can,
And teach him then it to amend,
That the lords' work be not spoiled,
And teach him easily it to amend,

With fair words, that God thee hath lent;
For his sake that sit above,
With sweet words nourish his love.

Twelfth point.

The twelfth point is of great royalty,
There as the assembly held shall be,
There shall be masters and fellows also,
And other great lords many more;
There shall be the sheriff of that country,
And also the mayor of that city,
Knight and squires there shall be,
And also aldermen, as you shall see;
Such ordinance as they make there,

They shall maintain it all together
Against that man, whatsoever he be,
That belongeth to the craft both fair and free.
If he any strife against them make,
Into their custody he shall be taken.

Thirteenth point.

The thirteenth point is to us full lief,
He shall swear never to be no thief,
Nor succour him in his false craft,
For no good that he hath bereft,
And thou must it know or sin,
Neither for his good, nor for his kin.

Fourteenth point.

The fourteenth point if full good law
To him that would be under awe;
A good true oath he must there swear
To his master and his fellows that be there;
He must be steadfast and true also
To all this ordinance, wheresoever he go,
And to his liege lord the king,
To be true to him over all thing.
And all these points here before
To them thou must need be sworn,
And all shall swear the same oath

Of the masons, be they lief be they loath,
To all these points here before,

That hath been ordained by full good lore.
And they shall enquire every man
Of his party, as well as he can,
If any man may be found guilty
In any of these points specially;
And who he be, let him be sought,
And to the assembly let him be brought.

Fifteenth point.

The fifteenth point is full good lore,
For them that shall be there sworn,
Such ordinance at the assembly was laid
Of great lords and masters before said;
For the same that be disobedient, I know,
Against the ordinance that there is,
Of these articles that were moved there,
Of great lords and masons all together.
And if they be proved openly
Before that assembly, by and by,
And for their guilts no amends will make,
Then must they need the craft forsake;
And no masons craft they shall refuse,
And swear it never more to use.
But if that they will amends make,
Again to the craft they shall never take;
And if that they will not do so,
The sheriff shall come them soon to,

And put their bodies in deep prison,
For the trespass that they have done,
And take their goods and their cattle
Into the king's hand, every part,
And let them dwell there full still,
Till it be our liege king's will.

Another ordinance of the art of
geometry.

They ordained there an assembly to be hold,
Every year, wheresoever they would,
To amend the defaults, if any were found
Among the craft within the land;
Each year or third year it should be held,

In every place wheresoever they would;
Time and place must be ordained also,
In what place they should assemble to.
All the men of craft there they must be,

And other great lords, as you must see,
To mend the faults the he there spoken,
If that any of them be then broken.
There they shall be all sworn,
That belongeth to this craft's lore,
To keep their statutes every one
That were ordained by King Althelstane;
These statutes that I have here found

I ordain they be held through my land,
For the worship of my royalty,
That I have by my dignity.
Also at every assembly that you hold,
That you come to your liege king bold,
Beseeching him of his high grace,
To stand with you in every place,
To confirm the statutes of King Athelstane,
That he ordained to this craft by good reason.

The art of the four crowned ones.

Pray we now to God almighty,
And to his mother Mary bright,

That we may keep these articles here,
And these points well all together,
As did these holy martyrs four,
That in this craft were of great honour;
They were as good masons as on earth shall
     go,
Gravers and image-makers they were also.
For they were workmen of the best,
The emperor had to them great liking;
He willed of them an image to make
That might be worshipped for his sake;
Such monuments he had in his day,
To turn the people from Christ's law.

But they were steadfast in Christ's law,
And to their craft without doubt;
They loved well God and all his lore,
And were in his service ever more,
True men they were in that day,
And lived well in God's law;
They thought no monuments for to make,
For no good that they might take,
To believe on that monument for their God,
The would not do so, though he was furious;
For they would not forsake their true faith,

And believe on his false law.
The emperor let take them soon anon,
And put them in a deep prison;

The more sorely he punished them in that place,
The more joy was to them of Christ's grace.
Then when he saw no other one,
To death he let them then go;
By the book he might it show
In the legend of holy ones,
The names of the four crowned ones.

Their feast will be without doubt,
After Hallow-e'en eighth day.
You may hear as I do read,
That many years after, for great dread
That Noah's flood was all run.
The tower of Babylon was begun,
As plain work of lime and stone,
As any man should look upon;
So long and broad it was begun,
Seven miles the height shadoweth the sun.
King Nebuchadnezzar let it make
To great strength for man's sake,

Though such a flood again should come,
Over the work it should not take;
For they had so high pride, with strong boast
All that work therefore was lost;
An angel smote them so with divers speech,
That never one knew what the other should tell.
Many years after, the good clerk Euclid
Taught the craft of geometry full wonder wide,
So he did that other time also,
Of divers crafts many more.
Through high grace of Christ in heaven,
He commenced in the sciences seven;

Grammar is the first science I know,
Dialect the second, so have I bliss,
Rhetoric the third without doubt,
Music is the fourth, as I you say,

Astronomy is the fifth, by my snout,
Arithmetic the sixth, without doubt,
Geometry the seventh maketh an end,
For he is both meek and courteous.
Grammar forsooth is the root,
Whoever will learn on the book;
But art passeth in his degree,
As the fruit doth the root of the tree;

Rhetoric measureth with ornate speech among,
And music it is a sweet song;

Astronomy numbereth, my dear brother,
Arithmetic sheweth one thing that is another,
Geometry the seventh science it is,
That can separate falsehood from truth, I know
These be the sciences seven,
Who useth them well he may have heaven.
Now dear children by your wit
Pride and covetousness that you leave it,
And taketh heed to good discretion,
And to good nurture, wheresoever you come,
Now I pray you take good heed,

For this you must know needs,
But much more you must know,
Than you find here written.
If thee fail therto wit,
Pray to God to send thee it;
For Christ himself, he teacheth us
That holy church is God's house,
That is made for nothing else
But for to pray in, as the book tells us;
There the people shall gather in,

To pray and weep for their sin.
Look thou come not to church late,
For to speak harlotry by the gate;

Then to church when thou dost fare,
Have in thy mind ever more
To worship thy lord God both day and night,
With all thy wits and even thy might.
To the church door when thou dost come
Of that holy water there some thou take,
For every drop thou feelest there
Quencheth a venial sin, be thou sure.
But first thou must do down thy hood,
For his love that died on the rood.
Into the church when thou dost go,
Pull up thy heart to Christ, anon;

Upon the rood thou look up then,
And kneel down fair upon thy knees,
Then pray to him so here to work,
After the law of holy church,

For to keep the commandments ten,
That God gave to all men;
And pray to him with mild voice
To keep thee from the sins seven,
That thou here may, in this life,
Keep thee well from care and strife;

Furthermore he grant thee grace,
In heaven's bliss to have a place.

In holy church leave trifling words
Of lewd speech and foul jests,
And put away all vanity,
And say thy pater noster and thine ave;
Look also that thou make no noise,
But always to be in thy prayer;
If thou wilt not thyself pray,
Hinder no other man by no way.
In that place neither sit nor stand,
But kneel fair down on the ground,
And when the Gospel me read shall,

Fairly thou stand up from the wall,
And bless the fare if that thou can,
When gloria tibi is begun;
And when the gospel in done,
Again thou might kneel down,
On both knees down thou fall,
For his love that bought us all;
And when thou hearest the bell ring
To that holy sacrament,
Kneel you must both young and old,
And both your hands fair uphold,
And say then in this manner,

Fair and soft without noise;
"Jesus Lord welcome thou be,
In form of bread as I thee see,
Now Jesus for thine holy name,
Shield me from sin and shame;
Shrift and Eucharist thou grant me both,
Ere that I shall hence go,
And very contrition for my sin,
That I never, Lord, die therein;
And as thou were of maid born,
Suffer me never to be lost;
But when I shall hence wend,

Grant me the bliss without end;
Amen! Amen! so mote it be!
Now sweet lady pray for me."
Thus thou might say, or some other thing,
When thou kneelest at the sacrament.
For covetousness after good, spare thou not
To worship him that all hath wrought;

For glad may a man that day be,
That once in the day may him see;
It is so much worth, without doubt,
The virtue thereof no man tell may;

But so much good doth that sight,

That Saint Austin telleth full right,
That day thou seest God's body,
Thou shalt have these full securely:
Meet and drink at thy need,
None that day shalt thou lack;
Idle oaths and words both,
God forgiveth thee also;
Sudden death that same day
Thee dare not dread by no way;
Also that day, I thee plight,
Thou shalt not lose thy eye sight;
And each foot that thou goest then,

That holy sight for to see,
They shall be told to stand instead,
When thou hast thereto great need;
That messenger the angel Gabriel,
Will keep them to thee full well,
From this matter now I may pass,
To tell more benefits of the mass:
To church come yet, if thou may,
And hear the mass each day;
If thou may not come to church,
Where that ever thou dost work,
When thou hearest the mass toll,

Pray to God with heart still,
To give thy part of that service,
That in church there done, is.
Furthermore yet, I will you preach
To your fellows, it for to teach,
When thou comest before a lord,
In hall, in bower, or at the board,
Hood or cap that thou off do,
Ere thou come him entirely to;
Twice or thrice, without doubt,
To that lord thou must bow;
With thy right knee let it be done,

Thine own worship thou save so.
Hold off thy cap and hood also.
Till thou have leave it on to put.
All the time thou speakest with him,
Fair and amiably hold up thy chin;
So, after the nurture of the book,
In his face kindly thou look.
Foot and hand thou keep full still,
For clawing and tripping, is skill;
From spitting and sniffling keep thee also,
By private expulsion let it go.
And if that thou be wise and discrete,

Thou has great need to govern thee well.
Into the hall when thou dost wend,
Amongst the gentles, good and courteous,
Presume not too high for nothing,
For thine high blood, nor thy cunning,
Neither to sit nor to lean,
That is nurture good and clean.
Let not thy countenance therefore abate,
Forsooth good nurture will save thy state.
Father and mother, whatsoever they be,
Well is the child that well may thee,
In hall, in chamber, where thou dost go;

Good manners make a man.
To the next degree look wisely,
To do them reverence by and by;
Do them yet no reverence all in turn,
Unless that thou do them know.
To the meat when thou art set,
Fair and honestly thou eat it;
First look that thine hands be clean,
And that thy knife be sharp and keen,
And cut thy bread all at thy meat,
Right as it may be there eaten.
If thou sit by a worthier man,
Then thy self thou art one,
Suffer him first to touch the meat,
Ere thyself to it reach.
To the fairest morsel thou might not strike,
Though that thou do it well like;
Keep thine hands fair and well,
From foul smudging of thy towel;
Thereon thou shalt not thy nose blow,
Nor at the meat thy tooth thou pick;
Too deep in cup thou might not sink,
Though thou have good will to drink,
Lest thine eyes would water thereby—

Then were it no courtesy.
Look in thy mouth there be no meat,
When thou beginnest to drink or speak,
When thou seest any man drinking,
That taketh heed to thy speech,

Soon anon thou cease thy tale,
Whether he drink wine or ale,
Look also thou scorn no man,
In what degree thou seest him gone;
Nor thou shalt no man deprave,
If thou wilt thy worship save;
For such word might there outburst.

That might make thee sit in evil rest.
Close thy hand in thy fist,
And keep thee well from "had I known."
In chamber, among the ladies bright,
Hold thy tongue and spend thy sight;
Laugh thou not with no great cry,
Nor make no lewd sport and ribaldry.
Play thou not but with thy peers,
Nor tell thou not all that thou hears;
Discover thou not thine own deed,
For no mirth, nor for no reward;
With fair speech thou might have thy will,
With it thou might thy self spoil.

When thou meetest a worthy man,
Cap and hood thou hold not on;
In church, in market, or in the gate,
Do him reverance after his state,
If thou goest with a worthier man
Then thyself thou art one,
Let thy foremost shoulder follow his back,
For that is nurture without lack;
When he doth speak, hold thee still,
When he hath done, say for thy will,
In thy speech that thou be discreet,
And what thou sayest consider thee well;
But deprive thou not him his tale,
Neither at the wine nor at the ale.
Christ then of his high grace,
Save you both wit and space,
Well this book to know and read,
Heaven to have for your reward.
Amen! Amen! so mote it be!
So say we all for charity.

The Regius Poem
Original Text

Hic inciplunt constitucines artis
gemetriae secundum Eucyldem.

Whose wol bothe wel rede and loke,
He may fynde wryte yn olde boke
Of grete lordys, and eke ladyysse,
That had mony chyldryn y-fere, y-wisse;
And hade no rentys to fynde hem wyth,
Nowther yn towne, ny felde, ny fryth:
A cownsel togeder they cowthe hem take,
To ordeyne for these chldryn sake,
How they myzth best lede here lyfe
Withoute gret desese, care, and stryge;
And most for the multytude that was
   comynge
Of here chyldrn after here zndynge.
(They) sende thenne after grete clerkys,
To techyn hem thenne gode werkys;

And pray we hem for our Lorsys sake,
To oure chyldryn sum werke to make,
That they myzth gete here lyvnge therby,
Bothe wel and onestlyche, ful sycurly.
Yn that tyme, throzgh good gemetry,
Thys onest craft of good masonry
Wes ordeynt and made yn thys manere,
Y-cownterfetyd of thys clerkys y-fere;
At these lordys prayers they cownterfetyd
   gemetry,
And zaf hyt the nane of masonry,
For the moste oneste craft of alle.
These lordys chyldryn therto dede falle,
To lurne of hym the craft of gemetry,
The wheche he made ful curysly;

Throzgh fadrys prayers and modrys also,
Thys onest craft he putte hem to.
He that lernede best, and were of oneste,
And passud hys felows yn curyste;
Zef yn that craft he dede hym passe,
He schulde have more worschepe then the
   lasse.
Thys grete clerkys name was clept
   Euclyde,
Hys name hyt spradde ful wondur wyde.
Zet thys grete clerke more ordeynt he
To hym that was herre yn thys degre,
That he schulde teche the symplyst of
   (wytte)
Yn that onest craft to be parfytte;
And so uchon schulle techyn othur,
And love togeder as syster and brothur.

Forthermore zet that ordeynt he,
Mayster y-called so schulde he be;
So that he were most y-worschepede,
Thenne sculde he be so y-clepede:
But mason schulde never won other calle,
Withynne the craft amongus hem alle,
Ny soget, nu servant, my dere
   brother,
Thazht he be not so perfyt as ys another;
Uchon sculle calle other felows by cuthe,
For cause they come of ladyes burthe.
On thys maner, throz good wytte of
   gemetry,
Bygan furst the craft of masonry:
The clerk Euclyde on thys wyse hyt fonde,
Thys craft of gemetry yn Egypte londe.

Yn Egypte he tawzhte hyt ful wyde,
Yn dyvers londe on every syde;
Mony erys afterwarde, y understonde,
Zer that the craft com ynto thys londe.
Thys craft com ynto Englond, as y zow
   say,
Yn tyme of good kynge Adelstonus day;
He made tho bothe halle and eke bowre,
Any hye templus of gret honowre,
To sportyn hym yn bothe day and nyzth,
An to worschepe hys God with alle hys
   myzth. Thys goode lorde loved thys craft
   ful wel,
And purposud to strenthyn hyt every del,
For dyvers defawtys that yn the craft he
fonde; He sende about ynto the londe

After alle the masonus of the crafte,
To come to hym ful evene strazfte,
For to amende these defautys alle
By good consel, zef hyt mytzth falle.
A semble thenne he cowthe let make
Of dyvers lordis, yn here state,
Dukys erlys and barnes also.
Kynzthys, sqwyers, and mony mo,
And the grete burges of that syte,
They were ther alle yn here degre;
These were uchon algate,
To ordeyne for these masonus astate.
Ther they sowzton by here wytte,
How they myzthyn governe hytte:

Fyftene artyculus they ther sowzton,
And fyftene poyntys ther they wrozton.

Hic incipit articulus primus.

The furste artycul of thys gemetry:—
The mayster mason moste be ful securly
Bothe stedefast, trusty, and trwe,
Hyt schal hum never thenne arewe:
And pay thy felows after the coste,
As vytaylys goth thenne, wel thou woste;
And pay them trwly apon thy fay,
What that they deserven may;
And to her hure take no more,
But what they mowe serve fore;
And spare, nowther for love ny drede,

Of nowther partys to take no mede;
Of lord ny felow, whether he be,
Of hem thou take no maner of fe;
And as a jugge stonde upryzth;
And thenne thou dost to bothe good ryzth;
And trwly do thys whersever thou gost,
Thy worschep, thy profyt, hyt shcal be most.

Articulus secundus.

The secunde artycul of good masonry,
As ze mowe hyt here hyr specyaly,
That every mayster, that ys a mason,
Most ben at the generale congregacyon,
So that he hyt resonably z-tolde
Where that the semble schal be holde;

And to that semble he most nede gon,
But he have a resenabul skwsacyon,
Or but he be unbuxom to that craft,
Or with falssehed ys over-raft,
Or ellus sekenes hath hym so stronge,
That he may not come hem amonge;
That ys a skwsacyon, good and abulle,
To that semble withoute fabulle.

Articulus tercius.

The thrydde artycul for sothe hyt ysse,
That the mayster take to no prentysse,
But he have good seuerans to dwelle
Seven zer with hym, as y zow telle,
Hys craft to lurne, that ys profytable;

Withynne lasse he may not ben able
To lordys profyt, ny to hls owne,
As ze mowe knowe by good resowne.

Articulus quartus.

The fowrthe artycul thys moste be,
That the mayster hym wel be-se,
That he no bondemon prentys make,
Ny for no covetyse do hym take;
For the lord that he ys bonde to,
May fache the prentes whersever he go.

Zef yn the logge he were y-take,
Muche desese hyt myzth ther make,
And suche case hyt myzth befalle,
That hyt myzth greve summe or alle.

For alle the masonus tht ben there
Wol stonde togedur hol y-fere.
Zef suche won yn that craft schulde dwelle,
Of dyvers desesys ze myzth telle:
For more zese thenne, and of honeste,
Take a prentes of herre degre.
By olde tyme wryten y fynde
That the prentes schulde be of gentyl
kynde; And so symtyme grete lordys blod
Toke thys gemetry, that ys ful good.

Articulus quintus.

The fyfthe artycul ys swythe good,
So that the prentes be of lawful blod;
The mayster schal not, for no vantage,

Make no prentes that ys outrage;
Hyt ys to mene, as ze mowe here,
That he have hys lymes hole alle y-fere;
To the craft hyt were gret schame,
To make an halt mon and a lame,
For an unperfyt mon of suche blod
Schulde do the craft but lytul good.
Thus ze mowe knowe everychon,
The craft wolde have a myzhty mon;
A maymed mom he hath no myzht,
Ze mowe hyt knowe long zer nyzht.

Articulus sextus.

The syzte artycul ze mowe not mysse,

That the mayster do the lord no
pregedysse, To take of the lord, for hyse
    prentyse,
Also muche as hys felows don, yn all vyse.
For yn that craft they ben ful perfyt,
So ys not he, ze mowe sen hyt.
Also hyt were azeynus good reson,
To take hys hure, as hys felows don.
Thys same artycul, yn thys casse,
Juggythe the prentes to take lasse
Thenne hys felows, that ben ful perfyt.
Yn dyvers maters, conne qwyte hyt,
The mayster may hls prentes so enforme,
That hys hure may crese ful zurne,

And, zer hys terme come to an ende,
Hys hure may ful wel amende.

Articulus septimus.

The seventhe artycul that ys now here,
Ful wel wol tell zow, alle y-fere,

That no mayster, for favour ny drede,
Schal no thef nowther clothe ny fede.
Theves he schal herberon never won,
Ny hym that hath y-quellude a mon,
Wy thylike that hath a febul name,
Lest hyt wolde turne the craft to schame.

Articulus octavus.

The eghte artycul schewet zow so,
That the mayster may hyt wel do,
Zef that he have any mon of crafte,
And be not also perfyt as he auzte,
He may hym change sone anon,
And take for hym a perfytur mon.
Suche a mon, throze rechelaschepe,
Myzth do the craft schert worschepe.

Articulus nonus.

The nynthe artycul schewet ful welle,
That the mayster be both wyse and felle;
That no werke he undurtake,
But he conne bothe hyt ende and make;
And that hyt be to the lordes profyt also,
And to hys craft, whersever he go;
And that the grond be wel y-take,
That hyt nowther fle ny grake.

Artculus decimus.

The then the artycul ys for to knowe,
Amonge the craft, to hye and lowe,
There schal no mayster supplante other,
But be togeder as systur and brother,
Yn thys curyus craft, alle and som,
That longuth to a maystur mason.
Ny he schal not supplante non other mon,
That hath y-take a werke hym uppon,
Yn peyne therof that ys so stronge,
That peyseth no lasse thenne ten ponge,
But zef that he be gulty y-fonde,
That toke furst the werke on honde;
For no mon yn masonry
Schal not supplante othur securly,
But zef that hyt be so y-wrozth,
That hyt turne the werke to nozth;
Thenne may a mason that werk crave,
To the lordes profzt hyt for to save;
Yn suche a case but hyt do falle,
Ther schal no mason medul withalle.
Forsothe he that begynnth the gronde,
And he be a mason goode and sonde,
For hath hyt sycurly yn hys mynde

To brynge the werke to ful good ende.

Articulus undecimus.

The eleventhe artycul y telle the,
That he ys bothe fayr and fre;
For he techyt, by hys myzth,
That no mason schulde worche be nyszth,
But zef hyt be yn practesynge of wytte,
Zef that y cowthe amende hytte.

Articulus duodecimus.

The twelfthe artycul ys of hye honeste
To zevery mason, whersever he be;
He schal no hys felows werk deprave,
Zef that he wol hys honeste save;
With honest wordes he hyt comende,

By the wytte that God the dede sende;
But hyt amende by al that thou may,
Bytwynne zow bothe withoute nay.

Articulus xiijus.

The threttene artycul, so God me save,
Ys zef that the mayster a prentes have,
Enterlyche thenne that he hym teche,
And meserable poyntes that he hym reche,
That he the craft abelyche may conne,
Whersever he go undur the sonne.

Articulus xiiijus.

The fowrtene artycul, by good reson,
Scheweth the mayster how he schal don;
He schal no prentes to hym take,
Byt dyvers curys he have to make,
That he may, withynne hys terme,
Of hym dyvers poyntes may lurne.

Articulus quindecimus.

The fyftene artycul maketh an ende,
For to the mayster he ys a frende;
To lere hym so, that for no mon,
No fals mantenans he take hym apon,
Ny maynteine hys felows yn here synne,
For no good that he myzth wynne;
Ny no fals sware sofre hem to make,
For drede of here sowles sake;
Lest hyt wolde turne the craft to schame,
And hymself to mechul blame.

Plures Constituciones.

At thys semble were poyntes y-ordeynt mo,
Of grete lordys and maystrys also,
That whose wol conne thys craft and com
   to astate,
He most love wel God, and holy churche
   algate,

And hys mayster also, that he ys wythe,
Whersever he go, yn fylde or frythe;
And thy felows thou love also,
For that they craft wol that thou do.

Secundus punctus.

The secunde poynt, as y zow say,
That the mason worche apon the werk day,
Also trwly, as he con or may,

To deserve hys huyre for the halyday,
And trwly to labrun on hys dede,
Wel deserve to have hys mede.

Tercius punctus.

The thrydde poynt most be severele,
With the prentes knowe hyt wele,
Hys mayster conwsel he kepe and close,
And hys felows by hys goode purpose;
The prevetyse of the chamber telle he no
     man,
Ny yn the logge whatsever they done;
Whatsever thou heryst, or syste hem do,
Tells hyt no mon, whersever thou go;
The conwesel of halls, and zeke of bowre,

Kepe hyt wel to gret honowre,
Lest hyt wolde torne thyself to blame,
And brynge the craft ynto gret schame.

Quartus punctus.

The fowrthe poynt techyth us alse,
That no mon to hys craft be false;
Errour he schal mayntelne none
Azeynus the craft, but let hyt gone;
Ny no pregedysse he schal not do
To hys mayster, ny hys felows also;
And thazth the prentes be under awe,
Zet he wolde have the same lawe.

Quintus punctus.

The fyfthe poynte ys, withoute nay,
That whenne the mason taketh hys pay
Of the mayster, y-ordent to hym,
Ful makely y-take so most hyt byn;
Zet most the mayster, by good resone,
Warne hem lawfully byfore none,
Zef he nulle okepye hem no more,
As he hath y-done ther byfore;
Azeynus thys ordyr he may not stryve,
Zef he thenke wel for to thryve.

Sextus punctus.

The syxte poynt ys ful zef to knowe,
Bothe to hye and eke to lowe,

For suche case hyt myzth befalle;
Am nge the masonus, summe or alle,
Throwghe envye, or dedly hate,
Ofte aryseth ful gret debate.
Thenne owyth the mason, zef that he may,
Putte hem bothe under a day;
But loveday zet schul they make none;
Tyl that the werke day be clene a-gone;
Apon the holyday ze mowe wel take
Leyser y-nowzgth loveday to make,
Lest that hyt wolde the werke day
Latte here werke for suche afray;
To suche ende thenne that ze hem drawe,

That they stonde wel yn Goddes lawe.

Septimus punctus.

The seventhe poynt he may wel mene,
Of wel longe lyf that God us lene,
As hyt dyscryeth wel opunly,
Thou schal not by thy maysters wyf ly,
Ny by thy felows, yn no maner wyse,
Lest thy craft wolde the despyse;
Ny by thy felows concubyne,
No more thou woldest he dede by thyne,
The peyne thereof let hyt be ser,
That he be prentes ful seven zer,
Zef he forfete yn eny of hem,
So y-chasted thenne most he ben;
Ful mekele care myzth ther begynne,
For suche a fowle dedely synne.

Octavus punctus.

The eghte poynt, he may be sure,
Zef thou hast y-taken any cure,
Under they mayster thou be trwe,
For that poynt thou schalt never arewe;
A trwe medyater thou most nede be
To thy mayster, and thy felows fre;
Do trwly al....that thou myzth,
To both partyes, and that ys good ryzth.

Nonus punctus.

The nynthe pount we schul hym calle,
That he be stwarde of oure halle,
Zef that ze ben yn chambur y-fere,
Uchon serve other, with mylde chere;
Jentul felows, ze moste hyt knowe,
For to be stwardus alle o rowe,
Weke after weke wihoute dowte,
Stwardus to ben so alle abowte,
Lovelyche to serven uchon othur,
As thawgh they were syster and brother;
Ther schal never won on other costage
Fre hymself to no vantage,
But every mon schal be lyche fre

Yn that costage, so moste hyt be;
Loke that thou pay wele every mon algate,
That thou hast y-bowzht any vytayles ate,
That no cravynge be y-mad to the,
Ny to thy felows, yn no degre,
To mon or to wommon, whether he be,
Pay hem wel and trwly, for that wol we;
Therof on thy felow trwe record thou take,
For that good pay as thou dost make,
Lest hyt wolde thy felowe schame,
Any brynge thyself ynto gret blame.
Zet good acowntes he most make
Of suche godes as he hath y-take,

Of thy felows goodes that thou hast
   spende,
Wher, and how, and to what ende;
Suche acowntes thou most come to,
Whenne thy felows wollen that thou do.

Decimus punctus.

The tenthe poynt presentyeth wel god lyf,
To lyven withoute care and stryf;
For and the mason lyve amysse,
And yn hys werke be false, y-wysse,

And thorwz suche a false skewysasyon
May sclawndren hys felows oute reson,
Throwz false sclawnder of suche fame

May make the craft kachone blame.
Zef he do the craft suche vylany,
Do hym no favour thenne securly,
Ny maynteine not hym yn wyked lyf,
Lest hyt wolde turne to care and stryf;
But zet hym ze schul not delayme,
But that ze schullen hym constrayne,
For to apere whersevor ze wylle,
Whar that ze wolen, lowde, or stylle;
To the nexte semble ze schul hym calle,
To apere byfore hys felows alle,
And but zef he wyl byfore hem pere,

The crafte he moste nede forswere;
He schal thenne be chasted after the lawe
That was y-fownded by olde dawe.

Punctus undecimus

The eleventhe poynt ys of good
   dyscrecyoun,
As ze mowe knowe by good resoun;
A mason, and he thys craft wel con,
That syzth hys felow hewen on a ston,
And ys yn poynt to spylle that ston,
Amende hyt sone, zef that thou con,
And tech hym thenne hyt to amende,
That the lordys werke be not y-schende,
And teche hym esely hyt to amende,

With fayre wordes, that God the hath
   lende;
For hys sake that sytte above,
With swete wordes noresche hyn love.

Punctus duodecimus.

The twelthe poynt of gret ryolte,
Ther as the semble y-hole schal be,
Ther schul be maystrys and felows also,
And other grete lordes mony mo;
There schal be the scheref of that contre,
And also the meyr of that syte,
Knyztes and sqwyers ther schul be,
And other alderman, as ze schul se;
Suche ordynance as they maken there,

They schul maynte hyt hol y-fere
Azeynus that mon, whatsever he be,
That longuth to the craft bothe fayr and
   free.
Zef he any stryf azeynus hem make,
Ynto here warde he schal be take.

Xlljus punctus.

The threntethe poynt ys to us ful luf.
He schal swere never to be no thef,
Ny soker hym yn hys fals craft,
For no good that he hath byraft,
And thou mowe hyt knowe or syn,
Nowther for hys good, ny for hys kyn.

Xllljus punctus.

The fowrtethe poynt ys ful good lawe
To hym that wold ben under awe;
A good trwe othe he most ther swere
To hys mayster and hys felows that ben
   there;
He most be stedefast and trwe also
To alle thys ordynance, whersever he go,
And to hys lyge lord the kynge,
To be trwe to hym, overalle thynge,
And alle these poyntes hyr before
To hem thou most nede by y-swore,
And alle schul swere the same ogth
Of the masonus, ben they luf, ben they
   loght,
To alle these poyntes hyr byfore,

That hath ben ordeynt by ful good lore.
And they schul enquere every mon
On his party, as wyl as he con,
Zef any mon mowe by y-fownde gulty
Yn any of these poyntes spesyaly;
And whad he be, let hym be sowzht,
And to the semble let hym be browzht.

Quindecimus punctus.

The fiftethe poynt ys of ful good lore,
For hem that schul ben ther y-swore,
Suche ordynance at the semble wes layd
Of grete lordes and maysters byforesayd;
For thylke that ben unbuxom, y-wysse,
Azeynus the ordynance that there ysse
Of these artyculus, that were y-meved
    there,
Of grete lordes and masonus al y-fere.
And zef they ben y-preved opunly
Byfore that semble, by and by,
And for here gultes no mendys wol make,
Thenne most they nede the craft forsake;
And so masonus craft they schul refuse,
And swere hyt never more for to use.
But zef that they wol mendys make,
Azayn to the craft they schul never take;
And zef that they nul not do so,
The scheref schal come hem sone to.

And putte here bodyes yn duppe prison,
For the trespasse that they hav y-don,
And take here goodes and here cattelle
Ynto the kynges hond, every delle,
And lete hem dwelle there full stylle,
Tyl hyt be oure lege kynges wylle.

Alia ordinacio artis gemetriae.

They ordent ther a semble to be
    y-holde
Every zer, whersever they wolde,
To amende the defautes, zef any where
    fonde
Amonge the craft withynne the londe;
Uche zer or thrydde zer hyt schuld be
    holde,

Yn every place whersever they wolde;
Tyme and place most be ordeynt also,
Yn what place they schul semble to.
Alle the men of craft ther they most ben,
And other grete lordes, as ze mowe sen,
To mende the fautes that buth y-spoke,
Zef that eny of hem ben thenne y-broke,
Ther they schullen ben alle y-swore,
That longuth to thys craftes lore,
To kepe these statutes everychon,
That ben y-ordeynt by kynge Aldelston;
These statutes that y have hyr y-fonde

Y chulle they ben holde throzh my londe,
For the worsche of my rygolte,
That y have by my dygnyte.
Also at every semble that ze holde,
That ze come to zowre lyge kyng bolde,
Bysechynge hym of hys hye grace,
To stone with zow yn every place,

To conferme the statutes of kynge
    Adelston,
That he ordeydnt to thys craft by good
    reson.

Ars quatuor coronatorum.

Pray we now to God almyzht,
And to hys moder Mary bryzht,

That we mowe keepe these artyculus here,
And these poynts wel al y-fere,
As dede these holy martyres fowre,
That yn thys craft were of gret honoure;
They were as gode masonus as on erthe
    schul go,
Gravers and ymage-makers they were
    also.
For they were werkemen of the beste,
The emperour hade to hem gret luste;
He wylned of hem a ymage to make,
That mowzh be worscheped for his sake;
Such mawmentys he hade yn hys dawe,
To turne the pepul from Crystus lawe.

But they were stedefast yn Crystes lay,
And to here Craft, withouten nay;
They loved wel God and alle hys lore,
And weren yn hys serves ever more,
Trwe men they were yn that dawe,
And lyved wel y Goddus lawe;
They thozght no mawmetys for to make,
For no good that they myzth take,
To levyn on that mawmetys for here
    God,
They nolde do so, thawz he were
    wod;
For they nolde not forsake here trw fay.

An beyleve on hys falsse lay,
The emperour let take hem sone anone,
And putte hem ynto a dep presone;
The sarre he penest hem yn that
    plase,
The more yoye wes to hem of Cristus
    grace.
Thenne when he sye no nother won,
To dethe he lette hem thenne gon;
By the bok he may kyt schowe,
In the legent of scanctorum,
The names of quatuor coronatorum.

Here fest wol be, withoute nay,
After Alle Halwen the eyght day.
Ze mow here as y do rede,
That mony zeres after, for gret drede
That Noees flod wes alle y-ronne,
The tower of Babyloyne was begonne,
Also playne werke of lyme and ston,
As any mon schulde loke uppon;

So long and brod hyt was begonne,
Seven myle the hezghte schadweth the
    sonne,
Kyng Nabogodonosor let hyt make,
To gret strenthe for monus sake,

Thazgh suche a flod azayne schulde come,
Over the werke hyt schulde not nome;
For they hadde so hye pride, with stronge
    bost,
Alle that werke therefore was y-lost;
An angele smot hem so with dyveres
    speche,
Tht never won wyste what other
    schuld reche.
Mony eres after, the goode clerk Euclyde
Tazghte the craft of gemetre wonder
    wyde,
So he deed that tyme other also,
Of dyvers craftes mony mo.
Throzgh hye grace of Crist yn heven,
He commensed yn the syens seven;

Gramatica ys the furste syens y-wysse,
Dialetica the secunde, so have y blysse,
Rethorica the thrydde, withoute nay,
Musica ys the fowrth, as y zow say,

Astromia ys the V, by my snowte,
Arsmetica the VI, withoute dowte
Gemetria the seventhe maketh an ende,
For he ys bothe make and hende.
Gramer forsothe ys the rote,
Whose wyl lurne on the boke;
But art passeth yn hys degre,
As the fryte doth the rote of the tre;

Rethoryk metryth with orne speche
    amonge,
And musyke hyt ys a swete song;
Astronomy nombreth, my dere brother,
Arsmetyk scheweth won thyng that ys
    another,
Gemetre the seventh syens hyt ysse,
That con deperte falshed from trewthe y-
    wys.
These bene the syens seven,
Whose useth hem wel, he may han heven.
Now dere chyldren, by zowre wytte,
Pride and covetyse that ze leven, hytte,
And taketh hede to goode dyscrecyon,
And to good norter, whersever ze com.
Now y pray zow take good hede,

For thys ze most kenne nede,
But much more ze moste wyten,
Thenne ze fynden hyr y-wryten.
Zef the fayle therto wytte,
Pray to God to send the hytte;
For Crist hymself, he techet ous

That holy churche ys Goddes hous,
That ys y-mad for nothynge ellus
But for to pray yn, as the bok tellus;
Ther te pepul schal gedur ynne,
To pray and wepe for here synne.
Loke thou come not to churche late,
for to speke harlotry by the gate;

Thenne tho churche when thou dost fare,
Have yn thy mynde ever mare
To worschepe thy lord God bothe day and
    nyzth,
With all thy wyttes, and eke thy myzth.
To the churche dore when thou dost come,
Of that holy water ther sum thow nome,
For every drope thou felust ther
Qwenchet a venyal synne, be thou ser.
But furst thou most do down thy hode,
For hyse love that dyed on the rode.
Into the churche when thou dost gon,
Pulle uppe thy herte to Crist, anon;

Uppon the rode thou loke uppe the,
And knele down fayre on bothe thy knen;
Then pray to hym so hyr to worche,
After the lawe of holy churche,

For to kepe the comandementes ten,
That God zaf to alle men;
And pray to hym with mylde steven
To kepe the from the synnes seven,
That thou hyr mowe, yn thy lyve,
Kepe the wel from care and stryve,
Forthermore he grante the grace,
In heaven blysse to hav a place.

In holy churche lef nyse wordes
Of lewed speche, and fowle bordes,
And putte away alle vanyte,
And say thy pater noster and thyn ave;
Loke also thou make no bere,
But ay to be yn thy prayere;
Zef thou wolt not thyselve pray,
Latte non other mon by no way.
In that place nowther sytte ny stonde,
But knele fayre down on the gronde,
And, when the Gospel me rede schal,

Fayre thou stonde up fro the wal,
And blesse the fayre, zef that thou conne,
When gloria tibi is begonne;
And when the gospel ys y-done,
Azayn thou myzth knele adown;
On bothe thy knen down thou falle,
For hyse love that bowzht us alle;
And when thou herest the belle rynge
To that holy sakerynge,
Knele ze most, bothe zynge and olde,
And bothe zor hondes fayr upholde,
And say thenne yn thys manere,

Fayr and softe, withoute bere;
"Jhesu Lord, welcom thou be,
Yn forme of bred, as y the se.
Now Jhesu, for thyn holy name,
Schulde me fro synne and schame,
Schryff and hosel thou grant me bo,
Zer that y schal hennus go,
And very contrycyon of my synne,
Taht y never, Lord, dye therynne;
And, as thou were of a mayde y-bore,
Sofre me never to be y-lore;
But when y schal hennus wende,

Grante me the blysse withoute ende;
Amen! amen! so mot hyt be!
Now, swete lady, pray for me."
Thus thou myzht say, or sum other
     thynge,
When thou knelust at the sakerynge.
For covetyse after good, spare thou nought
To worschepe hym that alle hath wrought;

For glad may a mon that day ben,
That onus yn the day may hym sen;
Hyt ys so muche worthe, withoute nay,
The vertu therof no mon telle may;
But so meche good doth that syht,

As seynt Austyn telluth ful ryht,
That day thou syst Goddus body,
Tou schalt have these, ful securly:—
Mete and drynke at thy nede,
Non that day schal the gnede;
Ydul othes, an wordes bo,
God forzeveth the also;
Soden deth, that ylke day,
The dar not drede by no way;
Also that day, y the plyht,
Thou schalt not lese thy eye syht;
And uche fote that thou gost then,

That holy syht for to sen,
They schul be told to stonde yn stede,
When thou hast therto gret nede;
That messongere, the angele Gabryelle,
Wol kepe hem to the ful welle.
From thys mater now y may passe,
To telle mo medys of the masse:
To churche come zet, zef thou may,
And here thy masse uche day;
Zef thou mowe not come to churche,
Wher that ever thou doste worche,
When thou herest to masse knylle,

Pray to God with herte stylle,
To zeve the part of that servyse,
That yn churche ther don yse.
Forthermore zet, y wol zow preche
To zowre felows, hyt for to teche,
When thou comest byfore a lorde,

Yn halle, yn bowre, or at the borde,
Hod or cappe that thou of do.
Zer thou come hym allynge to;
Twyes or thryes, withoute dowte,
To that lord thou moste lowte;
With thy ryzth kne let hyt be do,

Thyn owne worschepe thou save so.
Holde of thy cappe, and hod also,
Tyl thou have leve hyt on to do.
Al the whyle thou spekest with hym,
Fayre and lovelyche berte up thy chyn;
So, affter the norter of the boke,
Yn hys face lovely thou loke.
Fot and hond, thou kepe ful stylle
From clawynge and trypynge, ys sckylle;
From spyttynge and synftynge kepe the
     also,
By privy avoydans let hyt go.
And zef that thou be wyse and felle,

Thou hast gret nede to governe the welle,
Ynto the halle when thou dost wende,
Amonges the genteles, good and hende.
Presume not to hye for nothynge,
For thyn nye blod, ny thy connynge,
Nowther to sytte, ny to lene,
That ys norther good and clene,
Let not thy cowntenans therfore abate,
Forsothe, good norter wol save thy state.
Fader and moder, whatsever they be,
Wel ys the chyld that wel may the,
Yn halle, yn chamber, wher thou dost gon;

Gode maneres maken a mon.
To the nexte degre loke wysly,
To do hem reverans by and by;
Do hem zet no reverans al o-rowe,
But zef that thou do hem know.
To the mete when thou art y-sette,
Fayre and onestelyche tou ete hytte;
Fyrst loke that thyn honden be clene,
And that thy knyf be scharpe and kene;
And kette thy bred al at thy mete,
Ryzth as hyt may be ther y-ete.
Zef thou sytte by a worththyur mon,

Then thy selven thou art won,
Sofre hym fyrst to toyche the mete,
Zer thyself to hyt reche,
To the fayrest mossel thou myzht not strike,
Thaght that thou do hyt well lyke;
Kepe thyn hondes, fayr and wel,
From fowle smogynge of thy towel;
Theron thou schalt not thy nese snyte,
Ny at the mete thy tothe thou pyke;
To depe yn the coppe thou myzght not
synke,
Thagh thou have good wyl to drynke,
Lest thyn enyn wolde wattryn therby—

The were hyt no curtesy.
Loke yn thy mowth ther be no mete,
When thou begynnyst to drynke or speke.
When thou syst any mon drynkynge,
That taketh hed to thy carpynge,
Sone anonn thou sese thy tale,
Whether he drynke wyn other ale.
Loke also thou scorne no mon,
Yn what degre thou syst hym gon;
Ny thou schalt no mon deprave,
Zef thou wolt thy worschepe save;
For suche worde myzht ther outberste,

That myzht make the sytte yn evel reste.
Close thy honde yn thy fyste,
And kepe the wel from "had-y-wyste."
Yn chamber, amonge the ladyes bryght,
Holde thy tonge and spende thy syght;
Lawze thou not with no gret cry,
Ny make no ragynge with rybody.
Play thou not but with they peres,
Ny tel thou not al that thou heres;
Dyskever thou not thyn owne dede,
For no merthe, ny for no mede;

With fayr speche thou myght have the wylle,
With hyt thou myght thy selven spylle.

When thou metyst a worthy mon,
Cappe and hod thou holle not on;
Yn churche, yn chepyns, or yn the gate,
Do hym reverans after hys state.
Zef thou gost with a worthyor mon
Then thyselven thou art won,
Let thy forther schulder sewe hys backe,
For that ys norter withoute lacke;
When he doth speke, holte the stylle,
When he hath don, sey for thy wylle,
Yn thy speche that thou be felle,
And what thou sayst avyse the welle;
But byref thou not hym hys tale,
Nowther at the wyn, ny at the ale.
Cryst them of hys hye grace,
Zeve sow bothe wytte and space,
Wel thys boke to conne and rede,
Heven to have for zowre mede,
Amen! amen! so mot hyt be!
Say we so alle per charyte.

Appendix II

The Charges from the Roberts Constitutions

The early masonic initiation consisted largely of reading a list of "charges," to which the new member was expected to subscribe. The "Book" to which they refer was apparently a Bible, on which the initiate placed his hand while the charges were read.

Later versions of these charges, such as those in Anderson's *Constitutions*, reveal the fraternal and speculative nature the organization had assumed. Earlier versions, such as those in Roberts' *Constitutions*, show indications that they were originally formulated to serve an operative craft.

The version presented here is the so called *Roberts Constitutions*, which was first published in 1722. It appeared in serial form in a newspaper, *The Post Man and The Historical Account*, and later as a pamphlet. The two are basically the same but differ slightly in content. An examination of their texts indicates that they were copied independently of each other from a copy of the Gothic Constitutions that was transcribed around 1660.

Since non-operative Masons are first documented around 1600, it appears that this version of the charges came down relatively unchanged from the operative period but was used by the early speculative Masons. Thus it shows us something of the state of the Craft during the transition period.

The text reproduced here is drawn from McLeod's *The Old Gothic Constitutions* and Knoop, et al, *Early Masonic Pamphlets*. Both works feature commentary as well as the texts of this and other early documents, and readers are referred to them for more information.

The Charges From
The Roberts Constitutions

My loving and respected Friends and Brethren, I humbly beseech you, as you love your Soul's eternal Welfare, your Credit, and your Country's Good, to be very Careful in Observation of these Articles that I am about to read to this Deponent; for ye are obliged to perform them as well as he, so hoping of your Care herein, I will, by God's Grace, begin the Charge.

I. I am to admonish you to honour God in his holy Church; that you use no Heresy, Schism and Error in your Understandings, or discredit Men's Teachings.

II. To be true to our Sovereign Lord the King, his Heirs and lawful Successors; committing no Treason, Misprision of Treason, or Felony; and if any Man shall commit Treason that you know of, you shall forthwith give Notice thereof to his Majesty, his Privy Counsellors, or some other Person that hath Commission to enquire thereof.

III. You shall be true to your Fellows and Brethren of the Science of *Masonry*, and do unto them as you would be done unto.

IV. You shall keep Secret the obscure and intricate Parts of the Science, not disclosing them to any but such as study and use the same.

V. You shall do your Work truly and faithfully, endeavouring the Profit and Advantage of him that is Owner of the said Work.

VI. You shall call *Masons* your Fellows and Brethren, without Addition of Knaves, or other bad Language.

VII. You shall not take your Neighbor's Wife Willinously, not his Daughter, nor his Maid or his Servant, to use ungodly.

VIII. You shall not carnally lye with any Woman that is belonging to the House where you are at Table.

IX. You shall truly pay for your Meat and Drink, where you are at Table.

X. You shall not undertake any Man's Work, knowing yourself unable or unexpert to perform and effect the same, that no Discredit or Aspersion may be imputed to the Science, or the Lord or Owner of the said Work be any wise prejudic'd.

XI. You shall not take any Work to do at excessive or unreasonable Rates, to deceive the Owner thereof, but so as he may be truly and faithfully serv'd with his own Goods.

XII. You shall so take your Work, that thereby you may live honestly, and pay your Fellows the Wages as the Science doth require.

XIII. You shall not supplant any of your Fellows of their Work, (that is to say) if he or any of them hath or have taken any Work upon him or them, or he or they stand Master or Masters of any Lord or Owner's Work, that you shall not put him or them out from the said Work, altho' you perceive him or them unable to finish the same.

XIV. You shall not take any Apprentice to serve you in the said Science of *Masonry*, under the Term of Seven Years; nor any but such as are descended of good and honest Parentage, that no Scandal may be imputed to the said Science of *Masonry*.

XV. You shall not take upon you to make any one *Mason*, without the Privity or Consent of six, or five at least of your Fellows, and not but such as is Freeborn, and whose Parents live in good Fame and Name, and that his right and perfect Limbs, and able of Body to attend to the said Science.

XVI. You shall not pay any of your Fellows more Money than he or they have deserv'd, that you be not deceiv'd by slight or false Working, and the Owner thereof much wrong'd.

XVII. You shall not slander any of your Fellows behind their Backs, to empair their Temporal Estate or good Name.

XVIII. You shall not, without very urgent Cause, answer your Fellow doggedly or ungodly, but as becomes a loving Brother in the said Science.

XIX. You shall duly reverence your Fellows, that the Bond of Charity and mutual Love may continue stedfast and stable amongst you.

XX. You shall not (except in *Christmas* time) use any lawless Games, as Dice, Cards or such like.

XXI. You shall not frequent any Houses of Bawdery, or be a Pander to any of your Fellows or others, which will be a great Scandal to the Science.

XXII. You shall not go out to drink by Night, or if Occasion happen that you must go, you shall not stay past Eight of the Clock, having some of your Fellows, or one at the least, to bear you Witness of the honest Place you were in, and your good Behaviour, to avoid Scandal.

XXIII. You shall come to the Yearly Assembly, if you know where it is kept, being within Ten Miles of your Abode, submitting your self to the Censure of your Fellows, wherein you have erred to make Satisfaction, or else to defend by Order of the King's Laws.

XXIV. You shall not make any Mould, Square, or Rule to mould Stones withal, but such as are allowed by the Fraternity.

XXV. You shall set Strangers at Work, having Employment for them, at least a Fortnight, and pay them their Wages truly, and if you want Work for them, then you shall relieve them with Money to defray their reasonable Charges to the next Lodge.

XXVI. You shall truly attend your Work, and truly end the same, whether it be Task or Journey-Work, if you may have the Payment and Wages according to your Agreement made with the Master or Owner thereof.

All these Articles and Charge, which I have now read unto you, you shall well and truly observe, perform and keep to the best of your Power, and Knowledge, So help you God, and the true and Holy Contents of this Book.

And moreover I, A.B. do here in the Presence of God Almighty, and of my Fellows and Brethren here present, promise and declare, That I will not at any Time hereafter by any Act or Circumstance whatever, directly or indirectly, publish, discover, reveal or make known any of these Secrets, Privities or Councils of the Fraternity or Fellowship of Free Masons, which at this time, or at any time hereafter shall be made known unto me. So help me God, and the true and holy Contents of this Book.

Appendix III

The Grand Mystery Of Free-Masons Discover'd

Although the *Grand Mystery* was published only two years after the *Roberts Constitutions* (see Appendix II), it shows a much more fraternal character. In it, we have an indication of what Freemasonry had become by the time the Grand Lodge of England was formed.

It is likely that the catechism at the beginning of the *Grand Mystery* was the ritual used to open lodge meetings. Several of its questions and answers are similar to those used for the same purpose in the modern ritual.

It is interesting that the Word given in the last question and answer is, "Adieu," the French word for "farewell." The literal meaning of this word is "to God," giving it a dual meaning that would have made it especially well suited to ritual use.

The text presented here is from a photographic reproduction of the original.

THE GRAND

MYSTERY

OF

FREE-MASONS

DISCOVER'D.

WHEREIN

Are the feveral QUESTIONS put to them at their Meetings and In-ftallations:

AS ALSO

Their OATH, HEALTH, SIGNS, and POINTS, to know each other by.

As they were found in the Cuftody of a FREE-MASON who Dyed fuddenly.

AND

Now Publifh'd for the Information of the PUBLICK.

Ambubajarum collegia, Pharmacapolæ,
Mendici, Medici, balatrones, hoc genus omne.

HORAT.

- - - - - - *Mulus fcabit Mulum.* - - - - - -

LONDON:
Printed for T. PAYNE near *Stationer's- Hall.* 1724.
(Price Six Pence.)

The Grand Mystery
of Free-Masons Discover'd

PREFACE.

This Piece having been found in the Custody of a FREE-MASON, who died suddenly, it was thought proper to publish it in the very Words of the Copy, that the Publick may at last have something Genuine concerning the Grand Mystery of *Free-Masons*.

There was a Man at *Lovain* who publish'd he had, with great Toil and Difficulty, found out, overcome, and tamed, and was now ready at his Booth, to shew at the Rate of six Stivers a-piece, the most hideous and voracious Monster, the Common Disturber of Mankind, especially in their Adversity.

People flock'd from all Parts to see this Monster: They went in at the Fore-Door; and after they had seen the Creature, went out at the Back-Door, where they were ask'd whether the Monster was worth seeing. And as they had, at their Admittance into the Booth, promised to keep the Secret, they answer'd, it was a very wonderful Creature; which the Man found his Account in. But by some Accident it was divulged, that this wonderful Creature prov'd to be a LOUSE.

The Free-Mason's SIGNS.

A Gutteral

A Pedestal

A Manual

A Pectoral

THE
Grand MYSTERY
OF
FREE-MASONS
DISCOVER'D

Peace be here.

Answer. I hope there is.

Q. What a-Clock is it?

A. It's going to Six, or going to Twelve.

Q. Are you very busy?

A. No.

Q. Will you give, or take?

A. Both; or which you please.

Q. How go Squares?

A. Straight.

Q. Are you Rich, or Poor?

A. Neither.

Q. Change me that.

A. I will.

Q. In the Name of, &c. are you a Mason? What is a Mason?

A. A Man begot of a Man, born of a Woman, Brother to a King.

Q. What is a Fellow?

A. A Companion of a Prince.

Q. How shall I know you are Free Mason?

A. By Signs, Tokens, and Points of my Entry.

Q. Which is the Point of your Entry?

A. I Hear and Conceal, under the Penalty of having my Throat cut, or my Tongue pull'd out of my Head.

Q. Where was you made a Free-Mason?

A. In a just and perfect Lodge.

Q. How many make a Lodge?

A. God and the Square, with five or seven right and perfect Masons, on the highest Mountains, or the lowest Valleys in the World.

Q. Why do Odds make a Lodge?

A. Because all Odds are Mens Advantage.

Q. What Lodge are you of?

A. The Lodge of St. *John.*

Q. How does it stand?

A. Perfect East and West, as all Temples do.

Q. Where is the Mason's Point?

A. At the East-Window, waiting at the Rising of the Sun, to set his Men at Work.

Q. Where is the Warden's Point?

A. At the West-Window, waiting the Setting of the Sun, to Dismiss the Entred Apprentices.

Q. Who rules and governs the Lodge, and is Master of it?

A. Irah,

          } or the Right Pillar.

Iachin,

Q. How is it govern'd?

A. Of Square and Rule.

Q. Have you the Key of the Lodge?

A. Yes, I have.

Q. What is its Virtue?

A. To open and shut, and shut and open.

Q. Where do you keep it?

A. In an Ivory Box, between my Tongue and my Teeth, or within my Heart, where all my Secrets are kept.

Q. Have you the Chain to the Key?

A. Yes, I have.

Q. How long is it?

A. As long as from my Tongue to my Heart.

Q. How many precious Jewels?

A. Three; a square Asher, a Diamond, and a Square.

Q. How many Lights?

A. Three; a Right East, South and West.

Q. What do they represent?

A. The Three Persons, Father Son, and Holy Ghost.

Q. How many Pillars?

A. Two; *Iachin* and *Boaz.*

Q. What do they represent?

A. A Strength and Stability of the Church in all Ages.

Q. How many Angles in St. *John's* Lodge?

A. Four, bordering on Squares.

Q. How is the Meridian found out?

A. When the Sun leaves the South, and breaks in at the West-End of the Lodge.

Q. In what Part of the Temple was the Lodge kept?

A. In *Solomon's* Porch at the West-End of the Temple, where the two Pillars were set up.

Q. How many Steps belong to a right Mason?

A. Three.

Q. Give me the Solution.

A. I will. —The Right Worshipful, Worshipful Masters, and Worshipful Fellows of the Right Worshipful Lodge from whence I came, greet you well.

A. That Great God to us greeting, be at this our Meeting, and with the Right Worshipful Lodge from whence you came, and you are.

Q. Give me the *Jerusalem* Word.

A. *Giblin.*

Q. Give me the Universal Word.

A. *Boaz.*

Q. Right Brother of ours, your Name?

A. *N. or M.*

Welcome Brother M. or N. to our Society.

Q. How many particular Points pertain to a Free-Mason?

A. Three; Fraternity, Fidelity, and Tacity.

Q. What do they represent?

A. Brotherly Love, Relief, and Truth, among all Right Masons; for which all Masons were ordain'd at the Building of the Tower of *Babel*, and at the Temple of *Jerusalem.*

Q. How many proper Points?

A. Five; Foot to Foot, Knee to Knee, Hand to Hand, Heart to Heart, and Ear to Ear.

Q. Whence is an Arch derived?

A. From Architecture.

Q. How many Orders in Architecture?

A. Five; the *Tuscan, Dorick, Ionick, Corinthian,* and *Composit.*

Q. What do they answer?

A. They answer to the Base, Perpendicular, Diameter, Circumference, and Square.

Q. What is the right Word, or right Point of a Mason?

A. Adiue.

The *Free-Mason's* OATH.

You must serve God according to the best of your Knowledge and Institution, and be a true Liege Man to the King, and help and assist any Brother as far as your Ability will allow: By the Contents of the Sacred Writ you will perform this Oath. So help you God.

A *Free-Mason's* HEALTH.

Here's a Health to our Society, and to every faithful Brother that keeps his Oath of Secresy. As we are sworn to love each other. The World no Order knows like this our Noble and Antient Fraternity: Let them wonder at the Mystery.

Here, Brother, I Drink to thee.

SIGNS to know a True *Mason.*

1. To put off the Hat with Two Fingers and a Thumb.

2. To strike with the Right-Hand on the Inside of the Little Finger of the Left three Times, as if hewing.

3. By making a Square, *viz.* by setting your Heels together, and the Toes of both Feet straight, at a Distance, or by any other Way of Triangle.

4. To take Hand in Hand, with Left and Right Thumbs close, and touch each Wrist three Times with the Fore-Finger each Pulse.

5. You must Whisper, saying thus, The Masters and Fellows of the worshipful Company from whence I came, greet you all well.

The other will answer, God greet well the Masters and Fellows of the worshipful Company from whence you came.

6. Stroke two of your Fore-Fingers over your Eye-Lids three Times.

7. Turn a Glass, or any other Thing that is hollow, downwards, after you have drank out of it.

8. Ask how you do; and your Brothers drink to each other.

9. Ask what Lodge they were made Free-Masons at.

N.B. In the Third of King *Henry* the Sixth, an Act of Parliament was pass'd whereby it is made Felony to cause MASONS to confederate themselves in Chapiters and Assemblies. The Punishment is Imprisonment of Body, and make Fine and Ransom at the King's Will.

Finis.

Appendix IV

Ramsay's Oration

Freemasonry's Templar legend, at least in its modern form, started with an oration delivered by Andrew Michael Ramsay to the Grand Lodge of France in March, 1737. His words inspired the French Masons to embrace a chivalric legend, which the British Masons readily accepted, too. The result was the creation of Templar rituals that are still used in many of the "higher" degrees.

The oration survives in two versions. Ramsay is known to have delivered the first version at a lodge meeting in Paris in December, 1736. It attracted little notice but served as the basis for a substantially revised version, which he read at the Grand Lodge meeting a few months later.

Since the Grand Lodge Oration is credited with starting Templar Masonry, that it the version presented here. It is taken from an English translation in Gould's *History of Freemasonry*. A translation of both versions can be found in Volume 81 of the British Masonic journal, *Ars Quatuor Coronati*.

INITIATION
Ramsay gave the 18th Century Masons a tradition that made them heir to the
secret rituals of the *Crusaders.*

Ramsay's Oration

The Noble ardour which you, gentlemen, evince to enter into the most noble and very illustrious Order of Freemasons, is certain proof that you already possess all the qualities necessary to become members, that is, humanity, pure morals, inviolable secrecy, and a taste for the fine arts.

Lycurgus, Solon, Numa, and all political legislators have failed to make their institutions lasting. However wise their laws may have been, they have not been able to spread through all countries and ages, As they only kept in view victories and conquests, military violence, and the elevation of one people at the expense of another, they have not had the power to become universal, nor to make themselves acceptable to the taste, spirit, and interest of all nations. Philanthropy was not their basis. Patriotism badly understood and pushed to excess, often destroyed in these warrior republics love and humanity in general. Mankind is not essentially distinguished by the tongues spoken, the clothes worn, the lands occupied, or the dignities with which it is invested. The world is nothing but a huge republic, of which every nation is a family, and every individual a child. Our Society was at the outset established to revive and spread these essential maxims borrowed from the nature of man. We desire to reunite all men of enlightened minds, gentle manners, and agreeable wit, not only by love for the fine art, but much more by the grand principles of virtue, science, and religion, where the interests of the Fraternity shall become those of the whole human race, whence all nations shall be enabled to draw useful knowledge, and where the subjects of all kingdoms shall learn to cherish one another without renouncing their own country. Our ancestors, the Crusaders, gathered together from all parts of Christendom in the Holy Land, desired thus to reunite into one sole Fraternity the individuals of all nations. What obligations do we not owe to these superior men who, without gross selfish interests, without even listening to the inborn tendency to dominate, imagined such an institution, the sole aim of which is to unite minds and hearts in order to make them better, and form in the course of ages a spiritual empire where, without derogating from the various duties which different States exact, a new people shall be created, which, composed of many nations, shall in some sort cement them all into one by the tie of virtue and science.

The second requisite of our Society is sound morals. The religious orders were established to make perfect Christians, military orders to inspire a love of true glory, and the Order of Freemasons, to make men lovable men, good citizens, good subjects, inviolable in their promises, faithful adorers of the God of Love, lovers rather of virtue than of reward.

Polliciti servare fidem, sanctumque vereri
Numen amicitiae, mores non munera amare.

Nevertheless, we do not confine ourselves to purely civic virtues, We have amongst us three kinds of brothers: Novices of Apprentices, Fellows or Professed Brothers, Masters or Perfected Brothers. To the first are explained the moral virtues; to the second the heroic virtues; to the last the Christian virtues; so that our institution embraces the whole philosophy of sentiment and the complete theology of the heart. This is why one of our worshipful brothers has said—

> Freemason, illustrious Grand Master,
> Receive my first transports,
> In my heart the Order has given them birth,
> Happy I, if noble efforts
> Cause me to merit your esteem
> By elevating me to the sublime,
> The primaeval Truth,
> To the Essence pure and divine,
> The celestial Origin of the soul,
> The Source of life and love.

Because a sad, savage, and misanthropic philosophy disgusts virtuous men, our ancestors, the Crusaders, wished to render it lovable by the attractions of innocent pleasures, agreeable music, pure joy, and moderate gaiety. Our festivals are not what the profane world and the ignorant vulgar imagine. All the vices of the heart and soul are banished there, and irreligion, libertinage, incredulity, and debauch are proscribed. Our banquets resemble those virtuous symposia of Horace, where the conversation only touched what could enlighten the soul, discipline the heart, and inspire a taste for the true, the good, and the beautiful.

> O noctes coenaeque Deum . . .
> Sermo oritur, non de regnis dimibusve alienis
> . . . sed quod magis ad nos
> Pertinet, et nescire malum est, agitamus; utrumne
> Divitiis homines, an sint virtute beati;
> Quidve ad amicitias usus rectumve trahat nos,
> Et quae sit natura bond, summumque quid ejus.

Thus the obligations imposed upon you by the Order, are to protect your brothers by your authority, to enlighten them by your knowledge, to edify them by your virtues, to succour them in their necessities, to sacrifice all personal resentment, and to strive after all that may contribute to the peace and unity of society.

We have secrets; they are figurative signs and sacred words, composing a language sometimes mute, sometimes very eloquent, in order to communicate with one another at the greatest distance, and to recognize our brothers of whatsoever tongue. These were words of war which the Crusaders gave each other in order to guarantee them from the surprises of the Saracens, who often crept in amongst them to kill them. These signs and words recall the remembrance either of some part of our science, or of some mystery of the faith. That has happened to us which never befell any former Society. Our Lodges have been established, and are spread in all civilised nations, and, nevertheless, among this numerous multitude of men never has a brother betrayed our secrets. Those natures most trivial most indiscreet, least schooled to silence, learn this great art on entering our Society. Such is the power over all natures of the idea of a fraternal bond! This inviolable secret contributes powerfully to unite the subjects of all nations, and to render the communication of benefits easy and mutual between us. We have many examples in the annals of our Order. Our brothers, travelling divers lands, have only needed to make themselves known in our Lodges in order to be there immediately overwhelmed by all kinds of succour, even in time of the most bloody wars, and illustrious prisoners have found brothers where they only expected to meet enemies.

Should any fail in the solemn promises which bind us, you know, gentlemen, that the penalties which we impose upon him are remorse of conscience, shame at his perfidy, and exclusion from our Society, according to those beautiful lines of Horace—

> Est et fideli tuta silencio
> Merces; vetabo qui Cereris sacrum
> Vulgarit arcanum, sub iisdem
> Sit trabibus, fragilemque mecum
> Solvat phaselum . . .

Yes, sirs, the famous festivals of Ceres at Eleusis, of Isis in Egypt, of Minerva at Athens, of Urania amongst the Phenicians, and of Diana in Scythia were connected with ours. In those places mysteries were celebrated which concealed many vestiges of the ancient religion of Noah and the Patriarchs. They concluded with banquets and libations, and neither that intemperance nor excess were known into which the heathen gradually fell. The source of these infamies was the admission to the nocturnal assemblies of persons of both sexes in contravention of the primitive usages, It is in order to prevent similar abuses that women are excluded from our Order. We are not so unjust as to regard the fair sex as incapable of keeping a secret. But their presence might insensibly corrupt the purity of our maxims and manners.

The fourth quality required in our Order is the taste for useful sciences and the liberal arts. Thus, the Order exacts of each of you to contribute, by his protection, liberality, or labour, to a vast work for which no academy can suffice, because all these societies being composed of a very small number of men, their work cannot embrace an object so extended. All the Grand Masters in Germany, England, Italy, and elsewhere, exhort all the learned men and all the artisans of the Fraternity to unite to furnish the materials for a Universal Dictionary of the liberal arts and useful sciences, excepting only theology and politics.

The work has already been commenced in London, and by means of the union of our brothers it may be carried to a conclusion in a few years. Not only are technical words and their etymology explained, but the history of each art and science, its principles and operations, are described. By this means the lights of all nations will be united in one single work, which will be a universal library of all that is beautiful, great, luminous, solid, and useful in all the sciences and in all noble arts. This work will augment in each century, according to the increase of knowledge, and it will spread everywhere emulations and the taste for things of beauty and utility.

The word Freemason must therefore not be taken in a literal, gross, and material sense, as if our founders had been simple workers in stone, or merely curious geniuses who wished to perfect the arts. They were not only skilful architects, desirous of consecrating their talents and goods to the construction of material temples; but also religious and warrior princes who designed to enlighten, edify, and protect the living Temples of the Most High. This I will demonstrate by developing the history or rather the renewal of the Order.

Every family, every Republic, every Empire, of which the origin is lost in obscure antiquity, has its fable and its truth, its legend and its history. Some ascribe our institution to Solomon, some to Moses, some to Abraham, some to Noah, and some to Enoch, who built the first city, or even to Adam. Without any pretence of denying these origins, I pass on to matters less ancient. This, then is part of what I have gathered in the annals of Great Britain, in the Acts of Parliament, (which speak often of our privileges), and in the living traditions of the English people, which has been the centre of our Society since the eleventh century.

At the time of the Crusades in Palestine many princes, lords, and citizens associated themselves, and vowed to restore the Temple of the Christians in the Holy Land, and to employ themselves in bringing back their architecture to its first institution. They agreed upon several ancient signs and symbolic words drawn from the well of religion in order to recognise themselves amongst the heathen and Saracens. These signs and words were only communicated to those who promised solemnly, and even sometimes at the foot of the altar, never to reveal them. This sacred promise was therefore not an execrable oath, as it has been called, but a respectable bond to unite Christians of all nationalities in one confraternity. Some time afterwards our Order formed an intimate union with the Knights of St. John of Jerusalem. From that time our Lodges took the name of Lodges of St. John. This union was made after the example set by the Israelites when they erected the second Temple, who whilst they handled the trowel and mortar with one hand, in the other held the sword and buckler.

Our Order therefore must not be considered a revival of the Bacchanals, but as an order founded in remote antiquity, and renewed in the Holy Land by our ancestors in order to recall the memory of the most sublime truths amidst the pleasures of society. The kings, princes, and lords returned from Palestine to their own lands, and there established divers Lodges. At the time of the last Crusades many Lodges were already erected in Germany, Italy, Spain, France, and from thence in Scotland, because of the close alliance between the French and the Scotch. James, Lord Steward of Scotland, was Grand Master of a Lodge established at Kilwinning, in the West of Scotland, MCCLXXXVI., shortly after the death of Alexander III., King of Scotland, and one year before John Baliol mounted the throne. This lord received as Freemasons into his Lodge the Earls of Gloucester and Ulster, the one English, the other Irish.

By degrees our Lodges and our rites were neglected in most places. This is why of so many historians only those of Great Britain speak of our Order. Nevertheless it preserved its splendour among those Scotsmen to whom the Kings of France confided during many Centuries the safeguard of their royal persons.

After the deplorable mishaps in the Crusades, the perishing of the Christian armies, and the triumph of Bendocdar, Sultan of Egypt, during the eighth and last Crusade, that great Prince Edward, son of Henry III, King of England, seeing there was no longer any safety for his brethren in the Holy Land from whence the Christian troops were retiring, brought them all back, and this colony of brothers was established in England. As this prince was endowed with all heroic qualities, he loved the fine arts, declared himself protector of our Order, conceded to it new privileges, and then the members of this fraternity took the name of Freemasons, after the example set by their ancestors.

Since that time Great Britain became the seat of our Order, the conservator of our laws, and the depository of our secrets. The fatal religious discords which embarrassed and tore Europe in the sixteenth century caused our Order to degenerate from the nobility of its origin. Many of our rites and usages which were contrary to the prejudices of the times were changed, disguised, suppressed. Thus it was that many of our brothers forgot, like the ancient Jews, the spirit of our laws, and only retained the letter and shell. The beginnings of a remedy have already been made. It is only necessary to continue, and to at last bring everything back to it's original institution. This work cannot be difficult in a State where religion and the Government can only be favourable to our laws.

From the British Isles the Royal Art is now repassing into France, under the reign of the most amiable of Kings, whose humanity animates all his virtues, under the ministry of a Mentor, who has realised all that could be imagined most fabulous. In this happy age when love of peace has become the virtue of heroes, this nation [France] one of the most spiritual of Europe, will become the centre of the Order. She will clothe our work, our statutes, and our customs with grace, delicacy, and good taste, essential qualities of the Order, of which the basis is the wisdom, strength, and beauty of genius. It is in future in our Lodges, as it were in public schools, that Frenchmen shall learn, without travelling, the characters of all nations, and that strangers shall experience that France is the home of all peoples. *Patria gentis humanae.*

NOTE: The text of Ramsay's oration indicates that he did not translate the Latin quotations for his audience. Since it was customary for well educated people of the day to study Greek and Latin, most of his listeners would have understood the words, as well as the cultural references, contained in these passages.

The three Latin verses in this version of the oration, loosely translated, read:

"Having promised to keep faith, and to revere the sacred name of friendship, to value character more than wealth."

"Oh the nights and the dinners of the gods ... The talk begins, not about foreign kingdoms and palaces ... but about things that concern us more, and would hurt us not to know. We discuss whether men are made happy by riches or by virtue, or what draws us into friendship – its utility or its rectitude – and what is the nature of good, and what is the greatest good."

"And there is a certain reward for steadfast silence; I will not allow anyone who divulges the holy secrets of Ceres to be under the same roof or to set out in the same boat with me."

Appendix V

The Anti-Masonic Declaration of Independence

The *Anti-Masonic Declaration of Independence* was adopted and signed at an adjournment of the Convention of Seceding Masons which met at Le Roy, New York on July 4, 1828. The date of the meeting was selected to coincide with the anniversary of the signing of the United States' *Declaration of Independence* in 1776.

This *Declaration* is neither as extreme nor as brutal as many examples of anti-Masonry. Nevertheless, it is a revealing expression of the sentiment expressed by the fraternity's detractors. Its tone reflects the zeal that characterizes most serious attacks on Freemasonry, while the argument it presents includes the critics' standard objections to the fraternity.

Of special interest is the list of seventeen particulars, which outline Masonry's alleged offenses against religion and society. These items provide insight into both the moral values of the anti-Masons and their perception of the fraternity's character.

Special thanks to Caroline Spicer of the Reference Dept., John M. Olin Library, Cornell University for assistance in reproducing this document.

PROCEEDINGS

OF A

Convention of Delegates

OPPOSED TO

FREE MASONRY,

WHICH MET AT

LE ROY, GENESEE CO. N. Y.

MARCH 6, 1828

ROCHESTER :
WEED & HERON, PRINTERS.
1828

Anti-Masonic
Declaration of Independence

At an adjourned meeting of the Convention of Seceding
Masons held at Le Roy, July 4th, 1828, SOLOMON SOUTHWICK,
President, and REV. DAVID BERNARD, *Clerk*.

AUGUSTUS P. HASCALL, Chairman of the Committee appointed
to draft a DECLARATION OF INDEPENDENCE, from the Masonic
Institution, reported the following which was accepted and
signed.

When men attempt to dissolve a system which has influenced and governed part of community, and by its pretensions
to antiquity, usefulness and virtue, would demand the respect of all, its proper to submit to the consideration of a
candid and impartial world the causes which impel them to
such a course. We seceders from the masonic institution,
availing ourselves of our natural and unalienable rights, and
the privileges guaranteed to us by our constitution, freely to
discuss the principles of our government and laws, and to
expose whatever may endanger the one, or impede the due
administration of the other, do offer the following reasons for
endeavouring to abolish the order of Freemasonry, and
destroy its influence in our government.

In all arbitrary governments free inquiry has been restricted
as fatal to the principles upon which they were based. In all
ages of the world tyrants have found it necessary to shackle
the minds of their subjects to enable them to control their
actions; for experience ever taught that the free mind exerts
a moral power that resists all attempts to enslave it. However
forms of governments heretofore have varied, the right to act
and speak without a controlling power, has never been

permitted Our ancestors, who imbibed principles of civil and religious liberty, fled to America to escape persecution; and when Britain attempted to encroach upon the free exercise of those principles, our fathers hesitated not to dissolve their oaths of allegiance to the mother country, and declare themselves free and independent, and exulting millions of freemen yet bless their memories for the deed. A new theory of government was reduced to practice in the formation of the American republic. It involved in its structure principles of equal rights and privileges, and was based upon the eternal foundation of public good. It protects the weak and restrains the powerful, and extends its honors and emoluments to the meritorious of every condition. It should have been the pride of every citizen to preserve this noble structure in all its beautiful symmetry and proportions. But he principle of self aggrandizement, the desire to control he destinies of others, and luxuriate on their spoil, unhappily still inhabits the human breast. Many attempts have already been made to impair the freedom of our institutions and to subvert our government. But they have been met by the irresistible power of public opinion and indignation, and crushed. In the mean time the masonic society has been silently growing among us, whose principles and operations are calculated to subvert and destroy the great and important principles of the commonwealth. Before and during the revolutionary struggle, masonry was but little known and practiced in this country. It was lost amid the changes and confusion of the conflicting nations, and was reserved for a time of profound peace to wind and insinuate itself into every department of government, and influence the result of almost every proceeding. Like many other attempts to overturn governments and destroy the liberties of the people, it has chosen a time when the suspicions of men were asleep, and with a noiseless tread, in the darkness and silence of the night, has increased its strength and extended its power. Not yet content with its original powers and influence, it has of late received the aid of foreign and more arbitrary systems. With this accumulation of strength it arrived at that formidable crisis when it bid open defiance to the laws of our country in the abduction and murder of an inoffending citizen of this republic. So wicked was this transaction, so extensive its preparation, and so openly justified, that it roused the energies of an insulted people whose exertions have opened the hidden recesses of this abode of darkness and mystery, and mankind may now view its power, its wickedness and folly.

That it is opposed to the genius and design of this government, the spirit and precepts of our holy religion, and the welfare of society, generally, will appear from the following considerations.

It exercises jurisdiction over the persons and lives of citizens of the republic.

It arrogates to itself the right of punishing its members for offences unknown to the laws of this or any other nation.

It requires the concealment of crime and protects the guilty from punishment.

It encourages the commission of crime by affording the guilty facilities of escape.

It affords opportunities for the corrupt and designing to form plans against the government and the lives and characters of individuals.

It assumes titles and dignities incompatible with a republican government, and enjoins an obedience to them derogatory to republican principles.

It destroys all principles of equality by bestowing its favors on its own members, to the exclusion of others equally meritorious and deserving.

It creates odious aristocracies by its obligations to support he interest of its members in preference to others of equal qualifications.

It blasphemes the name and attempts the personification of the Great Jehovah.

It prostitutes the sacred scriptures of morality and religion by the multiplication of profane oaths and immoral familiarity with religious forms and ceremonies.

It discovers in its ceremonies an unholy commingling of divine truth with impious human inventions.

It destroys a veneration for religion and religious ordinances, by the profane use of religious forms.

It substitutes the self righteousness and ceremonies of masonry for vital religion and the ordinances of the gospel.

It promotes habits of idleness and intemperance, by its members neglecting their business to attend its meetings and drink its libations.

It accumulates funds at the expense of indigent persons, and the distress of their families, too often to be dissipated in rioting and pleasure, and in its senseless ceremonies and exhibitions.

In contracts the sympathies of the human heart for all the unfortunate, by confining its charities to its own members; and promotes the interest of the few at the expense of the many.

An institution, fraught with so many and great evils, is dangerous to our government, and the safety of our citizens, and is unfit to exist among a free people. We, therefore, believing it the duty we owe to God, our country and posterity, resolve to expose its mystery, wickedness, and tendency, to public view, and we exhort all citizens how have a love of country and a veneration for its laws, a spirit of our holy religion and regard for the welfare of mankind, to aid us in the cause which we have espoused—an appealing to Almighty God for the rectitude of our motives we solemnly absolve ourselves from all allegiance to the masonic institution and declare ourselves free and independent. And in support of these resolutions, our government and laws, and the safety of individuals against the usurpations of all secret societies, and open force, and against the "vengeance" of the masonic institution, "with a firm reliance on the protection of Divine providence, we mutually pledge to each other, our lives, our fortunes, and our sacred honor."

July 4, 1828

Bibliography

Aylmer, G.E. and Cant, Reginald. *A History of York Minster*. Oxford: Clarendon Press, 1977.

Barber, Malcolm. *The Trial of the Templars*. Cambridge: Cambridge University Press, 1978.

Baring-Gould, Rev. S. *The Lives of the Saints*. Edinburgh: John Grant, 1914.

Bede. *Historical Works*, translated by J. E. King. London: William Heinemann, 1930.

Bellot, Hugh H.L. *The Temple*. London: Methuen & Co. Ltd., 1914.

Benson, Edwin. *Life in a Medieval City*. Illustrated by York in the XVth Century. London: Society for Promoting Christian Knowledge, 1920.

Bingham, Caroline. *The Crowned Lions – The Early Plantagenet Kings*. London: David and Charles, 1978.

Blair, Peter Hunter. *The World of Bede*. London: Secker & Warburg, 1970.

Bridge, Antony. *The Crusades*. New York: Franklin Watts, 1982.

Burman, Edward. *The Templars – Knights of God*. Crucible, 1986.

Butler, Rev. Alban. *The Lives of the Fathers, Martyrs, and Other Principal Saints*. New York: D. & J. Sadlier, 1846.

Butler, R. M. *Medieval York.* York: The Yorkshire Architectural and York Archaeological Society, 1982.

Cameron, Sir Charles A. "On the Origin and Progress of Chivalric Freemasonry in the British Isles." *Ars Quatuor Coronatorum.* XIII, 1900.

Campbell, G.A. *The Knights Templars – Their Rise and Fall.* London: Duckworth, 1937.

Campbell, John. "Death and Taxes." *Investors Chronicle.* 95/1212 (March 22-28, 1991) 16-7.

Herbermann, Charles G., *et al,* eds. *The Catholic Encyclopedia.* New York: The Encyclopedia Press, Inc., 1907.

Clarke, J.R. "External Influences on the Evolution of English Masonry." *The Collected Prestonian Lectures 1961 – 1974.* London: Lewis Masonic, 1983.

Clutton-Brock, A. *The Cathedral Church of York – A Description of its Fabric and a Brief History of the Archi-Episcopal See.* London: George Bell & Sons, 1899.

Coil, Henry Wilson. *Coil's Masonic Encyclopedia.* New York: Macoy, 1961.

Coil, Henry Wilson. *Freemasonry Through Six Centuries.* Richmond: Macoy, 1968.

Colliers Encyclopedia. New York: The Macmillan Educational Company, 1985.

Conder, C.R. *The Latin Kingdom of Jerusalem.* London: The Committee of the Palestine Exploration Fund, 1897.

Cooke, Jean; Kramer, Ann and Rowland-Entwistle, Theodore. *History's Timeline.* New York: Crescent Books, 1981.

Covey-Crump, W.W. "Medieval Master Masons and Their Secrets." *The Collected Prestonian Lectures 1925 – 1960.* Shepperton: Lewis Masonic, 1965.

Crawley, W.J. Chetwode. "The Templar Legends in Freemasonry." *Ars Quatuor Coronatorum.* XXVI, 1913.

Crowe, Fred J.W. "The 'Charta Transmissionis' of Larmenius." *Ars Quatuor Coronatorum.* XXIV, 1911.

Currer-Briggs, Noel. *The Holy Grail and the Shroud of Christ.* Maulden: ARA Publications, 1984.

——— *The Shroud and the Grail.* New York: St. Martin's Press, 1987.

Darrah, Delmar Duane. *The Evolution of Freemasonry.* Bloomington, Illinois: The Masonic Publishing Company, 1920.

Davis, J.D. *Davis Dictionary of the Bible.* Grand Rapids, Michigan: Baker Book House, 1980.

Dickinson, P.L. *An Outline History of Architecture of the British Isles.* London: Butler & Tanner, Ltd., undated.

Doyle, Leonard, J. (trans). *St. Benedict's Rule for Monasteries.* Collegeville, Minnesota: The Liturgical Press, 1948.

Duncan, Malcolm C. *Duncan's Masonic Ritual and Monitor.* Third edition. New York: David McKay Company, Inc., undated.

Edgell, Hugh A.R. *Champions of the Cross.* Norfolk, England: Hugh A.R. Edgell, 1983.

The Encyclopedia Americana, International Edition. Danbury, Connecticut: Grolier, Inc., 1984.

Farmer, D. H. (ed). *The Age of Bede.* New York, Penguin, 1983.

Ferguson, George. *Signs and Symbols in Christian Art.* Oxford: Oxford University Press, 1961.

Finucane, Ronald C. *Soldiers of the Faith – Crusaders and Moslems at War.* New York: St. Martin's Press, 1983.

Fletcher, Eric. *Benedict Biscop – Jarrow Lecture, 1981.* Jarrow, Durham: St. Paul's Church, 1981.

Gibb, Sir Hamilton, *The Life of Saladin.* Oxford: Oxford University Press, 1973.

Gies, Frances. *The Knight in History.* New York: Harper & Row, 1984.

Grant, Michael. *Dawn of the Middle Ages.* New York: Bonanza, 1981.

Green, John Richard. *The Conquest of England.* New York: Harper & Brothers Franklin Square, 1884.

Hoare, Rodney. *A Piece of Cloth – The Turin Shroud Investigated.* Wellingborough, Northamptonshire: The Aquarian Press, 1984.

Holy Shroud Guild. *Proceedings of the 1977 United States Conference of Research on the Shroud of Turin.* New York: Holy Shroud Guild, 1977.

Horne, Alex. *The York Legend in the Old Charges.* London: A. Lewis, Ltd., 1978.

Howarth, Stephen. *The Knights Templar.* New York: Antheneum, 1982.

Hughan, W.J. "Origin of Masonic Knight Templary in the United Kingdom." *Ars Quatuor Coronatorum.* XVIII, 1905.

Jackson, A.C.F. *English Masonic Exposures 1760 – 1769.* London: Lewis Masonic, 1986.

Jamieson, John, D.D. *An Etymological Dictionary of the Scottish Language.* 4 vols. Paisley: Alexander Gardner, 1879.

Johnson, Paul. *A History of Christianity.* New York: Antheneum, 1977.

Kay, Billy. *Scots – The Mother Tongue.* Edinburgh: Mainstream Publishing Company, 1986.

King, Colonel E.J. *The Knights Hospitallers in the Holy Land.* London: Methuen & Co., Ltd., 1931.

Kingsley, Rose G. *The Order of St. John of Jerusalem.* London: Skeffington & Son Ltd., 1918.

Knight, Stephen. *Jack the Ripper: The Final Solution.* Chicago: Academy Chicago Publishers, 1986.

Knoop, Douglas. "The Mason Word." *The Collected Prestonian Lectures 1925 – 1960.* Shepperton: Lewis Masonic, 1965.

Knoop, Douglas; Jones, G.P. and Hamer, Douglas. *The Early Masonic Catechisms.* London: Quatuor Coronati Lodge, 1963.

––– *Early Masonic Pamphlets.* London: Quatuor Coronati Correspondence Circle, Ltd., 1978.

Laing, Lloyd and Laing, Jennifer. *Anglo-Saxon England.* London: Granada, 1982.

Mackay, Charles, LL.D. *A Dictionary of Lowland Scotch.* London: Whittaker and Co., 1888.

Macleod, Isabel. *Pocket Guide to Scottish Words.* Glasgow: Richard Drew Publishing, 1986.

Maher, Robert W. *Science, History, and the Shroud of Turin.* New York: Vantage Press, 1986.

Martin, Edward J. *The Trial of the Templars.* London: George Allen & Unwin, Ltd., 1928.

The Masonic Service Association. "The Morgan Affair," *Short Talk Bulletin* Vol. XI, No. 3. Silver Spring, Maryland: The Masonic Service Association, March, 1933.

——— *The Regius Poem — Freemasonry's Oldest Document.* Silver Springs, Maryland: The Masonic Service Association, 1987 printing.

——— *The Three Degrees and Great Symbols of Masonry.* Washington: The Masonic Service Association, 1924.

McCarthy, Charles. "The Antimasonic Party," *Annual Report of the American Historical Association for the Year 1902.* Washington: Government Printing Office, 1903.

Mitchell, Ann. *Cathedrals of Europe.* Feltham, England: Hamlyn, 1968.

Mitchison, Rosalind. *A History of Scotland.* London: Methuen and Co. Ltd., 1970.

Morgan, Capt. Wm. *Illustrations of Masonry.* Batavia, N.Y.: David C. Miller, 1827. (Reprinted by Charles T. Powner, Chicago, Ill., 1986.)

A Narrative of the Facts and Circumstances Relating to the Kidnapping and Murder of William Morgan. Batavia, N.Y.: D.C. Miller, 1827. (Reprinted by Ezra A. Cook, Chicago, Ill., 1965.)

Ness, J.A. *History of the Ancient Mother Lodge of Scotland.* Kilwinning, Scotland: Mother Kilwinning Lodge No. 0, 1979.

Newbury, George Albert and Williams, Louis Lenway. *A History of the Supreme Council, 33° of the Ancient Accepted Scottish Rite of Freemasonry for the Northern Masonic Jurisdiction of the United States of America.* Lexington, Massachusetts: Supreme Council, A.A.S.R., N.M.J., 1987.

Newby, P.H. *Saladin in His Time.* London: Faber and Faber, 1983.

New Catholic Encyclopedia. Washington: The Catholic University of America, 1967.

O'Donnell, James J. *Augustine.* Boston: Twayne Publishers, 1985.

Oldenbourg, Zoe. *The Crusades.* New York: Pantheon Books, 1966.

The Old Gothic Constitutions, with an introduction by Wallace McLeod. Bloomington, Illinois: The Masonic Book Club, 1985.

O'Rahilly, Alfred. *The Crucified.* Mount Merrion, County Dublin: Kingdom Books, 1985.

Palmer, John C. *The Morgan Affair and Anti-Masonry.* Washington: The Masonic Service Association of the United States, 1924.

Parker, Thomas W. *The Knights Templars in England.* Tucson: The University of Arizona Press, 1963.

Partner, Peter. *The Murdered Magicians — The Templars and Their Myths.* Crucible, 1987.

Payne, Robert. *The Dream and the Tomb — A History of the Crusades.* New York: Stein and Day, 1984.

Payne, T. *The Grand Mystery of Free-Masons Discover'd.* London, 1724.

Peters, F.E. *Jerusalem.* Princeton, New Jersey: Princeton University Press, 1985.

Pick, Fred L. and Knight, G. Norman (revised by Frederick Smyth). *The Pocket History of Freemasonry.* Seventh edition. London: Frederick Muller Limited, 1983.

Poole, Herbert. "Masonic Ritual and Secrets Before 1717." *Ars Quatuor Coronatorum.* XXXVII, 1924.

Purvis, the Rev Cannon J.S. "The Medieval Organization of Freemasons' Lodges." *The Collected Prestonian Lectures 1925 – 1960.* Shepperton: Lewis Masonic, 1965.

Quennell, Marjorie and Quennell, C.H.B. *Everyday Life in Roman and Anglo-Saxon Times.* New York: Dorset Press, 1959.

Ratner, Lorman (ed). *Antimasonry – The Crusade and the Party.* Englewood Cliffs, New Jersey: Prentice Hall, Inc., 1969.

Revised Knight Templarism Illustrated. Chicago: Ezra A. Cook Publications, Inc., 1975.

Ritual. The General Grand Chapter of Royal Arch Masons International, 46th edition. Baltimore, 1985.

Ritual. Grand Encampment of Knights Templar of the United States of America. Chicago, 1979.

Roberts, J. *The Old Constitutions Belonging to the Society of Free and Accepted Masons.* London, 1722.

Robinson, J. Armitage. *The Times of Saint Dunstan.* Oxford: The Clarendon Press, 1922.

Robinson, John J. *Born in Blood – The Lost Secrets of Freemasonry.* New York: M. Evans & Company, 1989.

The Secret History of the Free-Masons. London: Samuel Briscoe, 1724.

Shepard, Leslie (ed). *Encyclopedia of Occultism and Parapsychology.* Second edition. Detroit, Michigan: Gale Research Company, 1984.

Simon, Edith. *The Piebald Standard – A Biography of the Knights Templar.* Boston: Little, Brown and Company, 1959.

Smith, G. Gregory, M.A. *Specimens of Middle Scots.* Edinburgh: William Blackwood and Sons, 1903.

Stevenson, David. *The Origins of Freemasonry – Scotland's Century, 1590-1710.* Cambridge: Cambridge University Press, 1988.

Tuchman, Barbara W. *A Distant Mirror – the Calamitous 14th Century.* New York: Alfred A. Knopf, 1978.

Tuckett, J.E.S. "The Earliest Baldwyn K.T. Certificate." *Ars Quatuor Coronatorum.* XXIV, 1911.

Valance, Henry L. *Confession of the Murder of William Morgan as Taken Down by Dr. John L. Emery.* New York, 1849.

Van Rensselaer, Mrs. Schuyler. *Handbook of English Cathedrals.* New York: The Century Co., 1893.

Vaughn, William Preston. *The Antimasonic Party in the United States, 1826-1843.* Lexington: The University Press of Kentucky, 1983.

Vest, Deed Lafayette. *Pursuit of a Thread.* San Antonio: The Watercress Press, 1983.

Ward, Lt. Col. Eric. "In the Beginning Was the Word ..." *The Collected Prestonian Lectures 1961 – 1974.* London: Lewis Masonic, 1983.

Warrack, Alexander, M.A. *The Concise Scots Dictionary.* Alabama: University of Alabama Press, 1911.

Wines, Frederick Howard. *Punishment and Reformation.* New York: Thomas Y. Crowell Company, 1923.

Worley, George. *The Church of the Knights Templar in London – A Description of the Fabric and its Contents, with a Short History of the Order.* London: George Bell & Sons, 1907.

Yarker, John. "The Chivalric Orders." Notes and Queries, *Ars Quatuor Coronatorum.* XIV, 1901.

Index

About the Author

As a journalist and writer for more than twenty years, C. Bruce Hunter has produced work in fields as far ranging as religion, education, mysteries and science fiction.

Mr. Hunter's investigation of Masonic secrecy sprang from the numerous articles he wrote for the fraternity's magazines and a stint as editor of *The North Carolina Mason,* a Grand Lodge publication. He tried to learn more by joining such Masonic Research organizations as the Philalethes Society, Quatuor Coronati and the Illinois Lodge of Research, and by reading the Craft's literature. Emerging from those activities with more questions than answers, he was determined to learn the truth behind a cult of secrecy that has existed for nearly three centuries.

What began as a six-month project turned into three years of searching obscure sources for information that was forgotten, or in some cases concealed, hundreds of years ago. His quest for the origins of the Freemasons' secrets took him from the Library of Congress to Edinburgh's St. Giles Cathedral and the Louvre.